D0915946

A **PETER GZOWSKI** READER

A PETER GZOWSKI READER

Peter Gzowski

Compiled, selected and edited by Edna Barker

A DOUGLAS GIBSON BOOK

M&S

National Library of Canada Cataloguing in Publication Data

Gzowski, Peter
A Peter Gzowski reader
ISBN 0-7710-3695-7
I. Title.
PS8563.Z69A16 2001   081   C2001-901797-9
PR9199.3.G96A16 2001

We acknowledge the financial support of the Government of Canada through the Book Publishing Industry Development Program for our publishing activities. We further acknowledge the support of the Canada Council for the Arts and the Ontario Arts Council for our publishing program.

Typeset in Janson by M&S, Toronto
Printed and bound in Canada

A Douglas Gibson Book

McClelland & Stewart Ltd.
The Canadian Publishers
481 University Avenue
Toronto, Ontario
M5G 2E9
www.mcclelland.com

1   2   3   4   5   05   04   03   02   01

For R.A., K.L., B.F., R.F., R.G., G.R., H.B.
any many others who wrote as well as they edited,
and in both aspects of our craft set very high standards indeed.

A Peter Gzowski Reader
Compiled, selected and edited by Edna Barker

While it's true, as the line above suggests, that Edna Barker has been my friend as well as my right hand in the world of books for close to twenty years now (which is not bad considering she's left-handed), all errors of judgement, fact or historical accuracy are mine.

Although they span close to half a century, these pieces are not offered as a portrait of any particular time. They are simply people, places or events that caught my eye, and which I wrote about in a variety of newspapers, magazines, journals and books — and sometimes just presented as talks or amusements. One, as you'll see, is in fact a song Ian Tyson and I wrote one summer afternoon, but which to my delight a number of people still remember (better than I do) some thirty-five years later.

The order they appear in here bears no relation to the order in which I wrote them, although the discerning eye may discover they run more or less from the earliest part of my life in which I experienced them to the present. I hope you find some memories of your own among them, and that some of the pleasures I found in writing them — and in sharing their rediscovery with Edna — are there for you as well.

I'd also like to express my gratitude to Douglas Gibson at McClelland & Stewart for his support, and on Edna's behalf, say a word of thanks to Don McLeod; Bernadine Dodge, Jodi Aoki and Douglas Newman at the Trent University Archives; and Jonathan Webb.

Contents

A Perfect Place to Be a Boy

from the introduction to Images of Waterloo County, *1996*

When I was a kid, and the world was simpler, Waterloo County was the centre of the universe. Peter John Gzowski Brown, I would scribble on the flyleaves of my schoolbooks (my mother, divorced from Harold Gzowski and remarried, having added my stepfather's surname to mine), Upper Duplex, 24 Park Avenue, City of Galt, Township of North Dumfries, County of Waterloo, Province of Ontario, Dominion of Canada, Continent of North America, Western Hemisphere . . . and so on to the limits of imagined space.

At the epicentre was Dickson Park, which stretched from beneath the bay window of our duplex across the road and down the hill towards the railway tracks and the river. The park, named, as was the stately stone school where I went when the park was quiet, for one of the county's pioneer families, was truly a land for all seasons.

In spring, as soon as the creeks in the surrounding countryside — creeks were *cricks* in Waterloo County, although the pants we wore all winter, baggy-thighed but laced tight at the knee (and patched with leather if you were lucky) were *breeks* — had begun to run with their cheerful rivulets of icy water, we took to the park for the first sessions of what we called tibby. Tibby, or tippy, as it may have been spelled, was the simplest of games: a long piece of broomstick for a bat; a shorter one to hit with it; two holes in the muddy ground, a cricket pitch apart, for wickets. We played it until the grass in the park was firm enough for baseball — flies and grounders, at first, and then, when the diamonds were ready, scrub, which is what we called the game other parts of the world knew as work-up.

There were two diamonds in Dickson Park. The more impressive, where the mighty Terriers played their Inter-county League games, was directly across the road from our duplex, its playing surface shielded from my bird's-eye view only by the tar-papered roof of its rickety wooden grandstand, from which, one spring, we dropped homemade bombs whose ingredients I never knew. The other, where we played our games of scrub and, later, more formal matches between schools, was at the farthest reaches of the Terriers' outfield, with the back of its batting cage turned to the barns that held livestock during the fall fair. Although the outfields of the two diamonds shared the open greensward, the park was large enough that, so far at least as I can remember, there were no occasions when fielders from different games were confused by simultaneous home-run clouts rolling past each other.

In summer, the Terriers were our heroes. The Inter-county League — I remember, I think, Galt, Kitchener (I told you Waterloo County was the centre of the universe), Brantford, Stratford, London, Ingersoll and St. Thomas, although I'm sure my list is incomplete and that there were others over the years — was perhaps Class C in a flourishing minor-league system that went all the way up to AAA. But in the days before television it seemed big-time to us. Like most minor-league clubs in those days, the Terriers were built around itinerant players who would slip into town and supplement their baseball incomes with jobs in the mills and foundries. Sometimes, indeed, these players even included people we'd heard of — Goody Rosen, for example, who'd had a stint with the AAA Toronto Maple Leafs, or, for part of one unforgettable season, Mickey Owen, who'd caught in the majors, even though he was best remembered for having dropped a third strike in the World Series. But our real heroes were the local boys who'd made good: Moth Miller, as quick as an antelope in the outfield, with his pants tucked in like plus-fours, running down every ball he could see, which, considering his Coke-bottle eyeglasses, was a remarkable percentage; Red Cupples on the mound (Red's younger brother Gordie pitched in our games at the other end of the park, for St. Andrew's school against Dickson), and, the greatest of them all, Wiggy Wylie at shortstop. Although I was never sure where Wiggy's nickname came from (he was Bill Wylie, though no one ever called him that), I imagined it was from the way he set himself at the plate, twitching his bat and wiggling his hindquarters, for he not only played like a ballplayer, he walked like one, and for days after every Terriers game, we would shamble around our own diamond in emulation of his loose-limbed gait. "Are you *limping*?" my mother asked one summer morning, as, my glove freshly rubbed with dubbin (dubbin worked on high-cuts in the winters, too), the crook of my arm already tanned a golden brown, I set off for the fields of play, proving, I suppose, that there were some things mothers — even those who lived across the road from the centre of everything that mattered — would never understand.

The fall had a magic of its own, not only in the yellows and crimsons of the hills and woods — for we were never far from the countryside — or the sense of renewal that filled the wine-sweet air, but in the life of the park as well. Almost as soon as school began, workmen raised goalposts on baseball's overlapping outfields, and marked the yards with stripes of lime for football, and the park was home to the red, blue and gold-clad champions of the GCI — and VS, of course, although the full title didn't fit the rhythms of our cheers. We essayed some football ourselves, touch, mostly, since we lacked the pads (if not the will) for tackle, and on one memorable occasion assembled a team of six park denizens to play a squad from Kitchener, with rules that said, except on a pass, two players had to touch the ball before it crossed the line of scrimmage. We won, somewhat to our own astonishment, thanks largely to a kid named Bob Keachie who could run like quicksilver, and we chanted the score — which comes to me now as Galt 10, Kitchener 5 (touchdowns in those days being worth only a nickel) — all the way home on the trolley. But the reason the game and its accompanying fanfare

are still, for me, indelible, is more subtle than its outcome and, I'm afraid, more embarrassing.

A bunch of youngsters organizing something as adventurous as an out-of-town trip was, in those days, considered newsworthy in Galt, and one afternoon *The Reporter* — "The Rag," as we called it when it wasn't looking, though many of us earned pocket money by delivering it door to door — sent a photographer to pose us in the park. Without equipment, but with a boy's sense of drama, I decided to make myself look as tough as possible, and showed up for the photo session sporting Band-Aids across my nose and chin — badges, I hoped people would think, of some wounds of the game.

Even the thrills of football were set aside for the fall fair. For three magical days in September — though preparations began much earlier, under my watchful eye across the road — the park put on its autumn finery. A midway filled the baseball diamond and spilled over around the bandstand and onto our tibby pitch behind the backstop. Sheds and barns that stood unused for the rest of the year sprang to life. There were animals everywhere: sheep and pigs in pens along the hill; gleaming hunters and jumpers prancing around a show ring in front of the grandstand; sturdy Percherons and Clydesdales jingling with unaccustomed bells; sleek golden Jerseys and Guernseys and black and white Holsteins in their stalls. In the autumn air, the honkytonk of the midway barkers and the squeals of terrified rapture from the whirling rides mingled with the cries of roosters and the lowing of cattle, and the smell of candy-floss and frying hamburgers mixed with the sweet aromas of the barnyard.

Since long before I was lucky enough to move there, Galt had been an industrial city: a fortress, as was much of the county, of textile mills and furniture factories, of metal works and machine shops, symbolized, in Galt, by the sprawling plant of the firm we called Babcock-Wilcox, Goldie and McCulloch-cox. The industrial age surrounded us, and supported many of our families (my own stepfather was sales manager of the Narrow Fabrics Weaving and Dyeing Company Limited). But in the fall, when the fair came to Dickson Park, we were reminded of the richness of the landscape that was its setting, and of the variety and the ingenuity of the people who lived and worked along the county's tree-lined lanes and winding roads.

Winter was hockey, the most memorable season of all. After the midway had moved on to other counties and the farmers returned to the soil, boards would appear between the baseball back-stop and the exhibition hall, outlining the setting of our winter dreams. Metal light-standards ringed the perimeter, and with the first ice our games would begin at dawn — or so it seemed — and last till only the fear of punishment sent us home. There was, to be sure, a smaller rink as well, for "pleasure skating," as the park would have it, but, in our view, for girls.

On the real ice surface, we played forever, choosing up sides when the morning sessions began, amending the teams only to keep some semblance of equality as the day stretched on. Sometimes, in fact, there would be more than one game going on at the same time: one, for little kids, across the rink, one end-to-end between the snow-marked goals, and it was necessary to remember whose carved initials stood out in white on the puck you were supposed to be chasing. The rules were simple — no raising the puck, no body checking, no throwing your stick to bring down a fleeing break-away — and our costumes and equipment simpler still: toques and breeks and sweaters (the Leafs and Red Wings being about equal in our favour), heavy stockings with, yes, magazines for shin pads (sometimes affixed by garters cut from inner tubes), hockey gloves for the well-to-do, and sticks with tar-taped blades that lasted until we wore them down to toothpicks.

One day, the world froze around us. Spring was approaching. An overnight rain had fallen on the deep blanket of snow. Then a snap freeze created what mountaineers call *verglas*, a thick but solid coating of ice on top of everything. At first we didn't notice what had happened. But when the first puck flew over the boards, instead of sinking into the snow it skittered off across crusted surface. The boy who took off after it stayed on top as well, sliding the puck ahead of him and calling with delight. The rest of us followed, pouring over the boards and taking to the open land, the puck soon forgotten. Across the baseball diamond we flew, over Red Cupples' pitching mound and Wiggy Wylie's infield, and up the rise where I had posed in my unneeded bandages. For a while, we stayed on the hill, marking slalom courses with our up-turned hockey sticks and skimming among them like alpine skiers. But soon even that seemed ordinary. We took off again, climbing the park's weathered fence in our skates, sliding across Park Avenue, mounting the hill to Blair Road and off across the still-wintry fields, whooping and hollering as we went, as free as birds flying over the open land, moving in ever-expanding concentric circles from park to town to country, until, at last, we turned for home in the fading light.

I have thought, many times, of the metaphor of that joy-filled day.

As much as Dickson Park was our epicentre, we left it often. We took the trolley to Preston and Hespeler — skated, even (and with girls) on the rink behind the old Sulphur Springs Hotel. We hiked and rode our bikes among the surrounding pleasures: up Barrie's Cut, to Willow Lake and Puslinch, and through the Homer Watson landscape of Blair and Ayr and Doon. Later, and more adventurous, we rode as far afield as Kitchener and Waterloo, and my first memories of the Mennonites of the county's northern regions were from the seat of my shiny CCM. Even then, I realized there was a world beyond the park.

And, still later, there were other forces that matched the liberation of the *verglas*. When boyhood was over, so too was Galt, at least for me. My mother died. I moved to other galaxies.

Returning now, as I all too seldom do, I see the marks of progress everywhere. Galt itself, now folded into bustling Cambridge. Old street names swept away to avoid duplication with addresses in Hespeler and Preston. The murky river of my childhood returned to clean and sparkling life. At least one of the four banks that defined the corner of Water Street and Main now a chic restaurant. Many of the mills and foundries replaced by the humming prosperity of sophisticated technology — and one of them a restaurant too. Much of the countryside now scattered with subdivisions and shopping malls, with car-washes and fast-food franchises — the agricultural setting of my youth has given way to the growing, busy, modern world. At Dickson Park, the outdoor rink has disappeared, its place taken by a modern, enclosed arena, and on the Saturday morning I drove by, kids as young as my grandchildren flopped from their parents' cars, with duffel bags full of equipment slung from their shouldered sticks.

Are there still Terriers, I wonder, though Wiggy Wylie has long gone? Do boys still play tibby in the spring?

Yes, I think, forever. Waterloo County, the centre of the universe, was a homeland. It is one still, a place of people and memories, an anchor against the storms of change.

My Grandfather Leacock

from an unpublished address at the Leacock home, summer 1989

It would probably come as a surprise, even to people who have heard of us both, to learn that Stephen Leacock was my grandfather. Oh, I don't mean that he was my father's father — he'd be surprised by my last name if that were the case, I think — and I would certainly not presume to be his literary heir (although I did once make the short list for the award that honours his memory, for a book, alas, I hadn't intended to be funny) — but I have childhood memories of someone with white hair and twinkling eyes who could have been no other. The name he was using then was Young, McGregor Young, of what he liked to pretend was United Empire Loyalist stock from Prince Edward County, in what I sometimes heard him slip and call Upper Canada (a clue there, obviously), and it was as Young he raised his three children, one of whom, Margaret, was my mother. Now, with computers, scholars will easily be able to count the number of references in Leacock's published works to, and I quote, "the Young ones," and know to whom he is secretly referring.

The man who called himself Greg Young was a lawyer, and, I am told — for it mattered not at all to me when he was around — a very good one. In the days when the British Privy Council was the court of highest appeal for Canadian law his rate for a case (all this I found out later, you understand) was $400 a day from the time he strode up the gangplank on this side of the Atlantic until the time, usually some weeks later, when he strolled back down it. Even in his legal guise, however, he had little interest in money for its own sake — or if he did was unwilling to let his background in economics show — and would hand most of it over to his wife, the former Maude Williams of Peel Street, Montreal — another clue here for the discerning, although she claimed to have attended the University of Manitoba and not McGill, just to throw people off the scent. Maude, whom I called Grandma, used to invest his earnings in the flourishing stock market of the 1920s, and was doing very well indeed thank you, until exactly October 29 of 1929, a date that found her on a transatlantic steamship, quite a long way from her brokers, even those who hadn't yet jumped out of twelfth-storey windows, taking Margaret to enrol at St. Andrews University in Scotland, a trip which she began as a woman of some means, at least on paper, and ended as a still-proud but less ostentatious member of a slightly lower class. Margaret's tuition, fortunately, had been prepaid, and she was later able to use the education she acquired at St. Andrews as, first, a book clerk — *clark*, as I'm sure her father would have said — in the Eaton's book department in Toronto, and, later, a librarian in Galt, Ontario, where she was able to introduce me to the riches of literature, including the works of the man from Orillia whose link to herself, and thus to me, I only was able to deduce in retrospect, from the enthusiasm with which she brought his latest books home for me to peruse.

The man called Greg, meanwhile, continued to be interested only in the farm he had bought in Prince Edward County — I'm sure now it was yet another way to strengthen the impression that he actually came from there — and in the law. His enthusiasm for the farm took him each night into the den of the small house the family lived in in Toronto, where he would talk endlessly to the oldest son of the Prince Edward County family that tended it for him, discussing the price of baling twine, the choice between snake fences and barbed wire, the high cost of hayseed and the low price of whole milk, the wisdom of more livestock in shaky times. His love of the law came out not so much in the courtrooms, though he continued to appear there, but in the academic posts he held at both Osgoode Hall and the University of Toronto. He kept an office in the cloisters at University College, and when I went there myself many years later, I would picture him in his wrinkled, well-worn gown, walking under the ivied shelter of the granite structure, his thumbs stuck in his suspenders, thinking his thoughts and smiling his smile.

My memories of him are dim: a gentle, crinkly man, who would come to kiss me good night when my mother and I stayed with her parents for a while after her divorce. He would tell me a bed-time story if I was still awake — I remember something about going into banks, though the details have faded — and sometimes croon me a song, often from the works of Stephen Foster which, with their smiling darkies and hearts that were young and gay, would be as incorrect now as some of the more pointed passages from the works of his other persona. He was not known for his love of children — among adults, according to his obituaries, he was a popular after-dinner speaker — but in his times with me he was warm and gentle. Somehow he made me feel like a grown-up. I remember one night when I tried to see how close I could hold a candle to the curtains that billowed over my bed without setting them on fire. Not as close as that, I learned — surely all good science involves testing the limits. My mother and grandmother were upset to the point of hysteria when I called for some help in dousing the flames, it seemed to me, or would have seemed if I'd known what hysteria was, but the man called McGregor Young, lawyer, farmer, raconteur, just laughed and laughed, and though he pitched in to the impromptu family bucket brigade, seemed more concerned about my safety than that of the house.

I'm not sure exactly when he died. Whoever clipped the obituary I have neglected to note the date. But I remember I wore long pants to his funeral, and that not long afterward the war ended, so I'd be ten, I think, which would make it 1944. Once, much later, I went to check on his tombstone; there are indeed a lot of Youngs buried in Prince Edward County, and his remains may well be behind the little church in Hillier, down the road from his beloved farm.

But I was on my way to Picton to make a speech, I think — the details are hazy — and too rushed to do much more than drive up and down the highway a few times, a highway I had last travelled on the back of the truck carrying giant canisters of milk to the cheese factory, and peer at the fields where I thought I remembered eating lush tomatoes still warm from the sun, the juices dribbling down my hairless chin, and felt the prickle of straw as the men threshed the grain, and smelled the sweet intoxication of manure. And I could find no sign of the house I remembered from our occasional summer visits, and in Hillier itself even the lady at the general store couldn't tell me where the graveyard was.

There's another mystery that lingers, too. Word in our family was always that Greg Young and the other Leacock, contemporaries, academics, popular lecturers, were friends, though in all our family archives and even here at the Leacock home I can find no picture of them together. Once, in fact, my grandmother Maude, who outlived McGregor Young by more than twenty years, asked me if someday I'd like the collection of first edition Leacocks in her library, signed, she said, to Greg, with affection, Stephen. Of course, I said, not wanting to show my excitement at the prospect. But when she died, in the 1960s, we could find no such books among her estate. Someone said she'd donated them to Upper Canada College. I've never looked. But if they were there, that would be appropriate, don't you think?

Peter Brown's Schooldays

from the introduction to A Sense of Tradition, *1988*

The older we get, I sometimes think, the farther back we see.

I was fifteen when I first went to Ridley, with a boy's sense of time. The school was sixty. Now, of course, with my own sixtieth birthday just beyond the next onrushing hill, sixty years seems but a blink of history. From where I stand now, the people and events of six decades ago — Howie Morenz as the scoring champion of hockey, Lindberg safely across the Atlantic, Charlie Chaplin making movies that still make us laugh — appear merely as early images from the period of history we still occupy, part of the continuous flow that has led us to Wayne Gretzky and space shots and Woody Allen.

But in 1950, when I was fifteen, sixty years was beyond imagining. The lovely brick buildings, their ivy clinging through the gentle Niagara winter, had been there, surely, forever; the stone walls of the chapel must have stood since time began. Two Gzowskis, brothers of my grandfather, had been among Ridley's first boarders, and, indeed, my own father, who had driven me that afternoon along the Queen Elizabeth, had been a student there himself at the time of Morenz and Lindberg and Chaplin. But as I stood bewildered in the dark hall of Dean's House on the eve of my own first term, with a generation of fresh-faced boys spilling out from the trains and cars that had brought them back from the holidays, greeting each other by familiar nicknames, swapping lies about life at home, filling the rough wooden drawers of their dressers with stacks of striped pyjamas and woollen socks — two dark pairs for Sundays — the history that surrounded me, and my own place in it, were as remote from my awareness as the fact that General Brock had marched his troops along a road not far away, or Laura Secord tugged her unwitting cow towards immortality.

And then, nearly four decades later, grey-bearded and seasoned by time, I had a chance to go to Ridley again.

I began, as perhaps I ought to have begun much earlier, to consider some of the ways in which Ridley had set its mark on my life. The more I thought, the more I was intrigued. For one thing, I realized that for a professional life that had appeared to stray far from Ridley's traditions, mine seemed constantly to be leading me across the paths of other graduates. Often, these encounters took place in the least expected of circumstances, with the least predictable of people. To take a few recent examples, the manager of a bookstore where I was hawking my wares turned out to be an old Ridleian, and, just when we were commenting on that fact, so did the young lady who had stood in line to have a book autographed for her mother's Christmas. The unit manager of my most publicized excursion into television at the CBC had gone to Ridley, I learned one night, but so, it occurred to both of us at about the same time, had the man who had invented that program and had stood steadfastly and at some cost to himself behind it in the bastions of the bureaucracy. The president of the university that flattered me most recently with an honorary degree is a Ridley graduate, and so is the president of a small railway in Alberta I interviewed the next week on radio, a jolly, black-bearded entrepreneur who quoted Boris Pasternak while he told me about the joys of driving his own locomotive over tracks the corporate giants had abandoned.

I come across Ridleians everywhere. On an airplane coming back from England, I meet, the champions of Henley, the Ridley crew, and find myself caught up in the exultation of their victory. The man who presents the best case for an elected senate I have yet heard on *Morningside*, the CBC radio program I host, not only went to the school when I did but played left end on the football line when I was the right end. The director of Michel Tremblay's brilliant plays in English is a Ridley graduate, the chairman of Union Gas, the head of Business Administration at Ryerson, where my daughter studied journalism, the man who runs one of the hottest outfits on the Ontario thoroughbred racing circuit (and who figured in a book I wrote about the track), the lawyer who did my first mortgage, the young woman who comes on *Morningside* to talk about life as a Muslim, the man who arranges a ride on the roller coaster for a young deaf woman who has won a contest I conduct in a newspaper column, the owner of the country club where I hold a golf tournament to raise money for Frontier College — where other Ridley graduates have served a noble cause — and, as I can sometimes forget, the man, now a distinguished neurosurgeon and academic, whose friendship I have treasured longer than that of anyone else in my life and who was, and still talks with happy nostalgia of being, the quarterback on the same football team as Robin Dunbar and me and the elected-senate spokesman and, come to think of it, the man who arranged the roller-coaster ride.

Except for my too-infrequent dinners with the quarterback/neurosurgeon, my encounters with my fellow Ridleians do not come about because of the experience we share. In nearly every case, we meet each other for other reasons and discover our common background coincidentally. Often, the moment of discovery occurs in the form of a tentative "didn't you go to Ridley?" based on some half-forgotten passage in a quickly read *Tiger*, or prompted by a casual remark dropped into an otherwise irrelevant conversation. At other times, a comment about a favourite teacher, a question about the difficulty of deciding where to send one's own children to school, or the name of a mutual acquaintance, sparks a surprised "Don't tell me you went to . . . ?"

Many gardens have been tended, in this country and elsewhere, and many dogs walked, by middle-aged men in orange-and-black sweatercoats still emblazoned with the achievements of youth, but in our day-to-day lives we wear no badges of our background, we Ridleians, and exchange no secret handshakes. Still, somehow we find each other, and, when we do, barriers drop; formality dissolves; we smile. It is possible, I know, to make too much of this feeling of familiarity, to see it as unique to Ridley, or as a central, motivating factor in our lives. It is not unique. The alumni of every school in history, from Eton to Edgehill to Miss Edgar's and Miss Champ's, have shared common experiences and, to one degree or another, have taken pleasure in that sharing. And though there are those whose lives have never been as full again as they were in their days of school, I suspect that my own experience, of putting much of Ridley behind me as I moved on to the other stages of growing up, is not so rare as I might have supposed. Other graduates may have attended more reunions than I have, or engraved their names on chairs, but I imagine that even they have kept their memories where I have kept mine, on the back shelves of their adult minds, and that they too have taken them down only occasionally to dust them off and see what they now hold.

To say that, though, is to deny neither the special qualities of Ridley memories nor, however far back the shelves, their importance in our lives. The memories are special, I think, because they are of a special school, lovely in its setting, noble in its aims, aware of its traditions. When we were there, the haunting aesthetics of the buildings and the grounds, the nobility of the ambitions and the depth of the traditions seeped into us. And whether we have realized it or not, they have lingered on. They are important to us because of that. The effects are certainly different in every case, but it is also true, surely, that just as going to Ridley affected our young lives, so has having gone there affected our maturity. For a while, we belonged to a school, and whether we admit it or not later on, that sense of belonging has marked us indelibly.

• • •

A sense of belonging had been a very tentative part of the life that preceded my own going away to school. My father and mother were divorced shortly after I was born. My mother married again, to Reg Brown of Galt, Ontario, and, although Reg did not legally adopt me, for the ten years before I went to Ridley, largely to avoid awkward questions about a name different than my parents', I had been Peter Brown — or, as my grandmother defiantly addressed her regular letters to me, Peter John Gzowski Brown. PJGB's home life, never a happy one, had, in my teenage years, turned sour. After a promising start, I had an increasingly dismal academic career, and, by the middle of what the Galt Collegiate called grade eleven — it was still fifth form at Ridley, though I would not have known that then — I stood twenty-seventh in a class of twenty-seven. I left for Toronto, ostensibly for the Christmas holiday, but in fact hoping for a new start. My father, still putting his own life together in the post-war bustle of the city, had little space for a son he barely knew. But he was upset at my unhappiness in Galt and disappointed by my academic collapse. He had happy memories of his time at Ridley, where he had shone in the choir and revelled in an opportunity to follow the family's military tradition. He called Dr. Hamilton, then in his first term as headmaster, and made an appointment. A small bursary (I learned much later) was arranged. My father confiscated my draped pants and tubes of Brylcreem, and took me shopping for grey flannels, white shirts and a blue blazer. He suggested that I drop my extra patronym and return to his. I agreed enthusiastically. My grandmother, delighted, sewed name-tags into my stiff new clothes. When the holidays were over, my father and I drove out the snowy Queen Elizabeth, passing between the stone lions that were to become so familiar — I still cannot see them without thinking I am on my way to school — over the bridge at Hamilton and along the lines of brown grapevines to St. Catharines.

I remember how strange it seemed. The year before I enrolled, I had played basketball in the Ridley gym. Jim Chaplin, who had taken a year off from his Ridley career to go to Galt Collegiate and have a bad back treated nearer home, had taken a team down to test his old schoolmates. To the rest of us, Chaplin's recruits, the crowd that gathered to watch our game might as well have come from, if not a different planet, then at least a different age. It was all male, for one thing, dressed similarly and, certainly by high school standards, well; even the boys in their curious orange-and-black sweatercoats, I noticed, wore white shirts and ties. But Chaplin — Jim, as I had called him at Galt, but Chaplin as I think of him from later friendship — seemed to know everyone there, and to share with them the vocabulary and experiences that sounded so foreign to his pick-up team from the public high school: old boys, new boys, prefects, slobs, first teams and second teams, a Latin grace rattled at incomprehensible speed in the dining hall — "dining hall" itself falling awkwardly on my ears — "houses" without kitchens, "dorms," "permission, please" cried out as younger boys waited at doorways, chapel, caning, teachers called masters, boys called by their last names, sometimes with numerical suffixes, or with the odd designations of "major" or "minor." I envied Chaplin his familiarity, not so much with the words — many of which, of course, I have dredged from my own later knowledge, the impression from my first visit being only that everyone I met seemed to talk like someone from *Chum's* — as with the environment. Even after most of a year away, he was comfortable with all the students of Ridley in a way that, even in the small and congenial city I had grown up in I, Peter Brown, had been comfortable only with the small coterie of my closest friends. He felt at ease. He belonged. And now, on my own first evening among them, as I unpacked my baggage in the melee of the Dean's House dorm, thinking of the taillights of my father's borrowed Morris Minor hurtling along the Queen E back towards the lions, I wondered if I would ever fit in.

• • •

Perhaps six weeks later: Five-B is at evening study in School House. I am getting the hang of things, even this strange custom of returning to the classroom from 7:30 till 9:30, when in Galt I would be sipping a lemon Coke at Moffat's or trying to make a pink ball in the side at Nick's. I am grinding at my Latin verbs. I had wriggled out of Latin in Galt, but here, under the unbending guidance of the soft-voiced firebrand the boys call Matty — the only teacher . . . the only *person* . . . I have ever seen who can bound backwards to his desk from a two-footed standing start — it is beginning at last to make sense to me. My sweatercoat, though still embarrassingly stiff and bare of crests, now feels comfortable on my shoulders, and I have learned to knot a tie before retiring, so I can pull it over my sleepy head as I jog the cracked concrete from Dean's House to breakfast. I am absorbing the words to hymns and to "Come Fill Your Glasses Up." I call teachers — masters — "sir" without pausing to think, and wait at doors for permission from my betters. I know how to fake a shoeshine and where to slip down the Hog's Back for a butt before dinner. I have served an hour for lipping a duty boy, inked my name on a grey-and-white striped laundry bag, written home with the latest hockey scores (and a request for more money for the tuck shop), skated in the gloomy rink, tried squash and lain awake at night thinking of the girls I left behind.

Not all has gone smoothly. I am at least a year behind in French, and, though I am still wide-eyed at the thought that one of my dorm-mates comes from Maracaibo (in Galt, people from *Kitchener* were exotic), I am envious of the boys from South America who are allowed to substitute Spanish, which they speak more fluently than the master. I am still confused not only by the speed of the pre-meal grace but by the answer we are supposed to offer when role calls are taken, "*ad sum,*" which to my ear sounds like "absent."

And, in an especially sad moment, after being summoned eagerly by Dr. Bett, who was the choirmaster in my father's day and still revels in the memory of his voice, I have demonstrated, while that gentle man looked on with steadily mounting dismay — I can carry a tune about as well as I can carry water in my cupped hands — that musical talent does not necessarily pass from generation to generation with the colour of one's eyes. Poor Sid Bett. It was as if Howie Morenz Junior had showed up at hockey camp and couldn't skate.

But I am beginning to fit in here. Day by day, Peter Brown of Galt, Ontario, is becoming Peter Gzowski of Ridley College, just Gzowski in the classroom, pronounced as my great-uncles and my father pronounced it, Zoski, and in the dorm and dining hall and gym, Gzosk.

The master in charge of study this evening is Mr. Cockburn, Twink to us all as he was Twink in my father's time. Now, as the clock nears nine, he has stepped out. As I ponder my Latin verbs, a row of blue dots appears as if by magic across the conjugation of *docis, docere*. Shiggy Banks, a rising star of heavyweight boxing in the school (he will beat E. St. Elmo Taylor in the dramatic final of our graduating year), has lobbed a stream of ink across my bow. He has aimed two rows over, at Jimmy Conklin, who has been at Ridley since he was a toddler, having been sent to the lowest form of Lower School by his father Paddy Conklin, king of the Canadian carnival circuit. There is no malice in Shiggy's shot. It is simply that Mr. Cockburn has twinkled out of the room and Conklin has happened to be looking in the wrong direction. Banks has seen a target too inviting to resist. But he has fallen short.

Splat.

Splat-splat-splat-splat-splat-splat-splat.

Drops of dark blue Skrip spread across my verbs, stain the rough oak floor, scarred by two generations of polished black shoes, scuffed by Sissman's Scampers. The drops have climbed the leg of Conklin's flannels. The biggest is at the top. The remainder run down to his cuff, like tiddly winks displayed in descending order of value. Conklin, feeling nothing, continues to write his English composition on the pale ruled lines of his scribbler. Banks reloads from his inkwell, two-handed. He fires again. A line of the blue splotches breaks out on Conklin's cheek. More of the shortfall stains the verso of my text. Conklin feels the cold impact of Banks' accuracy. He turns to retaliate, pen upraised. Banks has his head down, trying to look innocent, but the tell-tale tracks across my Latin carry Conklin's eye back to the instigator. Conklin fires, a graceful overhead. Too high! Banks ducks. Conklin's return fire arcs over Shiggy's head and bisects the brush-cut of Monk Fisher. Fisher sees Conklin's guilty grin, but, reacting as creatively as he does on the football field, spreads the war to yet another front, his own roommate Roger Widdicombe.

By now, hostilities are spreading. Incidental skirmishes break out on the perimeter. Pens dip to inkwells. Pump, load, slurp, fire. No one is safe. The air is wet with ink. Faces, white shirts, brown desks, the orange trim of sweatercoats, the beige walls, the pale trim of the blackboards . . . everything is spattered with blue Rorschach stains and arpeggios of polka dots. It is a free-for all, as infectious and liberating as a Roy Rogers brawl, with every Son of a Pioneer choosing a partner or, failing to find one, lashing out at whoever's handy. And I am in the thick of it, happily splashing, happily splashed. I drench Freddy Lapp. Harry Malcolmson drenches me. Norrie Walker hits a double — Bob Broad and John Girvin with the same roundhouse swing. Broad gets me. I go for Walker. By the time Mr. Cockburn returns, the damage is done. We are the sons of Harlech, drenched in woad. Our pens and our inkwells are empty. Our energy is drained, and on the wall of the classroom that separates us from the corridor of School House is an image I will store on the shelves of my memory as long as I live: the profile of Fred Millman, clear as a Beardsley cameo, but instead of being black on white, in unsullied pale beige against a back-ground of thickly speckled blue, where Millman has taken a mass assault while standing sideways to the painted surface.

We are to be punished. Mr. Cockburn needs to consult the highest statutes of Ridley law, and we will be dealt with on the morrow. We are in for it, I know. But as I trudge back to Dean's House, trying to match John Girvin's long strides, I feel as if I am going to the place where I live.

Gzowski of Dean's House.

Gzosk.

• • •

I went back to Ridley on a Friday in May of 1987, thirty-seven years after the ink-fight in the School House corral. In the years that had passed, Shiggy Banks — Robin Banks — had risen to academic distinction at the University of Waterloo. Jimmy Conklin, who stayed on at Ridley until he graduated and, with a full thirteen years under his belt, ran up a record for student longevity that can never be broken, has taken up his father's mantle and was, in fact, the man who arranged the roller-coaster ride for my contest winner. Roger Widdicombe had become an important businessman in his native St. Catharines, Harry Malcolmson a lawyer. Norris Walker had taken over his family gravel business and had been active in school affairs. And John Girvin, whose friendship I still cherish, who had not yet played football at Ridley when the ink-fight broke out — fifth form was his first year at the school as it was mine — went on to become first Ridley's quarterback, then the University of Western Ontario's and, later, one of the most honoured neurosurgeons in the land (he played an important part in experiments that may lead to the development of an artificial eye), and now heads an important medical department at the university where he played. I had lost track of some of the others, but I knew that there was at least one psychiatrist who had been in that fight, a banker, an historian, a classicist and a substantial number of company presidents, mandarins and, if my own case is any example, grandfathers. But as I walked the School House halls, past the rows of football pictures with our own team's achievements now part of the gallery that stretched thirty-seven years beyond and included some of its sons, past the door of the old dining room that now leads into a modern library, and towards the new hall, whose opening we attended but whose chairs and honour roles now hold so many of their names, I thought of them all as they were then. Ridley boys of the school's sixtieth class, still on the thresholds of their lives.

I wanted to see if I could come to terms with Ridley after all the years, to see, in the end, what it stood for in my life, and I knew the place to do that was at the school itself. I put away the comfortable sweater that is my working uniform at *Morningside*, dug a shirt, tie and jacket from my cupboard and headed off once again between the lions. Just after the morning bells had rung, I pulled into a visitor's parking spot in the circle in front of School House, thinking of the times when it had seemed an impossible dream just to be able to use the front door.

I climbed the steps under the carved crest and entered the familiar hallway. Inside, I was overwhelmed by change. The student who had been assigned to meet me and take me to breakfast was a girl. Under the stately plaque that dedicated the dining hall to "THE GLORY OF GOD AND IN GRATEFUL MEMORY OF REUBEN WELLS LEONARD, 1860-1930 AND KATE ROWLAND LEONARD . . ." someone had posted a notice for the "First Annual Spring Rock Festival" ("What to bring: a friend . . . a blanket . . . a bandanna . . . and [for masters] . . . yourself and a hearing aid.") The airy space of the hall itself — still the new hall to me, but now, to the students who crammed its blond tables, I was sure, as ancient and permanent as the ivied brick walls outside had seemed to me — was scattered with boys — and girls! — of exotic complexions. To my eye, the informal dress was as unexpected as once the conservative clothes of the fifties had appeared when I visited from Galt. Every chair that I could see, once unadorned, now boasted the name of a generous graduate. (Partly in memory of the ink fight, I sat on N. W. Walker, '48-'52.) The battered metal pitchers for our milk had been replaced by sleek urns, dispensing their contents with the efficiency of an airport cafeteria. A splendid Varley portrait of Dr. Hamilton, somehow capturing his shy warmth and stern demeanour, had joined the ranks of the — to me — anonymous dignitaries who had stared down at the repasts of my youth. Chinese surnames had joined the ranks of outstanding scholars and winners of the Mason Gold, spelled out in gold on the black plaques high on the wall. Chatter filled the air.

Still under the aegis of my guide, I left for chapel. As I made my way along the hall, I resisted the impulse to explain to her how many memories rushed back as I passed each doorway, how many ghosts I saw in front of the classrooms (was that Norm Shipley outside what is now the master's study? Did I see the Burner scribbling trig equations on a blackboard?) or telling her how things had been in the days when the world was young.

I squeezed into a pew and edged along the polished oaken bench. I remembered the Sunday evening Barbara Ann Scott had attended church with us, and we had missed part of the wisdom of the Reverend Good — the Rabbi — craning our necks to catch a glimpse of her. Would the young people squeezing in beside me, I wondered, know who Barbara Ann Scott was?

My eye wandered over the unchanging memorials on the soaring stone walls. The men who had died in the Second War, I thought, the Ridley cadets of the 1930s and early '40s, were separated from my own time at school by fewer years than separated me from the students who were here this morning.

I had hit upon an unusual day to go back. A few days earlier, the school had held an auction to raise money for charity, and one of the prizes had been the role of headmaster for this Friday. The winning bidder, whom I had met when, begowned, he had made a ceremonial entrance into the dining hall, had relaxed discipline for the day. As a result, I'm sure — and even the auction was a symbol of the changed and changing times — the proceedings of the day I returned were a departure from the routine. Even discounting that, though, I was struck by the degree to which Ridley customs had changed since I had been a student. The young people who clattered down the old passageway to the chapel and dropped their voices as they entered wore clothes and sported haircuts Hammy would have caned them for. They included, as well as the girls, whose presence I still found remarkable, enough brown and black and yellow faces to reflect — as indeed they do — a different world. They were, I knew, preparing to attend classes I would not understand in classrooms made incomprehensible by computers. They were thinking of sports that would not have occurred to my contemporaries, and their heads rang, no doubt, with the rhythms of rock and punk and fusion from the ghetto-blasters in their rooms. I could think only of how much time had passed since I had last been here. But then the chaplain said "the Lord be with you," and the young congregation comfortably and casually echoed, "and with thy spirit."

And then they sang "Jerusalem" and I knew I had come home.

• • •

I spent the rest of that bright May Friday at Ridley, trying, as best a grey-beard could, to fade in among the students. I attended an English class given by the accomplished novelist Richard Wright, and watched six boys and five girls rise to give oral presentations on subjects as varied as *Alice in Wonderland*, Colombian coffee, and pollution in the Niagara River. I marvelled not only at the variety of their cleverness but at the informality and ease of their relationship with their teacher. I sat in on physics with Brian Martin. My head spun as, using a video camera, an oscilloscope and a computer, he moved from the abstract theory of resonance to a demonstration of how to tune a guitar. I attended a pep rally led by screaming, shirtless athletes, strutting on the tables of the dining hall, and, invited by hand-delivered letter on official stationery, I shared a formal lunch with the temporary headmaster. I watched a set of mixed-doubles tennis and wished good luck to a crew of rowers — a sport unknown in my time but now perhaps Ridley's greatest claim to fame — on their way to a regatta they were favoured to win.

And yet, haunted by my epiphany in the chapel, I could not escape the feeling that it was also all the same. Richard Wright's English class had taken me back to the lessons of a man called J. F. Pringle — Jim Pringle, as I was to learn later, a wounded war veteran who stopped only briefly at Ridley before moving on to Northern Ontario, and who may not be remembered by many other graduates, but who touched me and planted in me a desire to write clearly and well, as Wright was obviously touching the students whose presentations I witnessed. Brian Martin's physics experiments took me back to David Fensom — Fingers Fensom as a generation of boys called him — whose delight in his science illumined his laboratory. The half-dressed students in the dining hall led the students in the same songs I had sung, and only the memory of Sid Bett's look of horror kept me from joining in as I huddled along the wall. And the young athletes I saw, I realized, whatever games they were playing, were in a direct line of descent from the football teams of H. C. Griffith himself, who showed the school the meaning of striving for excellence.

I looked, that afternoon, on the portrait of Dr. Griffith in the dining hall. I saw him now as I had not seen him when he was alive. I never played for him — or not directly. He had retired from his coaching career, as well as the headmaster's office, when I arrived, and Dick Farley, who played at Western with the storied McFarlane brothers from Ridley, had taken up his mantle. But on the night before the first game I played in the stiff old canvas jerseys, he came to a team meeting, bent with age but with the fire of competition still blazing in his eyes, and made us feel part of the legacy he had built. Even without his physical presence, I think, that legacy has been passed on — a continuous line from the great old football teams to the international champions of rowing and to other sports as well, a heritage of pride, changed only in the manner of its expression.

In everything I had seen that day, I now realized, and in everything else I was noticing about the modern school, the traditions I had known as a student were reflected as clearly as Dr. Griffith's impact on the football teams was reflected in the achievements of the rowers, or the inspiration of all the teachers who had gone before them by the English lessons of Richard Wright or the scientific experiments of Brian Martin. They had been adapted to fit a changing world. But their essence, like the responses in the chapel, had remained constant. And though the students who had that morning responded so comfortably "and with thy spirit" had dressed differently, listened to different music and aspired to different accomplishments in their school, they were as clearly the inheritors of those traditions as the prefects who that evening would race through grace with the same breath-taking speed were the heirs of Jim Chaplin, or Tom Storm or Darcy McKeough or all the other prefects of my own day. The history of Ridley was not a series of separate stages, I realized, but one continuous stream, changing and turning every year, but still flowing steadily from the beginning into the present and towards the future, each year carrying something new but also carrying and being driven by everything that had gone before.

The farther we look back, the closer we seem to be. The boys in their Eton collars who had arrived in their horse-drawn cabs had faced the same unknowns — and written the same letters home when they found the answers to them — as we had in 1950. As Dr. Hamilton had taken over from Dr. Griffith in my time, and served for a while in his shadow — just as succeeding headmasters were to serve for a while in his — so had Dr. Griffith taken over from Dr. Miller. As I had watched Andy Iggulden succeed Cap, so had my father known Cap as the heir to Colonel Thairs.

From the perspective age now gave me, I saw at last how recent were the buildings that had seemed so old to me. I knew now that just as Arthur Bishop House — AB to the students I met on my return — seemed strange to me, so too had Merritt House seemed strange to my father, that the chapel was much younger than time, that the rink I knew as old was not the original, that boys had once gone down the Hog's Back not to smoke but to swim, that the men I knew by reputation or as corpulent middle-aged visitors had once been new boys too, and had once stood bewildered in the same places I had. I learned that the Ink Fight of Five-B was not the first outbreak of its kind and I knew that even in the age of ball-point pens it would probably not be the last, escapades that, however much they break the rules, bind the boys together as strongly as team victories or school plays or cadet inspections, and form the stuff of anecdote and memory.

I felt as if everyone who had ever been at Ridley had been there at the same time as everyone else, and that there is a sense of the tradition we shared when we went there and, I think, will share forever, understanding more every year, knowing the old a little better as we strive to figure out the new.

A Taste of the Wild Frontier

Maclean's, *November 2, 1963*

One September evening, while *Maclean's* photo editor Don Newlands and I were roughing it in the bush, I had an extra-dry Martini on the rocks, some snails *Bourgogne*, a bowl of pea soup, beef tenderloin with mushrooms, fresh hot rolls, Mexican corn and a carafon of Beaujolais. I would have had a chef's salad too, but they were out of lettuce. Nothing is perfect.

Later, Newlands and I walked across the street to watch the bowling and billiards, and then back to our hotel to see what was doing at a candlelight dance there. Not much was. I went upstairs to telephone my wife and settle down with that day's edition of the Montreal *Gazette*.

All this took place, believe it or not — and as a one-time construction worker in the north, I am not certain I believe it myself — in a town called Wabush, Labrador, some two hundred miles north of Seven Islands, Quebec, six hundred and fifty air miles from Montreal and about the same from St. John's. With its twin settlement of Labrador City, three miles around a corner of the shore of Wabush Lake, Wabush forms a new mining community in Canada's far, or at least fairly far, north. Labrador City, which started producing iron ore this year, has a population of about three thousand.

Wabush, which will not start producing anything until next winter, has a population of about two thousand, of which seventeen hundred people are workers and the rest are members of their families. This may not be Canada's ultimate last frontier — let us hope we press much farther north in years to come — but for the moment it can be called that. Three years ago, Wabush was bush: a rough, scraggly, nearly lifeless wilderness. The hills in summer echoed only with the whir of the blackfly. The only way for a man foolish enough to want to go there was to do so by seaplane. The bush, like so many of the parts of Canada that have yet to be opened, had to be broken and tamed, and the men who broke it — the last frontiersmen — are a breed apart.

One of the subspecies of this breed is the college student. Boots shining, his university's name emblazoned across the back of his windbreaker to shout "greenhorn" to the world, his first, soft beard struggling vainly to be seen, the student labourer is as much a part of the modern expansion of Canada as the bulldozer. I served three terms as one of these typically Canadian frontiersmen on the three biggest construction jobs of my time. In 1954 I worked on the St. Lawrence Seaway. In 1953 I spent a summer at Kildala, the powerline project that was to link Kitimat, the aluminum refinery on the coast of northern British Columbia, with Kemano, the hydroelectric station that supplied it from fifty miles inland. The summer before that, though, 1952, I worked on the QNS and L, the Quebec North Shore and Labrador Railway. This experience was gained in the same part of the world as Wabush, and it was hell. The QNS and L was — as it is now — the railway designed to carry iron ore from the vast wilderness deposits around Knob Lake, three hundred and fifty miles north of the St. Lawrence, to Seven Islands on the river's north shore. It was a tremendous task, costing more than two hundred and fifty million dollars and employing as many as seven thousand men at a time. After a tortuous passage through the hills and canyons of Quebec above Seven Islands, it crawls two hundred miles across the soggy muskeg of Labrador. Until the head of steel approached its last stage, there were many engineers — good men at their jobs — who said no one could build a railroad where the QNS and L was going.

For many weeks that summer I wished they had been right. Untrammelled by labour legislation in either Newfoundland or Quebec, the construction companies that built the QNS and L treated the men who did the work like serfs. Bold and aggressive in their engineering, they seemed — to us in the camps at least — coldly unaware that it was, in the end, men who were doing the job. We slept frequently in filth. We ate, while plentifully (any machine needs fuel), dismally. In B.C. and on the seaway, conditions were better. But never, in the bush camps around where I was working only a decade ago, could I have imagined the new life on the last frontier as it is now lived in Wabush.

The hotel where I ate so well on my first night in camp is the aspect of Wabush that separates it most strikingly from the kind of Labrador bush camp I worked in as a student. Except for the rugged scenery outside the window — a dirt road in the foreground and the sweeping hills of spruce and tamarack beyond — this hotel, the Sir Wilfred Grenfell, could as easily be in Montreal as in a mining town. It has a curvy hostess named Christine, several pretty wait-resses, a couple of switchboard girls, comfortable, carpeted rooms, room service — everything, in fact, except radio or television, the lack of which one housewife in Wabush told me was the roughest thing about living there. The roughest thing about the Grenfell hotel is the prices: twelve dollars for a small single room and eight-een for a double. You can do better than that at the Ritz Carlton in Montreal. The meal I described set me back about six dollars.

These prices, of course, keep most of the hotel's facilities well out of the financial range of the working men. But the men are still able to — and do — use the tavern in its basement; beer there costs forty-five cents, but is obviously welcome after a day of slugging on the job. On the QNS and L, when it would have been more welcome still, we would have been fired for smuggling it into the camps. After our supper, we either sat around and talked or read, or, drugged by fatigue, tumbled between our dirty sheets.

The sheets at Wabush are changed every week. A man living in one of the company dormitories — the only place he can live if he is just a working stiff — can also have all the laundry done he wants. The company charges him five dollars a month for laundry anyway, and most of the men seem to take advantage of the service. The single men's dormitories are not unlike houses at a good boys' boarding school: three storeys of long, monastic halls, with two or four men in each numbered room. This summer, the camp was more crowded with construction workers than it will be with miners when the ore is being shipped out, and many of the rooms were holding twice the number of occupants they had been planned for, in double bunks. To a man who had seen labour gangs living in boxcars at the head of steel, with one sheet each and no place to wash, these rooms still looked comfortable.

At Wabush, with its showers in every bunkhouse, its laundry services and its women to be seen, there is, as one company official put it, "no excuse for a man not to be clean," and although the men coming off the job still do not look as if they'd just been rehearsing with the Toronto Symphony Orchestra, the camp sports few unkempt beards and few grimy shirts. Newlands and I travelled to Wabush with a group of newspapermen from around Toronto, and when we got on the plane, I and the one other reporter — an old northern hand — who was wearing a sports shirt, talked condescendingly of the greenhorns around us who were going to appear in *Labrador* wearing jackets and ties. As it turned out, no one is even allowed into the Sir Wilfred Grenfell dining room unless he is wearing a jacket.

Both the costuming and the food are a little different at the company cafeteria, but not as much rougher as one might expect. The men, still in their working clothes, queue up to get to spanking-clean, glass-enclosed steam tables, and other men, in white (more than sixty men work in the cafeteria), serve them their choices. One evening meal that I sat in on included, among many other items, fried chicken legs, corn on the cob, and ice cream. Ice cream! The bread is baked in the cafeteria basement every night, and comes up fragrant in the morning. About the only concession the cafeteria makes to its remoteness from what we used to call civilization is that the milk is powdered instead of fresh.

After dining, a man can saunter over to the company-built recreation hall, and shoot a little pool, or bowl. Twice a week there is a movie — eighty-five cents admission — in the rec hall's auditorium, and any week night, the men at Wabush can take a bus or a taxi over to Labrador City for a commercial show or a change of grub. Mail comes in by train twice a week, and can come anytime by air mail, as the Montreal *Gazette* does, arriving on the evening of the day it is published. If a man gets too lonely for home, he can call any place in the world by a microwave setup. You can direct-distance-dial into Wabush, but not yet out of it. Isn't progress wonderful?

Aside from the pub and the availability of the telephone, the characteristic that brings Wabush a long step forward from my time in the bush is the presence of women. This time, progress *is* wonderful. During the summer I worked on the Quebec North Shore and Labrador, I saw roughly as many women as I did champagne cocktails, but in Wabush, women are as common as — as cocktails, come to think of it. As well as the hotel employees, there are about three hundred wives, mostly of senior or managerial personnel. (To answer a fairly obvious question: no, there is no prostitution in Wabush; since the camp is on private property, and access to it is limited, the company can and does prevent the import of fallen doves simply by not importing them. The company's temptation to stray from the paths of mining and construction must sometimes be strong; a pretty red-headed switchboard operator in the hotel told me she had been offered as much as seventy dollars for her favours.) Shopping in Wabush is not good — there is only one store — and the women mostly drive to Labrador City where there is a shopping centre. This means one needs a car, but doesn't one in Don Mills, Ontario? Perhaps the only difference is that it costs seventy-two dollars to ship a car to Wabush from Seven Islands and, once one has it, there is nowhere to go except back and forth to Labrador City.

Prices are outrageous. Forty-five cents for a quart of fresh milk. Twenty-nine for a handful of cottage cheese. Nearly two dollars a pound for steak. One woman, with no children, told me her grocery bill often topped forty dollars a week, and there is one family there with eleven children.

The families live in row housing which is certainly as comfortable as many places I've looked at in Don Mills. There is quite a rigid grade system for distributing tenants — the map in the camp manager's office frankly lists "Class A" and "Class B" houses — and if Wabush were much bigger it could properly be accused of segregating income groups. The sameness of the houses in the rows has been camouflaged a bit by painting the woodwork different colours. The company does not furnish the houses, but pays the shipping costs for old employees it transfers to Wabush. Anyone hired especially for Wabush pretty well has to get his own belongings in as best he can.

There are schools in Wabush. The school system now is a temporary building that will eventually be converted to a housing unit. Perhaps the showpiece of the whole camp is a new two-million-dollar school that will have, under Newfoundland's cumbersome system, one wing for Catholic students, one wing for "amalgamated" (everyone else) and a common central section for such secular items as labs and a gym. This building, high on a hill with a stirring view of Wabush Lake, will be opened next fall, and will look after students from grade one to grade eleven. The Newfoundland government paid for most of the school, but the company subsidized the construction, and even now, the temporary Wabush school with its seventy-one pupils has a higher teacher-to-student ratio than Newfoundland's present run-of-the-catch.

Throughout this report, I have used "company" as a kind of euphemism for the powers that be. In fact, the powers are multifarious, and although Wabush will eventually be a "company town" — one of those sometimes beneficial and occasionally malevolent institutions that dot the Canadian north — it is now under the hands of so many different people that it is impossible to explain who it was that changed the last frontier without giving a brief history of iron mining in Labrador.

Mining men have known since 1900 that there were iron deposits in the heart of the wilderness, the Labrador trough. But for years no one believed it could be brought out economically — if at all. Although most of the iron in Labrador lies so close to the surface that it can be mined by bulldozers, it runs in such low percentages — the best ore is only fifty-two per cent iron — that transportation becomes a big part of the price. By the 1940s, though, it was evident that the vast Mesabi range south of Lake Superior, which had been supplying most of North America's iron, was going to run out, and the last Mesabi reserves were scarcely higher in grade than the best at Labrador. That was when a number of bold men and bold steel companies banded together to form the Iron Ore Company of Canada, and set about building their impossible railway to the richest deposits in the trough, at Knob Lake, three hundred and fifty miles from the St. Lawrence. Ever since 1954 when the QNS and L went through, Knob Lake, or Schefferville as it is now known, has been sending from five to twelve million tons of ore a year down to Seven Islands, and thence to the steel mills of North America.

Since 1954, however, the people who work with iron ore have learned a lot more about it. New experiments, many of them conducted on the dwindling Mesabi reserves, showed how ore could be concentrated at the mine, and by the late fifties, it was evident that there were many places other than Knob Lake that would, with the new processes, yield ore profitably. John C. Doyle, the promoter, began developing some property he had acquired control of around Wabush Lake, more than a hundred miles closer to the St. Lawrence than Knob Lake, and only thirty-eight miles from the QNS and L. Shortly after, the Iron Ore Company, still working away around Schefferville, began developing another property it owned at Wabush. The ore in both IOC's and Doyle's land at Wabush is much lower in iron content than that at Knob Lake. Most of it runs about thirty-seven per cent. But with the new processes it can be worked up to as high as sixty-seven before it is shipped. This means that the ore shipped from around Wabush Lake will be richer than that from around Knob, as well as being closer to the port at Seven Islands.

Doyle began building a spur line from the QNS and L. Then he worked out a scheme with IOC for jointly financing the new line as far as Labrador City, where the IOC ore is, and paid for the remaining three miles to Wabush himself. IOC, because it was already an operating company, got the jump on Doyle in developing the new deposits by a couple of years, and when we arrived in Wabush to see what the last frontier looks like, Lab City, with its mine and its concentrating plant both working full blast, seemed already more of a town than a camp.

Doyle couldn't have financed his own developments by himself. Eventually, he worked out a consortium of American, Canadian and European steel companies to form a new company called Wabush Mines. Wabush Mines, in turn, will be run by Pickands Mather, a firm that acts as managing agents. And PM, as it is called, handed out contracts for constructing the mine and camp to a number of different construction firms, principally Henry J. Kaiser of Canada. These construction firms started work on Wabush only in 1960 and have already brought it along to the state I have tried to describe here.

For all the softness of life on the frontier compared to the camps I knew, no one has yet learned how to make it pleasant for the working man. No movie theatre, no bowling alleys, not even any beer parlour, can ease the brain-crushing monotony of labour in the north. No ice cream can compensate for the blackfly; no steam cafeteria for the slicing cold. They can bring in mail every hour on the hour, but a man who can't afford to get an airplane out or bring his family in is going to feel as isolated as if he were on the moon.

Life in the camps of the north has some things in common with the life of Ivan Denisovich. A whistle sounds at 5:00 a.m., and the men stumble groggily from their bunks. Breakfast ends at seven, and many of the men have to be on the job well before that. All day long they seem to be in queues, so many working machines with numbers. Unless they're among the first arrivals, they queue for breakfast in the cafeteria. They queue to catch buses or trucks to where they're working. At 11:30 (travel in and out of camp for lunch is on their own time), they come back in on the buses and queue for lunch, then queue again to go out on the job. Again to get a beer after work. Again for supper. Again for mail, or to pick up laundry. With the mixed tongues of Newfoundland, the Gaspé, Italy, Portugal and a score of other countries, men often spend hours alone with others they cannot talk to or comprehend. At night they lie around the bunkhouses, listening to someone's record of a cowboy tune or playing cards desultorily, or just lying there letting the fatigue drain out of their bones. They go to sleep early.

Men go north to make money, and now, as when I was in the camps, one hears grumbling about the lack of opportunity to work overtime. Wages have improved as much as fringe benefits in the last ten years, but a man slugging away with a pick or shovel at Wabush still gets only $1.65 an hour for ten hours a day, six days a week. Anything over that is time and a half. Even bulldozer operators make only $2.20 an hour; a general foreman $2.50. The company charges sixty dollars a month — two dollars a day — for eating at the cafeteria, and anywhere from fifteen to about thirty for the man's room. With laundry on top and without deducting taxes or his own incidental expenses, a labourer might clear three hundred and fifty dollars a month. The construction companies that have done most of the hiring so far have used Wabush as their point of hire, which means that a man must pay his own way in from Seven Islands or Montreal or St. John's. Wabush has an arrangement with the Newfoundland government to see that sixty per cent of the men employed here will be from Newfoundland and the camp echoes with the musical accents of the island, but Newfie labourers, as I remember from my own days in camp, get homesick very quickly. Nobody keeps figures on the turnover of labour but the airport at Wabush, which has three airlines servicing it, is busy most days with men coming in or going out. One can't help thinking that a lot of the men on their way out must be far short of the stake they hoped to get when they agreed to go to Labrador.

After a few days of living and observing the new soft life, Newlands and I boarded a passenger car at Labrador City to travel over to and then down the QNS and L to civilization and television. I had enjoyed our visit, and was impressed by the changes we had seen. But after a few days among the square, regimented living quarters that looked so like a concentration camp, I felt a tinge of exhilaration at escaping. On the train I got to talking with a general foreman who was on his way out with a bad back. He was a veteran of many construction campaigns in the north. I told him how impressed I'd been. "Yes," he said. "It's a good camp, the best I've ever been in. But they're all pretty much the same."

First Splashes of Printer's Ink

from The Private Voice, *1988*

I was born in 1934, in Toronto, where both sides of my family had roots. My parents were divorced soon after I arrived. My father, the Colonel's first child and only son, went wandering until war broke out, and my mother, the daughter of a successful and well-connected lawyer, remarried. My mother was a stylish woman, educated at Toronto private schools and in Switzerland and with an M.A. from St. Andrew's University in Scotland, which she acquired when she was nineteen. She was quite beautiful, too, or so I remember, tall and tranquil, given to the big, floppy hats of the time, with a taste for the verse of Dorothy Parker and the music of her jazz-age youth. In Galt, she became the children's librarian, and a minor star of the Little Theatre, but her life was not happy. She chafed and strained in her confining marriage. The tension affected me as well. My school marks, which had been respectable in the early grades — I could read before I went to kindergarten, thanks to her — plummeted in my teens. I developed terminal acne.

I took back my patronym, and, under the discipline of a private school, my marks picked up enough for me to win a couple of scholarships to university, where I proceeded in the fall of 1952. The university scholarships didn't work out. I couldn't decide what I wanted to study. I enrolled in arts but, free from the obligatory routines of private school, I studied fraternities at Zeta Psi and draft beer at "the KCR" — the King Cole Room of the Park Plaza. A couple of months into my second year, I realized I was going nowhere and dropped out. With some summer experience in heavy construction in Labrador and B.C. under my belt, I tried some surveying with half a mind to return to study the family profession of engineering — one of my scholarships had been in maths and physics — and then took off for Timmins.

That was the autumn of 1954. I can mark it by the descent of Hurricane Hazel on Toronto. I can still remember huddling in my grandparents' attic apartment on the night before I left, listening to the emergency on the radio and wondering what it would be like to be out there with a notebook, asking questions, jotting down history as it occurred, maybe even helping to rescue survivors — "Young Reporter's Courage Saves Child's Life." I remember, too, the devastation of the countryside outside the train windows the next morning.

In Timmins, I was a long way from writing for the front page.

I'm still not sure what pulled me into the career I chose, even though, now, I can't imagine having done anything else. Mostly, I think I wanted to be a writer, or at least to try it for a while. I'd written a bit as a student, mostly bad poems and clumsy short stories. I read voraciously, if not well, and many of the people whose work I enjoyed — Hemingway, Lardner, Runyon — had come from newspaper backgrounds. In Toronto, I had looked up Ed Mannion, an ad salesman who played badminton with my mother in Galt and who had been promoted to the national office of the Thomson chain. There was an opening in Timmins, he said, where Roy Thomson had started. It wasn't a reporter's job, but if I was prepared to sell ads for a few months — and who knows whether that might lead to something? — maybe I could move to the newsroom later on.

I was, I think, the worst salesman in Thomson history — an ambitious claim, I realize, in a chain where the news was often regarded as grey material to separate the ads, but one I'm prepared to justify. I couldn't sell anything. As the new boy on the block, I was given as my list of prospects everyone else's leavings, the deadbeats and the grouches, the merchants whose sisters-in-law's picture had been out of focus on last week's women's page. On top of that, I didn't believe in what I was selling. I was sure I'd never bought anything from an advertisement in my life, and I couldn't see how anyone else could have, either. Though I worked diligently with the Thomson training manuals and with books on salesmanship — "don't sell the steak sell the sizzle" — I couldn't subdue my doubts. Instead of applying the tricks, I used to believe the excuses my prospective clients offered. One haberdasher on Pine Street so overwhelmed me with his tales of woe that, instead of convincing him, as the manuals suggested, that the worse his business was going the more he ought to advertise, I bought a hat from him, a black homburg that set me back about a week's salary (forty dollars). I wonder now what a picture I must have presented in the weeks that followed, a weed of twenty, still not over the ravages of acne, pounding the pavements of the Porcupine in headgear that would have looked too pompous on Louis St. Laurent.

At nights and on weekends, and over drafts in the Double L — the Lady Laurier hotel, across the street from the *Daily Press* — I pestered the reporters and editors from the newsroom for a chance to show my stuff.

Some stuff. The first published piece in the oeuvre of Peter Gzowski, O.C., D.Litt., LL.D. (Hon. Caus.), is a five-paragraph account of a speech given to the Beaver Club of Timmins, Ontario, by someone whose name has mercifully been lost to history. In spite of the fact, however, that the putative author slaved for several hours over those paragraphs, pecking laboriously with the beginnings of the four-finger system that serves him still, the truth is that nearly every word in them was dictated — or typed impatiently while I looked on — by Robert Reguly, a rough-hewn ex-smoke-eater from Saskatchewan, who had worked on the *Winnipeg Free Press* before drifting in to Timmins, and who went on from there to win fame and national awards at the *Toronto Star* by tracking down Gerda Munsinger in Munich and Hal Banks on the docks of the eastern seaboard.

In certain circles, it is fashionable to decry the papers of the Thomson chain as, on the one hand, exploiters of young talent and, on the other, graveyards for the old. To a large extent, they are, or have been, both those things. In my own days in Timmins — and, later, in Moose Jaw and Chatham — I worked in newsrooms made up of odd mixtures of the unprepared young and the washed-up old, men with broken dreams, working their weary way around the country, from city room to city room. In between, on every paper where I worked, was a smattering of home-grown journeymen (the women were pretty well confined to the church socials and wedding announcements), capable enough, but uninspired and uninspiring.

But there was another pool on every paper as well: aspiring Ring Lardners like myself, starry-eyed and awkward at the typewriter, or immigrants from the British Isles or Australia or New Zealand, many of them graduates of the strict apprentice programs of their homelands, or good young pros like Reguly, putting the finishing touches on their own experience.

We were, all of us, studying a craft. From the veterans and the vagabonds, we picked up what we could in anecdote and experience. We read everything about newspapers we could put our hands on. We devoured magazines, and, in our spare moments, sent them overreaching queries, double-spaced and with self-addressed, stamped return envelopes, as we were told to do by *Writer's Digest*. We conducted post-mortems on each other's copy. We memorized the *Canadian Press Style Book* (you can spot us still, by our ability to spell accommodate or to differentiate between imply and infer). We worked long hours and talked longer ones. And, when we were ready, we moved on. Sure, the Thomson stories were true, or most of them: of pencil stubs that had to be turned in to justify a new issue, of bus tickets handed out grudgingly to dispatch reporters to fast-breaking news. But on daily newspapers that might not have stayed alive in a couple of dozen small Canadian cities without the

Thomson parsimony, and in the days before journalism schools, hundreds and hundreds of us got a chance to try our hands. Under-trained, under-rewarded and far, far under-qualified for what we were doing, we were, nevertheless, reporters. We sat in at the places where the news was made. We knew the heady thrill of spilling the inside stuff. And the intoxication of that feeling is with many of us still.

I remember my first by-line, some weeks after my Beaver Club report. To the relief of the advertising department, I'm sure, I had finally badgered my way onto the reportorial staff, and I occupied a desk in the city room, right next to Austin Jelbert, who knew every cop in the Porcupine by his first name. I wrote obituaries and service-club announcements, accident round-ups, and, when Jelbert was too busy, courtroom briefs. Tie loosened, a cigarette turning to ash against the gunmetal grey of the desk top, I rattled the keys of my Underwood with increasing speed and learned how to take a story on the typewriter with the phone cradled against my neck. And then, one day, I saw the city editor pencil my name in capitals across the first take of my copy:

By PETER GZOWSKI
Daily Press staff

The paper closed at eleven in the morning in those days — only the laity would have said "went to bed" — and it was our ritual to retire to a coffee shop on the main street after we'd wrapped it up. On the day I awaited seeing my name in print, we sat at a round table, and the waitress — whom our news editor later ran away with to San Francisco — came to take our orders.

"Coffee and french fries," said Reguly.

"Just coffee," said Jelbert.

"Chocolate milk shake," said Chris Salzen, now a news execu-tive on the prairies.

And so it went until she came to me.

"Yes?" she said expectantly.

"Peter Gzowski," I said, then changed it to a coffee and two doughnuts before I could add, "of the *Daily Press* staff."

Timmins.

I joined the Little Theatre, played the male lead in *Springtime for Henry*, opposite Denise Fergusson, who lives and works at Stratford now, and, when no one else was available, wrote the *Daily Press* review myself, finding myself adequate, but Denise (thank heaven, as I read the clipping now) much better. With growing confidence in my critical faculties, and, of course, a year and two months of higher education, I took over much of the cultural beat for the *Press*.

I won my photography award one weekend, when more senior reporters had better things to do. It was the spring of 1955. Forest fires were scorching Northern Ontario, and I was in charge not only of covering for emergencies, but of running around in the *Daily Press*'s fire-engine-red panel truck and taking pictures with the office Speed Graphic, which all of us had to master. I drove to the edge of a terrifying blaze. At its perimeter, I found a tree bearing a sign warning of the dangers of forest fire. On a second tree, not far away, was a second sign, this one on the dangers of smoking.

Aha! There was no one around, and, though the fire was licking steadily closer, I had time to remove the sign about cigarettes and tack it carefully just below the general warning: a matched pair framed on the trunk of a symmetrical spruce. I put a fresh four-by-five slide into the Speed Graphic and stood back.

Nothing.

The spruce stood unscathed.

I ran to the truck and moved it away from the encroaching wall of flame. I could see brown scorch marks on the red paint. I parked the truck in what appeared to be a safe spot and returned to my vigil.

Setting myself in position, I raised the Speed Graphic again and squinted into the view-finder.

Nothing again. My spruce stood in unspoiled symmetry, a cool green sentinel amid the onrushing inferno.

"Catch *fire!*" I screamed at it against the roar of the wind.

It stood.

The world grew hotter. The roar grew louder.

Every tree in creation seemed to be aflame. Except mine. I put the Speed Graphic on the ground, ran desperately to the very edge of the surrounding fire, ripped a small branch from a jackpine and plunged it into the flaming underbrush till it caught. Then I sprinted with my torch back to the tree I had prepared for fame and — how good it feels to tell the truth at last! — I set the perfect spruce alight myself.

The picture, with flames framing the warning signs in terrible irony, won the Canadian Press Photo of the Month Award for May 1955, and made, as I recall it, five columns that Monday on the front page of the *Telegram* in Toronto, the big time.

The Graduation of a Canadian Sex Symbol

University of Toronto Convocation Speech, June 19, 1995

Among the many things I learned in my brief newspaper adventures in Northern Ontario was how little I knew about everything. I went back to school, picking up more or less where I'd left off. I didn't quite graduate this time, either, but many chapters of my life later, the University of Toronto presented me with an honorary degree. Here are some of my remarks on that happy occasion — perhaps the proudest day of my life.

Madam Chancellor, President, Acting Principal, honoured guests, family members — including, I am delighted to say, my own — members of the faculty and — at last I get to say this — my fellow graduands.

This is a splendid day for all of us, isn't it, and, not least because it's taken me a bit longer to reach this stage than I dare say it has you — I wonder if I may be setting a record here for elapsed time between date of enrolment (1952 in my case) and graduation (1995) — I am honoured to be among you. I am also honoured — and moved — by Professor Clarkson's flattering citation, the more so, I'm sure, because it comes from someone who has so gracefully combined the rigours of scholarship and the skills of my own craft.

But as complete as your account was, Stephen, I wonder if I might just add a couple of details which, if you'd been aware of them, I'm sure you would have included yourself.

(1) I was the answer to 18 Across last month in the cryptic crossword in *Frank Magazine*, a publication I never read, of course, but whose contents I somehow remain aware of. The clue mentioned something about "going downhill" (as in "ski," you see), and called me the "tiresome broadcaster," which is as close as *Frank* gets to acclaim, and (2) — and I'm quite surprised that Professor Clarkson missed this — I am that rare creature, a Canadian sex symbol. Lest you doubt this obvious truth, let me point out only that this very morning, as I strolled about in my cap and gown, there was yet another encounter of a sort I have experienced all over this country. I was approached, as I have been so many times, by a winsome young woman, fair of countenance, gentle of bearing. As so many others of her description have done, she approached me shyly. "Excuse me," she said deferentially, "but aren't you Peter Gzowski," and when, equally shyly, I replied that yes indeed I was, she said, as say her counterparts from coast to coast to coast, "My mother is your greatest fan."

• • •

I did two very smart things early in my life. The first was to be born in 1934, a year in which almost no one else was being born — the Depression, you understand — and by the time I reached working age, in a booming, post-war economy, the competition was not for jobs but for bodies who could fill them. When I began in what is now called journalism (I thought it was just finding stuff out and telling people about it) you could — and we did — hold a meeting of all the people who were starting out with me in the roof bar of the Park Plaza. Now, as I constantly remind the two of my children who are, more or less, following in my footsteps and who are sometimes frustrated that their rise through the ranks appears — so far — to be a bit slower than their father's, you could pretty well fill the SkyDome with the people competing with them (which, come to think of it, is better than the Blue Jays have been able to do this year) and everyone in the Dome that day would be, as are my own children, smarter, better trained and better qualified than I was when I began — or, for that matter, am now.

The second clever thing I did was to come to this university. I came in the golden fall of 1952 — all falls are golden when you are eighteen — and the course of my passage here, and, I sometimes reflect, of my life ever since, was set by serendipity. The boys from the boarding school I had attended had traditionally gone, if they chose the University of Toronto, to the Anglican establishment bastion of Trinity College. But somewhere along the line, one of its more enlightened alumni had endowed a scholarship for a boy who would pick instead the more democratic University College — UC, as I came to know it. Needing whatever financial help I could get, I seized the opportunity — and the $300.

I quickly found myself in a situation I wasn't used to. For the first time in my sheltered life, I was in a minority. The college system on which this university had been built — a "community of communities," surely, before Joe Clark turned the phrase — was based, in those days at least, almost totally on religion. The Anglicans went to Trinity, the Catholics to St. Mike's, the Methodists and the Presbyterians to Victoria, and the rest to UC. In the 1950s — how remote this seems now — "the rest," in Toronto, meant largely Jewish, children of the immigrants who had worked their way up from what had been the ghetto of College and Spadina to Forest Hill and northward, and in 1952, as a saying of the time had it — and which may indeed have stuck in my mind this morning as I thought about the roof bar and the SkyDome — you could hold a meeting of all the gentiles in UC in the Junior Common Room phone booth.

For someone who had coasted through high school on a modest gift for last-minute study, it was an eye-opening place to be — the college, that is, and not the phone booth. I still remember watching in awe at the first session of a survey course of English literature, when the professor went round the room to see who had read what in preparation, and nearly every hand went up for nearly every work, from *Gulliver's Travels* to *The Love Song of J. Alfred Prufrock* — every hand, indeed, except mine, for the Book of Job. And so it went in every course I took. I was surrounded by students of an intellectual vigour I had never before seen. It was four generations since the first Gzowski had come to these shores, and the drive to excel that these children of immigrants brought to their studies was not part of my make-up. Being among them was both a privilege and an inspiration. And in the years since, as my classmates have risen to positions of power and influence — they have included the leader of at least one political party, the presidents of at least two universities, two deans of law, and more scholars, judges, bureaucrats and business leaders than I can recite — I have remembered the dedication with which they began their passage through life, and reflected often on the message of their success.

I have led, since I left these halls, a chequered career. In the first year I didn't graduate, when all of my friends who did went to Paris and London and Zagreb, I went to Moose Jaw, Saskatchewan. Since then, as they say in my business, I have pounded the same beat, from Pangnirtung to Prince George to Portugal Cove. I still haven't been to Paris, except the one on the Nith River in Ontario, where Wayne Gretzky's grandmother used to live, but I've been to Aklavik seven times. In my travels, and at the listening post I've been lucky enough to occupy on national radio, I've witnessed revolutionary change — in politics, in the work place, in the relationships between men and women, and, certainly in our cities, in the very nature of our population. And nothing has so invigorated me as the knowledge that the waves of immigration that have followed the people whose children I went to university with have also brought new energies and new visions to the land we share.

This is a great country, staggeringly beautiful, endlessly welcoming, constantly surprising. You have to know it as well as I have come to know it to know that no one will ever know it at all. Further, by the time some of you have a chance to stand here and challenge some graduands of the future — and to talk about how your class-mates have risen to the élite — it will have changed in ways we cannot now possibly foresee. But the course it moves on will be yours to set, and the hopes of those of us who pass it on to you are high.

I want to say one more thing about our common experience, yours and mine.

I loved it here — loved being young, loved being foolish (one of the wonderful things about having the privilege of editing *The Varsity* in those days was the opportunity to find out what not to do), loved the sense of beginning to learn. But it was not until many years later that it began to dawn on me what being here had really meant. For all the inspiration of my UC classmates, I was a casual scholar. Even after dropping out for a while, discovering how little I was prepared for the harshness of the real world — holding the rod on a survey crew, in case you haven't tried it, is very cold work — and then coming back, I wasted too many opportunities. In my final year, the first year I didn't graduate, the seductive pleasures of *The Varsity* kept me from too many lectures; I was writing while I should have read.

But for a while, I had been among greatness. I'd been on the campus of Northrop Frye and Marshall McLuhan, had been taught political science by C. B. MacPherson, history by Maurice Careless, economics by V. W. Bladen, philosophy by Emil Fackenheim. I may not have learned how to practise it, but I knew what scholarship was, and in the heady debates in our old residence at 73 St. George, and along fraternity row, and in Hart House and the JCR I saw and was beguiled by its results. I have, I hope, been beguiled ever since, and have had the lifelong pleasure of trying to answer my own curiosity.

The School of Heady Mistakes

from The Private Voice, *1988*

My time at *The Varsity*, from the fall of 1956 to May of '57, was as happy a sojourn as I've ever spent, a medley of golden autumn, frothy beer, Caraban weekends in Montreal, Belafonte songs, happily quarrelsome editorial conferences, self-indulgent crusades, carefree editorials and, at last, the glorious release of spring. On the university rolls, I was a third-year student in General Arts, headed for a degree, but in practice I went to no classes and wrote no essays. I was the editor of the student paper, and that was my life.

The Varsity of the time, a tabloid which appeared on campus every weekday morning, was the largest student daily, as we used to say, in the British Commonwealth. It had a long and distinguished tradition, having published, over the years, the early writings of Stephen Leacock, C. P. Stacey, Andrew Allan, and Johnny Wayne and Frank Shuster, among others. For all the past glories, though, it's hard to imagine that any editor could have walked into as promising a nest of aspiring journalists as I did. John Gray and Elizabeth Binks were junior reporters when I took over as editor; John is now the national editor of the *Globe and Mail*, and Elizabeth, who married him after graduation, is now the Liz Gray who has regularly beaten me for ACTRA awards at the CBC. Cathy Breslin, an American who was studying at St. Michael's College and who wrote a column for us, hit the best-seller ranks a while ago with a novel about, I think, the rape of a nun. John Brooks, who was the sports editor, is now an executive at the *Toronto Star*. Bill Eppridge, who walked into the office one day and offered to take pictures, went on to *Life* magazine and won honours for his work in Vietnam. And so on. Other people who worked on *The Varsity* when I did excelled later in other fields — most notably, I suppose, Michael Cassidy, the NDP MP from Ottawa — but it is the journalists I remember, and the excitement of trying our wings together.

We were creatures of our time. Not many years after we moved on, the university press turned earnest and political, and on many campuses, including Toronto's, the newspapers were focal points of what came to be called the New Left. But we were there in the fifties, when the world looked bright and secure. With rare exceptions — I remember, for example, a front-page editorial I wrote about the Soviet invasion of Hungary, which I entitled "Our Generation's Spain," and in which I urged my contemporaries to go overseas and fight to defend my freedom — the issues we tackled were mundane or callow. Canadian politics, with Uncle Louis at the helm, seemed dull to us, and, 1956 being an election year in the U.S., we took part in a campaign to run Pogo for president. We opposed student apathy and censorship in the rare-books room and stood foursquare for more parking and lower fees. We ran football stories on the front page and news of our own doings inside; Cathy Breslin, for heaven's sake, wrote one of her most memorable columns about me. But we got the paper out every night, even when one of us had to sit in our basement office making a column out of nothing while the rest stalled the printer's courier with the offer of an extra beer. We learned as we went, not only the seductive thrill of having a forum in which to speak our minds, but the effect of what we wrote on the life around us, and many of us, not only from *The Varsity*, have stayed in the business we discovered at school.

The generation that has followed us is far better trained. From the perspective of age, I sometimes wonder if I would have done things differently if I'd had more background than I had picked up in Timmins or at the *Tely* or in the basement of *The Varsity* before I assumed my first real command. But even in my most sombre moods, I know I wouldn't trade those heady days for anything. There is much to be said for learning by doing, and having a place to make mistakes on your own.

Besides which, I don't think I've ever had such fun.

The Editorial That Changed My Life

The Varsity, *Thursday, January 24, 1957*

Like most cities of comparable size, Toronto has established a few characteristics all its own. Smoky air, blinds-down Sundays, a too-short subway and Casa Loma are all unique to Toronto.

But probably its most extraordinary feature is its afternoon newspapers. Certainly nowhere in North America, and probably nowhere in the world, do two journals compete with such fierce intensity as do the *Telegram* and the *Daily Star*. Their competing headlines are flashed hourly across Canadian Press wires; their rivalry has become an institution.

Occasionally, this mutual jealousy acts in the interest of the Toronto newspaper reader. If the *Telegram* has reasonably complete coverage of a story, it is a certainty that *Star* readers will be treated to at least as full information within the next edition or two. If the *Star* buys a new feature for its readers, it is not long before the *Telegram* will come up with one of equal appeal.

But it is not always so. There is no need to list here examples of stories that have been driven to extremes by the interaction of the two newspapers.

Last Saturday, a five-year-old girl was brutally murdered in a Toronto ravine. According to even responsible journals, the crime was as fiendish as senior police officers could remember in this city's history.

The *Star* and the *Telegram* went to work. From every conceivable angle they wrote about the horrible crime, exposed the anguish of the parents, brought in similar crimes of the past two years, hunted descriptions of the killer. All these examples were within the realm of good — if sensational — journalism, and may have had no small part in the intensity and so-called success of the manhunt which took place.

The worst is yet to come.

Late Monday night an arrest was made and a seventeen-year-old schoolboy was charged with the murder. Charged, that is, and innocent until proven guilty. He is a suspect in the case and can be called no more until he is brought to fair trial under a Criminal Code, which applies as equally to sex maniacs as to newspaper editors.

The *Star* and the *Telegram* both ran pictures of the youth, and each tried to out-do the other in digging up his background. "This is Peter Woodcock," screamed the one. "Did the same murderer commit other crimes?" bellowed the other.

The libel laws of Canada are very broad indeed. Probably a reader could search and search through both newspapers without finding the actual statement that Peter Woodcock killed Carol Voyce. (Unless you could count the *Star*'s description of their artist's conception of the murderer as being in fact a picture of Peter Woodcock.) But every word in both papers was designed to show that the police had arrested the murderer.

We doubt if one single citizen who would qualify for jury duty could honestly state that he had not already made up his mind (or had it made up for him).

And worse, under the technical terms of the law, was the printing of the boy's picture before he had been sent through a line-up. What person who had perhaps seen someone near the recent murder scene could fail to pick young Woodcock from a line-up of fifty boys?

Competition is the spice of good journalism, as it is of almost any business: and we would be the last to suggest control of the press. But freedom to write the news has been hard-won and is a dearly cherished property of all who respect that profession.

We hope such clear defiance of good conduct — not to mention the law of the land — will not occur again in Toronto, and we hope that this performance is severely criticized in the courts.

If not, Peter Woodcock may be an innocent sacrifice on the altar of sensational news competition.

Postscript:
It did not occur to me when I published this little essay in The Varsity *how widely it would be read off campus. The Canadian Bar Association, meeting in Niagara Falls, read a copy into its proceedings, chastising the* Telegram *in particular, and the* Globe and Mail *reported the chastisement. Unfortunately for my short-term prospects, I had been earning a modest income for the* Telegram *to keep them supplied with campus news. They fired me. I would not have enough money to finish my school year. Fortunately for my long-term prospects, the Moose Jaw* Times-Herald *was looking for a young city editor, and I was at least affordable. Equally fortunately, Ralph Allen, the editor of* Maclean's, *also became aware of my scrape with the authorities, and made a note of my name. Later on when I had moved to another Thomson paper, this one in Chatham, Ontario, he remembered it, and called to ask if I was interested in a job at* Maclean's. *I thought that over for about a quarter of a second, and in the fall of 1958, set off to begin my life with magazines. I have often wondered since if I'd never written about the* Tely's *transgressions, I'd ever have gone to Saskatchewan or worked at* Maclean's.

Greenhorn in the Heartland

Maclean's, *July 25, 1964*

I realize that anyone who was there will find this a pretty naive thing to say, but I sometimes wish I had lived in — or at least got to know — Saskatchewan in the 1930s. The time I did live there was in 1957. I went to Moose Jaw in March, to take up a job on the local newspaper. During the three or four years before that I had worked and lived in most parts of the country, from Labrador to Kitimat, and I had begun to form some ideas about the size and shape of Canada. I wondered if the piece that was missing, the prairie, wasn't the most important one of all. Not since Alexis de Tocqueville has anyone attempted to understand America — the United States — without peering into its "heartland," the great midwest. But for some reason no one has ever examined our heartland as the same sort of touchstone to a nation, and I thought it would be interesting to have a look for myself.

In the nine months I lived there, I learned to enjoy Saskatchewan very much. Nearly every evening through the summer and fall I drove the forty open miles to Regina to court the girl I have since married, and on those long return trips across the changing, moody plains I think I felt something of the strong hold the prairie can exert on its settlers. The people of Saskatchewan seem to be close to the land in a way that no other non-French Canadians are, and the reason

I am in some ways sorry I missed the prairies of the 1930s is that the legacy of those years was, in 1957, one I couldn't share. No one who had not been there in the thirties — who couldn't say, "My son was four years old before he saw rain," and then smile ruefully — could ever really feel a part of the province in the 1950s. This is not to say a young man from elsewhere wasn't welcomed or made to feel at home. On the contrary. One of the reasons for the west's famous hospitality is simply that many westerners are strangers there themselves, so to speak, and the sense of pioneering in a province where civilization is not yet a century old is one that gives everyone something in common. But the dust and poverty of the Depression — a Depression that was a distant memory in the east by the middle fifties — had drawn its veterans together like the survivors of a foreign war. I remember talking during the federal election campaign of 1957 to a jolly farm matron from around Swift Current. "I still can't see a dust cloud anywhere without feeling terrified," she said. "The whole thing comes back so easily." The prairie holds in common with the sea the power to mould human beings.

For all these reasons, I never thought of the CCF government as particularly remarkable in Saskatchewan. Even to someone raised in southern Ontario, where "CCF" was commonly held to stand for "Cancel Canada's Future," the socialist experiment on the prairies — if that's what it was — seemed both inevitable and proper. The protest movements that had produced the Douglas government made sense not only as protests against the moneyed east and high tariffs, but against the harsh, bald land the people had settled only a generation or two before, and which had turned against them. Politics have always been very real in Saskatchewan, simply because the effects of government are so important to people so close to the land. Scattered over a quarter million square miles, a population less than half of Montreal's simply has to pull together, through government, to make do. And, just as they have grappled with their land, the people who settled Saskatchewan have had to grapple with ideas. While a farmer in Ontario could sell most of his crop to a local cannery, his colleague with a quarter section in Saskatchewan had to know about everything from the Crowsnest Pass differential to the likelihood of war in Europe, and the men with the red necks and the white foreheads had a long tradition of arguing economic theory and co-operative action before the CCF came along. The founding date of the Territorial Grain Growers' Association, which might be regarded as the great-grandfather of the CCF, is 1901.

There are three other impressions that Saskatchewan left on me as setting it apart from the other parts of the country I had got to know. The first was the complete absence of the kind of people sometimes known as "the families." In a city like Galt, Ontario, there are perhaps a dozen names that constitute a sort of municipal upper class: principally the factory owners, but also some of the larger merchants. And every child knows who they are and what kind of car they drive. But in Moose Jaw, which is almost exactly the same size, there is no comparable group. For one thing, there *are* no factories of any size, and such large enterprises as there are in town are mostly owned by absentees. Even in Regina, where no private industry employs nearly as many people as the Saskatchewan Power Corporation (whose presidency is not hereditary), the managers of many of the biggest businesses are men who may well be moved on to head another branch plant next month, and they are not institutions in the city, the way they would be in, say, Halifax.

The second impression I want to set down is a difficult one to document, since it involves so many unmeasurable qualities, but Saskatchewan always seemed to me more publicly Christian — at least more publicly Protestant — than any other place I had known. I don't mean necessarily that more people went to church (although that is possible too), but that the churches seemed to play a more important role in public life. The Protestantism that the early Methodist circuit preachers brought to the plains had been of a special kind. The true Christian, they had taught, was interested not only in salvation for himself, but in helping others, physically and spiritually, while he was still on earth: first you fill a man's stomach and then you save his soul. This worldly Christianity seemed to me — I will just have to take the risk of stepping on someone's toes by oversimplifying here — one turn of the theological dial from the absolute, fundamentalist, Get-Saved Protestantism that flourished elsewhere in America from the nineteenth century on, and it had sent down deep roots on the prairie. To take just one tiny example: anyone who doesn't dig sermons is well advised to leave his radio off at any hour of Sunday morning in Saskatchewan.

The third thing I want to say about the Canadian heartland is how completely Canadian it is, at least in the sense that it is not American. Nearly every other important population centre in Canada is twinned by geography to a large American city: Vancouver-Seattle, Toronto-Buffalo, etc. Calgary and Edmonton, two exceptions, have imported enough Americans not to have to go anywhere to hear someone ask for cawffee. But if you drive due south from Regina the distance between Saint John, New Brunswick, and Boston you end up on the outskirts of Ismay, Montana. Consequently you do not drive due south. If a Regina housewife wants to go to a larger city to shop, she is much more likely to go to Winnipeg or Calgary than to St. Paul. A by-product of this isolation is that no U.S. television reaches the province, and scarcely any U.S. radio; the most important cultural influence on Saskatchewan over the past few decades has probably been CBK, the powerful CBC radio station with, as anyone who has lived in the province for any time at all can recite, "studios in Regina and transmitter at Watrous." U.S. newspapers are as rare as mountains in Saskatchewan, and only the most popular magazines are on the newsstands. *Maclean's*, for instance, which has a Canadian circulation roughly double that of *Time's* Canadian edition, outsells *Time* by nearly four to one in Saskatchewan. And when a trend like the anti-eggheadism of the early 1950s sweeps the United States — even though, as that particular one did, it seems to have its mother lode in the American midwest — Saskatchewan can remain untouched, and Canadian.

Ross Thatcher, the son of a local hardware merchant, won a seat on the Moose Jaw city council in 1942, when he was only twenty-five and not long out of Queen's University in Ontario. He was a socialist, or at any rate a CCFer, when that party was just reaching its zenith everywhere in Canada. He was also, according to Moose Jaw people who remember his early career, an obvious comer in politics: glib, energetic and sporting an aggressive charm. Now, of course, his enemies dismiss him as an opportunist or a turncoat, and, indeed, it is easy to read simple personal ambition into everything he has done since. But it is just as easy to read sincere conviction and the courage to admit he has changed his beliefs. He says now that "the only thing wrong with socialism is that it doesn't work," and this year he was apparently able to convince a lot of people that he was right. In 1945, Thatcher sought and won the federal CCF nomination for Moose Jaw. In the general election of that year, he was the youngest of twenty-eight CCF MPs — eighteen of them from Saskatchewan — elected. In succeeding elections he built his majority in his home riding to a comfortable six thousand votes, although as the years wore on in Ottawa he sounded less and less like the fiery young socialist who had first entered the Commons. By 1955 he was making speeches about the Liberal government's over-generosity with welfare measures and suggesting corporation taxes were too high. In 1956 he crossed the floor and joined the government. At once, with his big cigars and three-piece suits, he looked as if he'd found his home. His desertion shocked the CCF in his home province and, in the way converts to Catholicism are usually the best Catholics, he became one of the country's most outspoken critics of socialism, particularly as it was practised in Saskatchewan.

Whatever opinion one might have held of Thatcher's political history, it was impossible for an observer of his campaign in the 1957 election not to admire his guts. He was unable to get the nomination in Moose Jaw (by this time Moose Jaw–Lake Centre) and instead moved one constituency south to Assiniboia to take on his old friend and Ottawa desk-mate Hazen Argue. Wherever Thatcher went in that campaign he was followed by carloads of his former workers from Moose Jaw, who jammed the back rows of his meetings and pestered him — with all the fury that a prairie election can engender — with quotations from his old speeches. Cigar in mouth, ever smiling, Thatcher would reply, "I changed my mind," and launch into one more counter-attack on the CCF. At one point he appeared to go too far, and Tommy Douglas, then the premier of Saskatchewan, and a man whose platform appeal reached beyond his own party, offered to take Thatcher on head-to-head. Thatcher agreed to debate with Douglas on the subject of the provincial government's Crown corporations, and they arranged a meeting at the community hall in Mossbank, halfway between Moose Jaw and Douglas's home territory of Weyburn. To the surprise of nearly everyone who was present, Thatcher emerged the winner. Douglas lunged bitterly and personally at Thatcher, while Thatcher stuck to facts and reasoned arguments. Thatcher's triumph — against Douglas it would have been a triumph just to come out whole — wasn't dimmed by his defeat by Argue in Assiniboia, and by 1959, having switched to provincial politics, he was the new leader of his party in Saskatchewan.

As much as it was the result of any single factor, the end of the CCF regime was Ross Thatcher's personal victory. He injected his flamboyant, driving personality into every aspect of the campaign, and his own energy inspired the wheat-roots organization he had built throughout the province after the 1960 election. So energetic did he appear, in fact, that when some advisers from MacLaren Advertising arrived in mid-campaign to help the Saskatchewan Liberals, their first and most important decision was to edit Thatcher's speeches and supervise his performance so he would appear dignified enough to lead a government, as well as dynamic enough to lead an opposition or conduct a whirlwind campaign.

The CCF had nothing to match Thatcher's *chutzpah*. By the admission of even their own cabinet ministers they had grown old in office. Douglas's successor, Woodrow Lloyd, a reflective, even philosophical former schoolteacher, suffers from what Canadian political historians may someday call the Pearson Problem: he is as lacklustre in public as he is witty and disarming in private. The CCF had fought to exhaustion in the medical care insurance battle of only two summers before. A whole new generation — eighteen-year-olds can vote in Saskatchewan elections — had grown up untouched by

the 1930s. The young people were uninspired by the memory of the
CCF's early goals, and the older leaders had been unable to set new
ones to excite them. Although the party signed enough new members
to top its 1944 figure for the first time, the organizers were unable to
attract the uncommitted. Thatcher's organizers had weakened the
CCF's farm support. The CCF held on to enough votes in the cities
to keep its vote within one percentage point of their 1960 victory,
but people who had voted Social Credit or Conservative before
flocked to Thatcher. The end was a whimper instead of a bang, but
the era that had begun in 1944 drew to a close in 1964.

In a pamphlet he called *Social Democracy in Canada*, George
Williams, a tinsmith's son who during the 1920s and early thirties
walked and hitchhiked through the farming area east of Saskatoon
preaching the new gospel of prairie protest, wrote: "This is not a
treatise on socialism according to Marx, Lenin, Stalin, Bellamy or
Engels . . . The people of Canada are not interested in ascertaining
whether a proposed economic system agrees with Marxism or any
other ism; they want to be reasonably sure that it will work."

Williams was elected to the legislature in 1934 — one of the original CCF "quints" who won seats against a Liberal landslide — and
went on to become the first CCF minister of agriculture. He died in
1945, a few months after assuming his portfolio, but the words of his
pamphlet, written in 1936, are as valid as if he'd lived to see the whole
history of the movement he'd helped to launch. A few doctrinaire
socialists provided a sort of focal point for the protest movements
out of which the CCF grew, perhaps, but at every step on the road to
power and after, their ideas were tempered by the realities of the
prairie. At first, for instance, the CCF talked of nationalizing the land:
the system would be known as "use-lease," and a farmer would have
life tenure on land the state owned. But cooler heads soon realized
how the proud, independent settlers of Saskatchewan would react to
that particular outrage, and "use-lease" disappeared in 1936. Even
the *Commonwealth*, the party's Saskatchewan newspaper, which
might have been expected to be brimming with attacks on the
"bloated capitalists of Bay Street" in the 1930s, contained scarcely

more invective than a *Toronto Star* editorial of the 1960s. The division between the CCF and the old-line parties never was one of class, partly because Saskatchewan, from its outset, was nearly a classless world. One member who entered the legislature with the CCF's second small wave (the "quints" were joined by six more CCF MLAs in the 1938 election) recalls losing every one of the ten polls in his riding where all the families were on relief.

By 1944 the CCF's triumph was inevitable — as inevitable, perhaps, as their 1964 defeat. The Liberals, grown fat in power, had postponed the election to extend their term to six years. The war to preserve the old order that many people had found wanting was nearly over. The CCF's bright promises were attracting new followers everywhere in Canada; it was to form the official opposition in Ontario the next year. Tommy Douglas had returned from Ottawa to lead the provincial party, and the bantam Baptist's magnetic oratory was the most popular show in the province. Thirty of the fifty-two CCF candidates in 1944 — of whom forty-seven were elected — were farmers, but Douglas named only five to his first cabinet. The ministry of health, where much of the government's first precedent-setting work was to be done, he kept for himself — he was, of course, a clergyman, with a master's degree in sociology. Three of the remaining portfolios, including the important one of provincial treasurer, he gave to school teachers, and this particular choice was the first evidence of a pattern that was to dominate the years of CCF rule: a trust in the intellectual. In the depression years of the west, many men who in more prosperous times might have gone on to post-graduate degrees and academic careers turned instead to the security of the prairie classroom. M. J. Coldwell, who was to become the national leader of the CCF, was one. Woodrow Lloyd, the CCF's first minister of education, and Clarence Fines, the provincial treasurer, were others.

The Douglas cabinet ministers brought with them implicit instructions from the party, if not from the electorate as a whole. Their platform, which had been drafted in open convention, pledged them to a score of general and, for the time, revolutionary, proposals, nearly all of which had been thrashed out by some of the party's thirty-five thousand dues-paying, vitally involved members. The question that the government now faced — exactly *how* all these measures were to be instituted — must have looked overwhelming. To help the cabinet translate these plans into concrete programs, the government began seeking out the first of the number of bright young men from all over Canada — and beyond — who came to Saskatchewan in the 1940s. These men, most of whom came out of the graduate schools of universities, became the machinery of CCF accomplishment for the next twenty years, and there is scarcely any area of provincial life that their trained minds have not touched. Saskatchewan was able to attract them in the 1940s by its atmosphere of hope and willingness to experiment. The province became, in a sense, a social and governmental laboratory. Many ideas and theories that almost certainly would have remained *only* ideological and theoretical were tested out among the rational, Christian, Canadian people of the prairie. The CCF was able to retain these men partly by giving them the freedom and co-operation they could scarcely expect from other governments, and partly by encouraging them — even assisting them financially — to go back to university and pursue further studies in the light of the practical experience they had attained in the meantime. The key men in the Saskatchewan civil service were a small group — perhaps no more than a dozen played truly important roles — but the effect they had on the province was enormous.

Even before these experts had arrived, though, the CCF set out on one of the most frenzied periods of action any government in Canada has ever undertaken. In the first eighteen months they passed 196 acts, established four new departments or agencies of the civil service, set up and heard reports from half a dozen royal commissions and opened eleven new government corporations.

The plunge into health insurance was typical of both the turmoil of the time and the government's eagerness to seek the advice of experts and to follow it. On September 8, 1944, Douglas, in his role as minister of health, appointed Dr. Henry Sigerist, a professor of medical history at Johns Hopkins University in the U.S., to head a survey commission. Dr. Sigerist immediately chose two other doctors, a dentist, a nurse and a hospital administrator to assist him, and began his hearings. The commission, in a burst of activity that seems incredible in view of what we have come to expect of all government commissions, reported less than thirty days later, on October 4. It recommended broad and fundamental changes in the province's health structure, among them the establishment of "health districts" — a program of regional preventive medicine in which Saskatchewan pioneered — as well as free treatment of cancer, free health services to all pensioners and an air ambulance system to serve the scattered farm communities. Here was the explicit rendering of the general policies of the CCF. Immediately, the government announced it would fulfill "the spirit of the report," and in November Douglas established a Health Services Planning Commission. Again, the pattern that became the hallmark of the CCF was clear. To take just one example, the new commission — which was to play a major role in Saskatchewan's remarkable record of health and welfare leg-islation — included in its membership T. H. McLeod, an economist, who was among the first of the bright young men to assume gov-ernment jobs. McLeod, unlike many of the men who came after him, had known Douglas earlier, in Weyburn, their common home town. Douglas had invited him to join the government as his eco-nomic adviser, and McLeod decided to stay in Saskatchewan. His role over the next decade was a varied and important one and at the same time typical of the men who have extended the influence of Saskatchewan's enlightened government into other fields or other parts of the world. Among other things, McLeod was an architect of the province's successful automobile insurance plan. In the course of his government career he picked up a Ph.D., and is now dean of arts and science at the Regina campus of the University of Saskatchewan.

The Health Services Planning Commission went to work eagerly in the fall of 1944, and by February of 1945 it was able to make specific proposals. But the impatient government had been unable to wait even that long. It had already passed legislation, along some of the lines Sigerist had set down, for such measures as medical and hospital care for the province's twenty-nine thousand pensioners. The committee, undaunted at being anticipated, settled into the role of long-range planning it followed in the future.

At the same time Woodrow Lloyd, who was thirty years old when he assumed the ministry of education, had been ramming through a school-reorganization plan that was as revolutionary as Douglas's measures in health. And Joe Phelps, a furiously energetic farmer from Saltcoats who had taken over natural resources and industrial development (and who was one of the exceptions, perhaps not incidentally, to the CCF's willingness to seek expert advice), was establishing some of the Crown corporations that led to so much controversy in later years. Inevitably, the pace slowed down after 1945. In the 1948 election, running on their record, the CCF very nearly went, as they say in Saskatchewan, belly up. But through the late forties and fifties, the new programs continued to emerge. Power and gas, distributed by a Crown corporation, were pushed to the outermost farms. A vast program of highway construction and paving was launched by government construction crews — to the consternation of private contractors. The government, with results varying from mildly successful to catastrophic, went into such businesses as insurance, shoes, fish, lumber, wool, transportation, paper boxes, tanning and potash. And the co-operative movement, which had begun to grow under the Liberals, flourished with the encouragement — and the custom — of the CCF government.

Over the years, the bureaucracy grew in stature, if not in wisdom. Occasionally it must have seemed to the voters of Saskatchewan that the government and the civil service were determined to do the right thing for them whether they liked it or not. Medicare, of course, was the most noticeable exhibition of what the CCF's opponents have described as contempt for the electorate; even now in Saskatchewan it seems impossible to find anyone from Ross Thatcher down who says medicare was a bad idea — only the way it was brought in was bad. But the signs of the same attitude were evident earlier. In 1959 Saskatchewan faced an invasion of trading stamps. To the CCF, the stamps were an instrument not only of capitalism, but of the devil. But simply prohibiting them would have raised delicate legal and constitutional questions. So, instead, the government passed a Retail Merchants Bill, which included several large cudgels — in the form of controlled financing and even controlled inventory — to hold over the merchants' heads. The bill, which infuriated every storekeeper in the province, was never proclaimed. But the implied threat was clear: if the stamps come into the province, the bill goes into effect. The end, it seemed to some observers, had justified a pretty frightful means.

Yet in many cases it was exactly the CCF's willingness to go beyond what the electorate might demand that took it into new and valuable fields of government participation. A case in point is the Centre for Community Studies at the University of Saskatchewan. In 1956 the government launched a royal commission on agriculture and rural life, under the chairmanship of W. B. Baker, a rural sociologist. (It was this royal commission, incidentally, that worked out, under Baker's direction, the system of open discussion that became the basis of the federal inquiry into biculturalism and bilingualism in 1963.) One of the commission's recommendations was for some sort of academic body that could examine what is happening to the small communities — principally in Saskatchewan of course, but with meaning for many other parts of the world too — in our quickly changing age. The government agreed, and Baker was appointed to head the Centre in Saskatoon, working with $135,000 a year in public funds and whatever it could get from other groups and organizations for freelance research. On the surface this was not an earth-shattering piece of progress, but in its own quiet way the Centre became a remarkably important institution. Scholars from all over Canada and the United States were attracted to it by the opportunities for research, and their work cast light on Saskatchewan — and Canada — that would otherwise have shone elsewhere. Similar centres in Australia and Africa were modelled on it, with the co-operation of people from Saskatchewan — and Canada's reputation, however slightly, was increased abroad. And, too, the Centre had some real effects on Saskatchewan, supervising among other things a settlement between the town of Esterhazy and the management of a nearby potash mine when hostility had broken out.

The work of the Centre, it has always seemed to me, summed up a great deal of what was good for Saskatchewan about the CCF: the willingness, in the prairie tradition, to learn, and to try things. The people of the CCF changed many aspects of their social environment, and, with the gas and power-lines and roads, they even made efforts at controlling their physical one. Their federal colleagues, of course, have won a great deal of praise for their prodding of other parties into social measures that we all now take for granted. In the same way, there are measures now in effect everywhere in Canada that can be traced directly to the experiments on the prairie.

I went back to Saskatchewan just after the government fell. Before I even began calling on the people I had gone out to see I could sense some differences between 1964 and the time I lived there. With the coming of cocktail bars the restaurant food has improved enormously; there are a couple of places in Saskatoon and at least one in Regina that now rank, in my opinion, with the best in Toronto, if not Montreal. The relaxed liquor laws somehow seem to spell the end of the great Christian tradition, with its overtones of puritanism. *Fanny Hill* is on sale in the drugstores, and I bought a couple of copies to take back to Toronto where it has been banned.

Some of the most important changes in the province show up statistically. Although its total population hasn't increased since the 1920s, Saskatchewan now has one of the highest *urban* rates of increase in the country; the people are moving off the farms and into the cities. The province now seems more typically North American and less distinctly Canadian.

Regina is now dominated by the Saskatchewan Power Corporation building — as handsome a piece of public architecture as I have seen in Canada. The Wascana project, thirteen hundred acres of parkland, university and government buildings, is well under way. Wascana is, to me, the most exciting piece of civic planning in Canada, and although some similar plans were sketched out under a Liberal government in 1908, Wascana seems a monument to the CCF. The planners hired the best architect they could find, Minoru Yamasaki, and they gave him his head, and in future the heart of Regina — which is almost an arbitrarily situated city — will be an international showplace.

I spent most of a day touring Wascana, for in a way it is a symbol of the new Saskatchewan. Although many of the men who helped to see its plans through were among that hard core of bright young academics who arrived in the 1940s and are now making plans to leave, there is no atmosphere of defeat among the Wascana staff. The Wascana Authority is a "statutory corporation" — the government cannot cut its finances out from under it, the way it cut away those of the Centre for Community Studies. The foundation has been laid. Wascana will, in a sense, now run itself.

Later on I made my way to the office of the leader of the opposition, and found Woodrow Lloyd looking as if he hadn't quite enough to do. We chatted for most of an hour about what the government had accomplished, and about how it had come to be defeated. At one point he said, lighting his pipe: "Sometimes we got so involved in the plumbing and the practicalities that we forgot we were a party of dreams and revolutions."

Portrait of an Intellectual Engagé

Maclean's, *February 24, 1964*

This was the very first of dozens of pieces I would write about Pierre Elliott Trudeau.

In a civilization where the influence of the thinking man is generally confined to his advice on filters for cigarettes, Quebec stands out as a place where the intellectual has had some part in a recent and vital political victory — the toppling, in June 1960, of the Union Nationale regime. How big the part was, of course, is impossible to know for sure. But it is quite obvious that the part of the liberal platform that appealed to uncommitted voters, and swung the balance of electoral appeal from the UN to the liberals, was the part inspired by a small group of men who were and are, undoubtedly, intellectuals.

A few of these men had been harping on the themes eventually picked up by the Liberal party — the themes, to oversimplify for a moment, of political and social reform — for as long as ten years before the actual changeover of power. The principal place where they were doing so was a small magazine called *Cité Libre*, which published its first edition on June 15, 1950.

Cité Libre began with a circulation of 500. By the election of 1960 it had passed 5,000, but its influence could never be measured in number. Shortly after its inception, the eminent and acerbic journalist André Laurendeau wrote in *Le Devoir* that *Cité Libre* was saying things "out loud" (about Duplessisism and Quebec) that until then "others have only whispered." By the mid-fifties, other people and other publications (including *Le Devoir*) were saying them too — but only after *Cité Libre* had shown the way. Its influence was so widespread that one reader remarked that if he hadn't known *Cité Libre* was published only four times a year (it's a monthly now), he would have thought from the frequency with which it was quoted that it was a daily newspaper. Some bishops forbade their charges to read it (though its editors were all Catholics) and many university professors refused to write for it on the privately admitted grounds that they were afraid they would lose their jobs if they did.

Yet, for all its influence, *Cité Libre* has always been an amateur magazine. Its first capital was $300, which was subscribed by the six men who started it. Those six men, and the four who joined the group shortly after its inception, were involved in other things as well. Some of them have since achieved some prominence: Pierre Juneau is executive director of the National Film Board; Roger Rolland is regional program director of French networks for the CBC; Charles-A. Lussier is in charge of Quebec House in Paris; Gérard Pelletier is editor of French Canada's foremost daily newspaper, *La Presse*. And all of the original ten have been very much the intellectuals *engagés*, being involved with the law or the labour movement, or writing in other publications and generally offering a strong contrast with the traditional English-Canadian intellectual who huddles in an office somewhere and writes occasional essays for the *Queen's Quarterly*.

One of *Cité Libre*'s original six, and the one who, with Pelletier, has been its moving force, is Pierre Elliott Trudeau, a wiry, gentle-spoken forty-two-year-old bachelor who at once typifies the group — and the thinking-man *engagé* — and breaks all its rules for membership. On the typical side, Trudeau is about as intellectual as one can get, having completed a bewildering number of courses in law, economics and political science at the universities of Montreal,

Harvard and Paris, and the London School of Economics, from which he graduated at a very erudite twenty-seven. He is, like most of the *Cité Libre* people, well left of centre in his politics, though he has never been, for one reason or another, a card-carrying member of either the CCF or the NDP. He has also, like most of the *Cité Libre* group, been called a communist, which he is not and never has been (nor have they). After a series of reports he wrote on Russia appeared in *Le Devoir* in 1952, an American priest published a "rebuttal" in the newspapers *Le Droit* and *l'Action Catholique* that all but painted him red. Trudeau threatened both newspapers with a libel suit and both backed down.

Trudeau is the author of what is generally regarded as *Cité Libre's* most important single article, *Un manifeste democratique* ("A democratic manifesto," published in October 1958), and the editor of *La Grève de L'Amiante* ("The Asbestos Strike"), a book published in 1956 under the imprint of *Les Editions Cité Libre*, which, in the guise of an examination of the events of 1949, directed a blistering attack on the status quo in Quebec: most blisteringly on clericalism, the education system and electoral practices.

*Un*like any of his *confrères* on the magazine, and unlike virtually all intellectuals, *engagés* or otherwise, Trudeau is a millionaire, or close to it. He is currently living with his mother in a large and very comfortably appointed house in the city of Outremont on Montreal island. Each morning, he drives either to his Sherbrooke Street law office, which has been described as a "free clinic for anyone with an interesting case," or to the University of Montreal, to whose staff he has recently been appointed, and when he leaves for work he chooses between a black Mercedes-Benz sedan and a 300 SL sports car. He is a brown belt at judo, master of three languages (French, English and Spanish) and jack of several others, world-traveller, skin-diver, skier and bad amateur pianist. He is a formidable debater and, as one of Montreal's most eligible bachelors, an authoritative judge of wine and women.

Where clothes are concerned — which is somewhere, in fashion-conscious Montreal — Trudeau is a creative thinker, whose costume varies between conservative Britishism and corduroy slacks and sandals. He has been observed swimming in a pool in Ste. Adèle while snow fell around him during a meeting of the Institut Canadien des Affaires Publiques, which he helped found, and he once tried to row a boat from the Florida Keys to Cuba. In the fall of 1960, Trudeau went on a tour of Red China with a group of French Canadians, and as an old China hand (he had left Shanghai just before the Communists crossed the Yangtze in 1949) was elected spokesman. He was performing this function one day, during one of the trip's innumerable guided tours, when to the astonishment of his official guide and the other members of his group, he leaped into the air and performed a perfect somersault, then unsmilingly picked up his questioning where he'd left off.

In 1952 Trudeau attended an international conference of economists in Moscow. There, to the great chagrin of his guide and interpreter, he was discovered throwing snowballs at the statue of Stalin. "I have since wondered if I should write Khrushchev and show him how far ahead of him I was," he says, "but then it was not the thing to do. However, I told them, truthfully, that I used to go to Ottawa all the time and throw snowballs at Laurier's statue, and I was let off with a warning."

Such tactics — whose results have not always been so amicable — have sometimes led to Trudeau's being dismissed as nothing more than a clown. He is, of course, much more. Democracy and democratic practices have few more eloquent spokesmen in Canada and, through what Trudeau calls "the dark years" of the forties and fifties, they probably had none more determined in the province of Quebec. Nevertheless, Trudeau himself admits that some part of his life as a social critic — "if you want to look at it psychoanalytically" — has been motivated by a desire simply to throw snowballs at authority.

Sometimes, "authority" has meant not so much the people in power as the reigning popular sentiment. Trudeau's willingness to be on the unpopular side has seldom been so evident as it is in French Canada this winter, when he is standing squarely against the wave of nationalism and separatism that is sweeping the province.

He is so convinced that this movement is dealing with a dead issue that he has virtually refused to discuss it in public. Even though at least one of his colleagues has been urging him to blast separatism in a published essay, the closest he has come has been in the final paragraphs of a piece called *La Guerre! La Guerre!* ("War! War!") which appeared in the December issue of *Cité Libre*, in which he roasted French-Canadian intellectuals for ignoring the great issues of war and peace and turning to what he has called many times "problems that were solved a century ago."

Asked a few weeks ago to expound on why he stands so strongly against separatism, even when he admits that the feeling may be stronger in French Canada now than it has ever been before, Trudeau said: "I am against any policy that is based on race or religion. Any such policy is a reactionary policy and — while the bases of race and religion don't necessarily lead to evil — it is true that for the last hundred and fifty years nationalism has been a retrograde idea. There may be some countries where separatism is the only solution to current problems, but Canada is not one of them. By a historical accident, Canada has found itself approximately seventy-five years ahead of the rest of the world in the formation of a multinational state and I happen to believe that the hope of mankind lies in multinationalism."

But surely it is not unhealthy for a minority group to express itself through separatism — particularly if that expression leads to a righting of some of the wrongs the minority has suffered?

"If I were an English-Canadian Machiavellian," Trudeau said, "I'd encourage the separatists. I'd give them as much publicity and pay as much attention to them — or have the public pay as much attention to them — as I could. I would think that if I could keep the bright young men coming out of the universities worrying about separatism, I could hold them back for another ten years. While they were arguing about separatism, my sons would be getting the kind of education that would help them in tomorrow's world, and when the next industrial revolution came along — the cybernetics revolution — it would be, once again, my sons who were equipped to be the effective leaders. A nation or people only has so much intellectual energy to spend on a revolution. If the intellectual energy of French Canada is spent on such a futile and foolish cause as separatism, the revolution that is just beginning here can never be brought about."

Trudeau's word for this kind of thinking is "constitutionalism," by which he means that it is more complex than simple anti-nationalism. "I do not mean that I do not get angry at slights to my language — I can get as mad as the next guy when I come back from a trip and the customs officer at Montreal is unable to understand when I say in French that all I have to declare is a few scarves. But I am far removed from what's commonly called nationalism. I always have been, though part of that may be just that I wanted to throw snowballs."

Part of it also may be that Trudeau is no less comfortable in English than in French, so that he misses completely the frustrations of having to use a language in which he is not at home when speaking with members of Canada's majority. His mother's native tongue was English, before her marriage to Charles Trudeau, a lawyer who made his fortune from a chain of service stations in the twenties, and the two languages were interchangeable in their home; they have remained so interchangeable that Pierre habitually speaks English to his sister, a Montreal matron, and French to his brother, an architect. As a student, he occasionally used his bicultural heritage as a home base for throwing snowballs at extreme nationalism.

"When I first entered *collège classique*," he recalls, "there was another Pierre Trudeau and I became Pierre-Phillipe. Phillipe was one of my baptismal names. But later on, I began signing Elliott, my mother's name, with which I was also baptized, and I won't deny that it was at least partly to spite the nationalists. You have to remember that those days, the thirties, were a time of pretty intense feelings about — there is just no other name for it than nationalism. The professors used to tell the stories about French-Canadian triumphs with great dramatic flair and when they would come to the climax of a battle that we won the students would burst into applause. That rather amused — and annoyed — me, and when we got to the result of the battle of the Plains of Abraham, I remember, I broke into applause myself. I was alone."

In the war years, Trudeau was neither so alone nor so removed from his French heritage that he could forgive the government for its conscription policy — a phase of political history that he is still bitter about — and like many young French Canadians of his eminently eligible age, he simply continued his schooling. Since then, however, he has seen his share of fighting. In 1948, after he had finished at the London School of Economics, he set out, at first with a motorbike and later simply with a knapsack, on a year-and-a-half's tour of the world. His itinerary during that time sounds like a catalogue of trouble spots. He was arrested in Jerusalem, in Arab dress and without papers, shortly after the assassination of Count Bernadotte; friends vouched for him, after some harrowing hours. He saw street fighting in the suburbs of Rangoon during the Burmese civil war and travelled across Cambodia and Vietnam in an army envoy at the height of the Indochinese wars. He was arrested — and later released — crossing the India-Pakistan line shortly after partition and he crossed the Khyber Pass while tribesmen from Afghanistan were conducting regular raids on Pakistani villages.

Whatever his early inclinations and whatever his odysseys, Trudeau says that the part of his life that gave him both his political convictions and the determination to make them public was his postgraduate education. "Even though I'd chosen to go outside Quebec after I'd got my law degree to learn something about the social sciences, I had no idea until I got to Harvard how far behind we were," he explains, and his voice has a tinge of rancour. "I'd thought that if I just went along and learned my Latin and Greek I'd be all right. But now I felt — well, gypped. Why, I had the right to practice law in Quebec and yet I'd been given no inkling of the philosophy of law, never even read the writings of the great jurists, like Coke. At Harvard, and later even more so, my eyes were opened to what we'd been missing in Quebec, and I didn't like what I saw."

In Paris, Trudeau met Gérard Pelletier, who had been an acquaintance at home and who was there with the World University Service — "giving American money to countries that were about to go Communist," as Pelletier puts it. The two of them, with occasional visits from other temporary expatriates, began talking about the need for change in Quebec, and out of those conversations came both the idea for *Cité Libre* — "we knew we needed a place to put our ideas forward, and we knew the traditional places wouldn't be open to us" — and the bases for the unconventional (for Quebec) ideas that have dominated Trudeau's thinking ever since.

Where Trudeau differs from the traditional left is that he is not yet convinced that French Canada is ready for a "social revolution." What he would like to see first, and what he has worked towards and preached for in all his writings, is a "democratic revolution," a revolution which he admits has now started. It is this desire — a desire to see such fundamental democratic practices as clean elections instituted in Quebec — that has been behind nearly everything he has been saying for the past ten years. "The ideas we were putting forward," he says, "may seem self-evident now — ideas like separation of church and state, electoral reform, a re-evaluation of our educational system — but they were not self-evident then, at least in Quebec." And it is the frustration he felt in trying to make his desire become a reality that has led to such petulant generalizations as this: "Historically, French Canadians have not really believed in democracy for themselves; and English Canadians have not really wanted it for others."

Armed with these convictions, or at least the beginnings of them, Trudeau returned to Canada in 1949, "determined," as he says, "to see how the cogs of democratic government worked." Through some academic connection in Ottawa, he was able to latch on to the very hub, the Privy Council, and for nearly three years worked there as an "economic adviser," summarizing interdepartmental arguments for cabinet decision and generally oiling the cogs. But those were also the first years of *Cité Libre*, to whose meetings

Trudeau was commuting regularly, and "although the work with the Privy Council was fascinating I knew that the place I wanted to be was Quebec."

Gérard Pelletier, who along with several other members of the *Cité Libre* was then in the labour movement, urged on Trudeau the notion that the unions in French Canada could use his legal and economic training, and in 1952 he moved to Montreal and opened a law office. He has kept one open ever since, and from it has offered advice — often free — to scores of people involved in everything from habeas corpus to property suits, but his chief interest through that time was labour legislation and labour-management bargaining. "I would not like to give the impression that I was trying to use the unions," he says, "but I felt that for the kind of change I wanted to see in Quebec — an awakening of democracy — the unions were the best vehicle. At the same time, because of my training, I was able to advise both the Catholic syndicates and the international unions, who were often at loggerheads, and I was able to act as a sort of bridge between them."

Trudeau prepared briefs, served as union nominee on arbitration boards and argued union cases before other arbitration boards. "It was amazing," he says, "how much technical advice the unions needed. Again, I blame the system, the lack of education. For years, the unions had been calling strikes just when the companies wanted them to, when supplies were stockpiled and the market was crowded. Without economic advice, the unions were often just suckers." Gérard Pelletier adds: "Trudeau was invaluable. In 1952 and '53, for instance, when there was so much talk of a railroad strike, we really hadn't the background to know what it was about, but Pierre was able to give us a detailed history, from his very precise knowledge of Canadian institutions, of the role the railways had played in Canada."

Through the fifties, *Cité Libre* increased in stature, if not in practical wisdom. Those who appeared regularly in its pages automatically cut themselves off from the political Establishment, and in those days the political Establishment reached everywhere. Trudeau's experience is as good an example of this phenomenon as anybody's.

Four times during the UN years, he was offered a job by the faculty of social sciences at the University of Montreal. Four times he accepted and four times the offer was retracted. Why he was not hired during this period, in spite of his obvious qualifications, was never clearly stated to him, but the inferences are obvious.

In 1956, Trudeau took his first direct political action: he was instrumental in the founding of a movement called Rassemblement, which was to be the basis of a "new and broadened left in Quebec." (The CCF had never attracted more than one and a half per cent of the vote.) Rassemblement lasted roughly two years as a political force. Its directors soon fell to bickering about who should be let in and how far, and by 1958 it had become an "educational movement." Trudeau remained as one of the main educators, but it was obvious that as a mechanism of his "democratic revolution," Rassemblement had broken down, and he was soon back at his ideological drawing board.

In October 1958, he emerged with *Un manifeste démocratique*. Its main thesis was this: It is still too soon for the socialist revolution in Quebec but the need for a democratic one has never been more evident; we must lick Duplessis now or watch the material we're trying to build on be rotted away. We *must* find a basis for fighting Duplessis on a democratic platform and whether the means of building that platform is a union of the provincial CCF and Liberals, or an agreement to stay out of one another's constituencies and form a coalition later, we must agree to work on the principals we have in common — and there are many of them. We can work out the differences later. Now, we must have a *union des forces democratiques*.

The idea began to catch on, but slowly — too slowly for the course of history. In the fall of '58, the provincial Liberal federation passed a resolution welcoming Trudeau's suggestion, saying, in effect, that the Liberals were willing to accept help from outside their own party in their effort to unseat Duplessis. But the CCF, still apparently unwilling to face the weakness of its own role in provincial affairs, was slower to come around. Then, in the summer of 1959, Maurice Duplessis died and Paul Sauvé ascended to power, bringing with him a clean breath of reform to the Union Nationale. But on January 2, 1960, Sauvé died and the UN seemed on the brink of a return to a Duplessis-type regime. The Liberals, realizing there was no route to power through orthodoxy, moved to outflank the UN on the left. In so doing, they attracted such small-l liberals as René Lévesque, now minister of resources. (They were, apparently, prepared to move even farther to the left: Gérard Pelletier and a couple of others as far left were offered a chance to run. Trudeau was not, perhaps because he had independent means. Unlike, for instance, Lévesque, who has been growing noticeably restless under the pressures of Liberals seeking to return to the old ways, Trudeau could bolt any job the party could offer him at no risk to his livelihood.)

After the defeat of the Union Nationale on June 22 the theories of Trudeau's *Manifeste démocratique* seemed borne out: the old regime was toppled by a single force; there were no CCF candidates nominated. Is the "democratic revolution" under way? "Of course," Trudeau said not long ago. "As one example, this province is obviously on its way to developing one of the best educational systems on the continent, if not the best. But the margin of victory was very narrow. We still do not know if democracy is firmly planted here. And think how much faster this revolution — for it is a revolution — would have gone, if there were more people like Lévesque in power, if *all* the forces of democracy were represented in the government now."

As for Trudeau himself, he is finally a member of the faculty at the University of Montreal. This fall he began work at the newly formed Institute of Public Law, where he will be conducting research. "What could be better for me? I am working in the field that I know best, and I would like a chance for a few years to read some books and replenish my stock of ideas."

The October We'll Never Forget

from Peter Gzowski's Book About This
Country in the Morning, *1974*

A year after it all happened, I am surprised at what has stuck in my mind and what has not. I do not, for example, remember exactly how it all began. A British diplomat, a trade commissioner whose name I had not heard before but now, of course, will never forget, had been kidnapped. In a curious way, that seemed more comic than tragic. A diplomat kidnapped in Canada? That's kind of nice, isn't it? It was as if we could take pride in having enough conflict in our normally dull country to inspire a real live drama. But surely it would all be over soon. After all, hadn't there been rumours about a plot to kidnap an Israeli diplomat in Montreal just a couple of weeks before? And there, surely, someone was kidding.

No, as it turned out, no one was kidding. Gradually, into our comprehension of the fact that one man — by now, a man with a name, James Cross — had been taken from his family, was being held somewhere, was, perhaps, injured or even dead — into that comprehension seeped also the knowledge that these people, these separatists, these *terrorists*, *had* set off bombs, *had* held up banks, *had* tried, however incredible it might seem to the rest of us, to ally themselves with a worldwide movement of violent revolution. And the joke remained a joke no longer.

That understanding, as I say, dawned slowly, and it is impossible, looking back now, to remember precisely when any of us understood precisely what. In any person's life, only a few moments of public history implant themselves in such a way that we carry forever the memory of just how we heard about them. For myself, I can remember riding my bicycle home from school on V-E Day as clearly as if it were last week. I can tell you the name of the boy who not long before that day had told me that Roosevelt was dead, and how he told me, and when. I remember the evening my oldest son came in from the television room to say that Martin Luther King had been killed — and I doubt if there is anyone who cannot recount in perfect detail the way he or she first heard that Jack Kennedy had been shot. It is, I'd suggest, no coincidence that nearly all those events of modern history are in fact events in the modern history of the United States. The U.S., we had been led to believe, was the place where such wrenches of political sanity took place. In Canada, we were spectators, moved, perhaps, and shaken, but spectators all the same. Even the Second World War, which we'd been fighting for more than two years before the U.S. was drawn in, had somehow, for those of us not directly involved, become Americanized. The movies, the songs, the propaganda — American. V-E Day? In public terms — and I thank God I am not among those for whom that war involved personal loss — in public terms, there was nothing especially Canadian about it; we simply happened to be part of the Allies.

And then, there it was, a year ago this month, a public event that would become an indelible and terrible Canadian memory. Tomorrow, October 16, is the anniversary of the implementation of the War Measures Act. That day was surely one of the most significant political occasions of our time, and yet I wonder if, even now, all of us realize precisely what it meant. In practice, the action taken that day may well have been effective; there is some reason to believe that separatism, revolutionary separatism, is weaker in French Canada now than it was a year ago; that a repressive act, in other words, repressed. And if Gallup polls are really any guide to what all Canadians thought, then eighty-three per cent of us — French and English — thought the War Measures Act was a good idea.

But if it is possible to talk about "some evidence" of a weakening movement, it is also possible to speculate that many people who had preached moderation were driven to consider immoderate means. Whatever it seemed to accomplish, the War Measures Act is still an awesome piece of legislation. Our government, acting in our name, arrested and incarcerated people not for what they had done and been convicted of, but for what the government thought they *might intend* to do. Before the events of last October had worked themselves out, more than four hundred people had been taken from their homes and put into jail, with no right to a trial, no right, for the moment at least, even to see a lawyer.

So the other side of a complex argument is simply that the law, as we understand it, is intended to be above men's judgement of what is wrong and what is right, and one interpretation of legislation such as the War Measures Act is that it says, "Okay, government, whatever you say — the usual rule of law is suspended." Can you imagine, for instance, what the editorials in the press of Canada — again, in French as well as English — would be like if the government of the United States were to give J. Edgar Hoover untrammelled rights to jail people he thought might do something dangerous in the future? Oh, how holy we can get about other people's transgressions. But when we move from the third row in the spectators' stand to centre ice, oh, how our attitudes change.

On that Friday evening a year ago, of course, none of those theories were clear to me. Then, I was still trying to cope with the knowledge that eleven days previously it would have been difficult, if not impossible, to consider that people would actually kidnap a total stranger for what they took to be political ends. So that while I was able to deplore the implementation of the act — to me it seemed a monumental overreaction — I was still willing to grant the government the benefit of my doubts. Pierre Trudeau might just know something I didn't know.

In the aftermath, of course, the implementation of the act has been proven unwarranted. There was, it is clear now, no state of "apprehended insurrection" in Quebec; a sad, sorry group of misguided, frustrated, disturbed people had committed a crime of cruelty and stupidity. That much, I think, is clear from the evidence. On October 16, 1970, we did not have that evidence; we were a confused and shaken nation, and we needed shoring up. But a year later, even such tough guys of the time as Jerome Choquette, Quebec's minister of justice, have questioned the wisdom of implementing that act, and now, on its anniversary, I find it sad that our Parliament has not yet examined the idea of taking it off the books, and replacing it with something that would still protect the rights of individuals in times of national crisis. Still, as deeply as I feel about that act, the memory of last October that has stuck with me most strongly is more personal.

• • •

We were playing bridge. My wife and I and two cherished friends. It was late on Saturday evening of that weekend, and the radio was playing softly in the background. The announcements came in bursts, at first confused, rumours, hints, confirmed, contradicted, reaffirmed . . . and finally, correct and indisputable. Pierre Laporte, a man I had met but once and really wouldn't recognize on sight, but a man . . . had been murdered. However one might sympathize with the cause of Quebec independence, whatever one might think of its ultimate goals, nothing, nothing could justify that. We stopped playing bridge. Our world, our country had changed. What had begun as a joke had become an obscenity. I thought that evening of Pierre Trudeau, a man so easy to condemn for those of us who thought that act was wrong, and yet alone that ugly night with his own thoughts. He had behaved as he believed right, and how easy it was then, and how much easier now, for those of us who believed him wrong to criticize him. But Pierre Laporte was a friend of his.

I have said before that if you had to boil down my love of this country to one word, that word would be "hope" — hope for the future, hope that we can work things out here. Neither the murder of Pierre Laporte nor the fact that we lived through a time in our lives when four out of every five Canadians thought civil liberties should be suspended — neither of those things can blunt that hope. But it is tempered, tempered by the fire of last October. This week we have been and this weekend we will be again, inundated with media re-hashes of all those events. Through it all I, as one Canadian, will remember the moment I heard Pierre Laporte was dead.

A Prince in the Revolution

Maclean's, *July 14, 1962*

The French and Catholic people of Quebec, in their by now famous quiet revolution, are changing faster than any group of people on this continent. What they are changing *from*, as much as anything else, is their consent to domination by the Catholic Church and clergy of their schools, their social ideas, and in some ways even their politics. It is this two-centuries-old grip of the church that has made it popular if imprecise for outsiders to describe Quebec as "priest-ridden." In Quebec's new mood, the church itself faces what John Foster Dulles called, in another context, an agonizing reappraisal. It must change with the times or try, as best it can, to stop the times from changing. Today, the dilemma divides Quebec's most influential churchmen.

One of the most powerful advocates of change in French Canada is Paul-Emile Cardinal Léger, Archbishop of Montreal. The influential *opponents* of change in Quebec include the bishops of Rimouski, Sherbrooke, Three Rivers and Gaspé — indeed, all the bishops outside Montreal with the exceptions of Ottawa, Quebec City and perhaps one or two others. The wing the cardinal leads, which is ready to give laymen a greatly increased voice in the church and the schools, can be described for lack of more precise terms as the "liberal" or "left" wing of the church. It is opposed, with conviction and mounting emotionalism among extremists, by a status-quo party that in these terms is the church's "conservative" or "right" wing.

This summer the argument between the left and the right in the church is growing louder. It may yet echo across the country. If it does, it will be well to keep one thing in mind: whatever their differences, and however bitterly these differences are expressed, they're still differences within the church. Both movements are, before everything else, Catholic movements. The left is the ecclesiastic left — something far different from the political position. And neither side intends to rend the church. Nevertheless, and that being said, the church in Quebec cannot move both ways at once. Only one of these forces can prevail. And, because the church and Quebec have always been and will surely continue to be inseparable in their development, the outcome of the struggle within the church will have a profound effect on the future of French Canada — and for that reason all Canada.

Already the left wing has effectively "liberalized" some aspects of the Catholic religion in Quebec. The wing draws its strength from both laymen and priests. Some of the laymen — like Gérard Pelletier, a brilliant forty-three-year-old former labour leader who is now editor of the big Montreal daily, *La Presse* — are devout Catholics who have spoken so frankly and often in past years about the need for change within the church that they have sometimes been accused of simple anti-clericalism. Most of the wing's priests are young. Most of them are well educated, many schooled abroad. A significant number are Dominicans.

The right wing, too, has lay support for its churchmen. In addition to the rural and small-city bishops, it includes many parish priests and some influential Jesuits. But its most extreme members, and the ones the liberals fear most, are adherents to a lay movement called Cité Catholique, which is of French origin and is just now rearing its head in Quebec. This movement is not unlike the John Birch Society in the U.S. It rigidly opposes *all* change. It holds as its principal enemies communism and what it calls *laïcisme*. In Cité Catholique terms, *laïcisme* is any school of thought that would reduce the clergy's role in anything, and Cité Catholique sees *laïciste* plots everywhere.

Recently, a couple of conservative French-Canadian newspapers printed what they claimed was a "secret document of great importance," which they had just discovered. The document, they contended, was a "plan of *laïcisation* prepared by enemies of the church." One step in the plan was to publish "anticlerical and free-thought articles in *La Presse* and *Le Devoir* and in the magazines *Cité Libre* and *Liberté* . . . and to publish caricatures and articles that ridicule the clergy, the religious communities, and the people of the right (*les gens de droite*)."

The French word for the ultraconservatism that produces this kind of nonsense is *intégrisme*, and the *intégristes'* chief target, the most important and interesting proponent of changes within the most monolithic of human institutions, is the Archbishop of Montreal. Cardinal Léger has not always been a liberal. When he became Archbishop of Montreal in 1950, many liberal Catholics were extremely wary of him, and for the first several years of his tenure their wariness seemed justified.

There were at least two reasons for the attitudes Léger brought with him. One was his background. Until he became a bishop, he had virtually no contact with liberal ideas. Born in 1904 in a town called Valleyfield, Quebec, first of two sons of a general storekeeper, Léger was raised and educated in St. Anicet and in Ste. Thérèse. A highly intelligent and bookish child (his mother surprised him one day, at the age of eight, making a speech on reciprocity to his mirror), he dreamed at twelve of being a missionary. At twenty he entered the grand seminary of Montreal, and after his ordination in 1929 he left for four years of teaching and further study in Paris. From Paris, after a brief visit home, Abbé Léger was sent to Japan and for the next six years his boyhood vocation was fulfilled. As part of his work there, he founded a seminary. Extracurricularly, he grew a rich black beard, which, coupled with his black eyes, gave him a sternly dramatic appearance in photographs taken before the war. In 1939, clean-shaven, he returned to teach sociology for a year at the

Séminaire de Philosophie de Montréal, and in 1940 he went back to Valleyfield as vicar-general.

In Valleyfield, his reputation as an efficient administrator grew, but his popularity among the "liberal" Catholics of Montreal did not. One of them, now a fervent admirer of Léger's, recently recalled that the young monsignor had seemed like "poison to what we were fighting for." In 1947, because of his growing reputation as a teacher and administrator, Léger was sent to Rome, where he became rector of the Pontifical Canadian college. Three years later he was appointed archbishop of Montreal, replacing Msgr. Joseph Charbonneau. In 1954 Léger was made a cardinal, and when he arrived back from Rome with his new red hat his words were such that they have stayed in the mind of a friend of mine for eight years, because, says my friend, of their "typical arrogance." "*Montréal*," said the new cardinal, "*o ma ville, tu as voulu te faire belle pour rècevoir ton Pasteur et ton Prince.*" (Rendered freely, this was his acknowledgement of Montreal's efforts to beautify itself in honour of its prince.)

The situation of his city during the early fifties was a second reason for Léger's early conservatism. This was the height of Duplessism, and liberal ideas, religious ones as well as political, were seldom if ever heard out loud. Msgr. Charbonneau, Léger's predecessor, had been a liberal in some ways — he had fought from his pulpit for Quebec's labour movement in the bitter asbestos strike of 1949. Charbonneau had been fired. The official explanation was that Charbonneau had "retired for reasons of health," but in Victoria, B.C., where he went after stepping down, he told a reporter he "felt fine" and was now "among friends." One of Léger's early official acts, and one that still makes liberals wince, was to take what they consider abusively unfair action to help crush a teachers' strike in Montreal.

But the liberal currents that were stirring, few as they were, began to reach the cardinal. He showed himself accessible to points of view he did not yet share. In the early 1950s, he invited to a personal audience two of the editors of *Cité Libre*, the very liberal little magazine that is and was the principal sounding board for many liberal Catholics. Léger was quick to learn the realities of life in

Catholic Montreal, against which, in his scholarly and often remote life, he simply had not brushed. His response was sometimes strong enough to arouse his emotions — he is, say those who know him, emotionally intense. One man who was an official of the lay movement Action Catholique in the 1950s recalls having a disagreement with Léger on a matter that concerned a source of gifts to his movement. He criticized the cardinal. Léger asked to see the layman and listened to an explanation of his position. Léger wept; he admitted he was wrong and asked only that in future the layman should bring criticism first to him.

"He is," says a Catholic who was not in those days among the cardinal's admirers, "a deeply religious man, a truly religious man. I would not say that of all the bishops of the church. I think it is this that is behind the tremendous change that has come over him. I can't see how, otherwise, a man of that age could change so much."

Something else behind the change has been the appointments Léger has made to his own staff. The men around him are, mainly, bright, highly trained young priests — one monsignor is still in his middle thirties — from such backgrounds as the universities and the labour movement. These men know they are expected to speak frankly and freely to His Eminence about the issues of the day.

The liberalism that these factors, and of course others, has produced is as varied in its applications as those issues. Like the present pope, John XXIII, Léger has taken a special interest in what the churchmen call the "ecumenical dialogue" — the discussion among all Christian faiths about possible unity — and he has become one of his church's leading spokesmen on the subject. He now spends ten days of every month in Rome, working on plans for John's upcoming Second Vatican Council, which, as Léger has said, "aims to facilitate the reconciliation and reunion of churches." Last winter, Léger asked all the Catholics in his archdiocese to pray for the World Council of (Protestant) Churches, then meeting in New Delhi. In traditionally rigid and nationalistic Quebec, this request made, as a writer for the U.S Jesuit magazine *America* noted, "a professional impression." The cardinal has also set up in Montreal a diocesan committee of priests and laymen, one of the first in the world, to pursue the ecumenical dialogue. In other fields, he has requested priests and monks to wear black clerical suits instead of cassocks or colourful robes as their street dress in Montreal. While this decision may have flattened a little of the city's special flavour for tourists, it has also given the clergy a considerably more up-to-date image to present to the world. (One neighbouring bishop, probably more conscious of tradition than of the tourist trade, quickly pointed out that the ruling didn't apply in *his* diocese.) On the Mass itself, the cardinal has written a pastoral directory that has been admired and followed as far away as Europe. As part of what Catholics call the "liturgical revolution" — which may one day result in the Mass being celebrated in living languages — he has helped further the practice of "dialogue services," in which the congregation answers the priest. "I now have parishes where a thousand people sing the Mass like angels," he told the magazine *America* with a touch of pride. Under his aegis, the Dominicans have established a "pastoral training institute" in Montreal, to help young priests bridge the gap between their unworldly seminary training and the sometimes cold sociological facts of the outside.

This sort of change, however, while certainly of the kind the liberals advocate, is not what has brought Cardinal Léger up hard against the *intégristes*. Education has done that.

Quebec, as nearly everyone must know by now, is in the middle of a thorough overhaul of its school system. Changes have been made already and there is now a provincial royal commission studying the question. Quebec is, in the next few years, likely to jump from having one of the continent's most backward systems of education to having one of its most advanced. Among the crucial decisions before that jump is completed is to what degree the schools will remain "confessional" — how much teaching, in other words, is going to be taken away from the "black robes," the priests and the brothers and nuns.

The *intégristes*, of course, would like the schools to remain exactly as they are, or better, as they were a few years ago. At the other extreme is a loose organization called Le Mouvement Laïque de Langue Française. The MLF was organized in the spring of 1961 to see what could be done about, among other things, providing more adequately for teaching children of French-speaking non-Catholics. Some of the MLF's members do favour a complete "neutralization" of the schools, but the movement as a whole does not. Instead, it has suggested a plan, modelled on one presented to it by Prof. Paul Lacoste of the University of Montreal, that would divide education in Quebec on a language basis rather than a religious one. Because of this plan, and even though the MLF's membership is at least half Catholic (including at least one priest), the movement has become a favourite target of the *intégristes*.

In May, for instance, the Fédération Nationale des Ligues du Sacré Cœur issued a ringing condemnation of the MLF (not to mention drinking on Sundays without meals, uncensored movies and a few other *laïciste* trends). In a phrase not untypical of the *intégriste* line on this question, the Reverend Wilfrid Gariépy, who had just been re-elected national director of the Ligues, called the MLF's position "a subversive affair." The Ligues claim a total membership of 192,000, and even though there were only seventy-five people at the convention that passed this resolution, their ideas presumably represent those of many Catholics in Quebec.

They do not represent those of the Archbishop of Montreal. The week after the Ligues' convention, about a thousand Ligueurs met in Montreal to hear their leaders report on what had gone on, and invited the cardinal to hear, too. After the announcement of the anti-*laïciste* motion, there was prolonged applause. Then Cardinal Léger stood up, "visibly troubled" as one reporter put it. He rapped the Ligueurs' knuckles. "Have you studied these questions?" he asked in a lengthy speech, which ended: "God has put into your hands, not a bludgeon, but charity."

Léger had not, of course, endorsed the Mouvement Laïque. But he has made it abundantly clear that he regards the desire of laymen to play a much greater role in the teaching of the Catholic children as both natural, at this moment in Quebec's history, and healthy.

In a remarkable speech at the seminar of Saint-Jean-de-Québec last summer, Léger explained that he did not see this desire as any sort of evil "*laïcisme*." He said that he thought laymen — *Catholic* laymen — could in fact be "leaven" in education in the province, and he pointed out that both Pope John and his predecessor, Pius XII, called for more lay participation in church affairs. Making his actions fit this view, Léger last year made his three appointments to the Montreal Catholic School Commission laymen; all three positions had always been filled by priests. He has appointed a layman as vice-chancellor of the University of Montreal. He has handed over St. Paul's College, a Montreal *collège classique* formerly directed and staffed by secular priests, to laymen, and he has pointed proudly to the fact that in his archdiocese up to seventy per cent of the teaching hours are now in the hands of the laity.

This leaves the cardinal still to the right of such movements as Le Mouvement Laïque, but within the church it places him a long way left of many of his clergy. "Where are the *colleges classique* that are the property of the laymen?" a priest wrote recently. "These colleges are *ours*."

The most important form of reaction to what is happening in the Quebec church today is Cité Catholique. Cité Catholique began in France in the 1940s. In anyone's terminology, it is ultra-right-wing. While no formal link has ever been established between Cité Catholique and France's terrorist Secret Army Organization, it is known that the two groups shared many followers. The man who has done most to draw Quebec's attention to its potential is the Rev. André Liégé, a French Dominican who has studied and fought against the movement in France and who spent this winter at the universities of Laval and Montreal. Father Liégé describes Cité Catholique as a "struggle against all the ideas and all the trends that characterize the modern world." In 1960, the Assembly of Cardinals and Bishops of France (the church in France, of course, is essentially liberal) issued a "*mise en garde*" — a warning — against Cité Catholique and the magazine it publishes, *Verbe*. One passage in that document explains why Cité Catholique is literally more Catholic than the pope. Cité Catholique's announced goals include uniting the church on both doctrine and temporal action. Said the French bishops: "Unity on doctrine is a matter for the church itself to decide; unity among Catholics on temporal matters is neither possible nor desirable. . . . The church gives its sons great liberty in the domain of concrete techniques in the social and political order. . . . The spirit of Cité Catholique is the spirit of counterrevolution. . . . There is (in that point of view) a grave danger for the true mission of the church."

The new target of this movement is Quebec, and the revolution it would like to counter is the quiet revolution here. This spring, the international director of Cité Catholique, a short, slim, mild-mannered Frenchman in his forties named Jean Ousset, took up residence in Quebec City. When he arrived, or how long he would stay, no one was saying; he was there in mid-May, at 42 Rue Saint-Famille, with a group of laymen who live like a religious community. He was not entertaining journalists. In April, a reporter named Evelyn Gagnon, of *La Presse*'s Quebec bureau, got in to see Ousset, and discovered that the only reason he had agreed to see her was that on the telephone he had understood her to say Labrecque, not *La Presse*. Miss Gagnon didn't discover much else. Cité Catholique is a secret movement. It works by a device similar to that of its enemy, communism. It organizes cells, often groups of people from the same office or belonging to the same club, who meet to discuss creeping *laïcisme* and what they can do to fight it. The movement's own phrase is "*action capillaire*."

How far this capillary action has already seeped into Quebec, no one knows. *Verbe* is being seen more and more around the province. Father Liégé told the *Nouveau Journal* that he thought more than three thousand copies of a book setting out the movement's aims, a nine-hundred-page tome called *Pour Qu'il Règne* (a more classical text on the same theme is called *Liberalism Is a Sin*), had been sold in Quebec.

How far it can seep in has many liberals — within and without the church — worried. The quiet revolution has as yet had little effect on the number of people in rural and artisan Quebec who tend to see things in black (or red) and white, as the phenomenal outbreak of Social Credit here has proved. "It would be utopian to think that Quebec, a milieu to a large extent still traditional and now undergoing rapid transformations, could remain aloof from *intégrisme*," a young Dominican wrote recently. At least one U.S. Catholic bishop has publicly deplored the fact that Catholics seem more ready than Protestants to join this sort of movement. There are already strong organizations, such as the Ligues du Sacré Cœur, with a strong leaning towards *intégrisme*. As Abbé Louis O'Neill, the young Quebec City priest who has become nationally known as a spokesman for democracy in his province, put it recently: "In Quebec, people of the right tend to be very far right."

There is talk that Cité Catholique has plans for a newspaper of its own here, and the talk mentions as editor Jean-Noel Tremblay, the nationalistic ultra-Catholic former Laval professor who sat as conservative MP for Robervalle from 1958 until June 18, and whom an Ottawa journalist once described privately as having "the best medieval mind in the House of Commons."

To the men who have been fighting Cité Catholique, priests and journalists mostly, Cardinal Léger has given tacit encouragement, but he has not yet condemned the movement publicly. Why not? Perhaps the most important reason is that he still has those other bishops to contend with. Already there are sounds of grumbling in the boondocks about the changes he has made — even a rumour that there has been a letter circulated among some bishops that would have Rome slow the cardinal down. To denounce *intégrisme* at this time would almost certainly set many of his fellow bishops squarely and bitterly against him. (There is virtually no chance, however, that Léger will suffer Msgr. Charbonneau's fate. For one thing, his own connections in Rome and his influence there are far stronger than those of any other Quebec bishop. For another, he is a superb administrator, which Charbonneau was not, and apologists for the church still quote Charbonneau's inept administration as a reason for his dismissal.)

Why is Cardinal Léger so much readier than most of his colleagues to accept and even institute change? Many people of whom

I asked that question went into various explanations of how Montreal, with its recent influx of immigration and its cosmopolitan nature, is far more ready to undergo modernization of its church — as of its other institutions — than rural and artisan Quebec. But as one Montreal Dominican said: "Rosemont and Hochelaga and Verdun — they are all in the archdiocese of Montreal and they are not different from Rimouski in their makeup."

Will the others catch up? Which way *will* the church in Quebec move? Abbé O'Neill says: "This province now is like a man in a canoe, going down a set of rapids. He can steer — he *must* steer, or he will crash on a rock — but he cannot get out, and he cannot turn around."

And the Man We'll Always Remember

from Trudeau Albums, *2000*

My admiration for Pierre Trudeau was well developed long before 1968, when he assumed the leadership of the party he had so unexpectedly chosen; in the six years that followed, that admiration was to undergo much metamorphosis. I had met him in Montreal, in 1961, where he was teaching law, writing for and helping to edit the influential journal *Cité Libre*. I was working as the Quebec editor of *Maclean's*, struggling, with my inadequate French, to capture some of the people and events making the profound changes that were coursing through the province. I used the words "Quiet Revolution" so many times in my dispatches that many people thought, with flattering inaccuracy, that I'd coined the term. (In fact, the first use I've ever been able to track down was, surprisingly enough, in the old Tory *Toronto Telegram*.) Though I hadn't yet met him, Trudeau's name kept cropping up in my research. He, or his writings, were in evidence in subjects as diverse as Paul-Emile Cardinal Léger, who turned out to be a closet supporter of *Cité Libre*, and Jacques Hébert, whose publishing company, Les Editions de l'homme, was carrying on its own fight against Duplessism. I decided to seek Trudeau out to see if he'd sit still for a *Maclean's* profile.

He was a reluctant subject, even then no fan of journalists or journalism. If he had any desire for the limelight, it was certainly not apparent to me. I persevered, pulling every string I could think of, Jacques Hébert, Gérard Pelletier, then the editor of *La Presse* and perhaps Trudeau's closest friend, and anyone else I'd met who might know him.

He eventually succumbed, and one morning that spring I found myself ringing the bell at his mother's stately home in Outremont. He answered the door himself and ushered me into the living room, dominated, as I remember, by a large, somewhat forbidding European painting — Braque would have been my guess, but I was too intimidated to offer it.

"Like a drink?" he said.

Wow, I thought as I accepted, these Montreal intellectuals, into the sauce at ten in the morning. *Quel panache.*

He brought me about four fingers of Scotch, neat, but, to my dismay, took nothing himself. Ah well, I thought, and proceeded to sip myself into a blissful fog, as we rambled through the first of what was to become the most challenging, stimulating and, in its own way, enjoyable series of conversations — nearly all of the later ones taking place, of course, on the radio — I have ever been lucky enough to be part of.

Interviewing him wasn't then — nor has it ever been — easy. He was as he has remained, as private as the Sphinx, apparently incapable of small talk, intolerant of pretence or stupidity, certain of his own opinions. But his mind was as penetrating as an épée and his erudition as formidable as a broadsword. He seemed to relish being challenged, provided you had thought your way through your question, and to delight in the Jesuitical adroitness of his response. As someone once said of Bobby Orr at his peak in the NHL, "he should play in a higher league."

My unabashedly admiring portrait of him ran in *Maclean's* under the title "Portrait of an Intellectual Engagé." It wasn't bad, I suppose, including, as it did, a prescient suggestion that if he ever entered politics he would be a force to be reckoned with, but I never did hear whether he liked it or even, come to think of it, whether or not he read it.

• • •

Given my earlier encounters with Trudeau, it was hard for me not to share in the excitement of his remarkable rise to victory: political unknown to MP to parliamentary secretary to justice minister in two years. And then, in 1968, Trudeaumania; he was elected prime minister, and would lead the country with a majority government.

To those of us who had been swept up in the American promise of John F. Kennedy and still mourned his death, Trudeau was especially inspiring. He was glamorous, he was sexy and he was ours — the perfect symbol of the newly invigorated Canada that had emerged from Expo and the centennial celebrations. From the outset, it was clear that high among Prime Minister Trudeau's priorities was a diffusion of the forces of Quebec nationalism. Quickly, any suspicions that his role in the intellectual circles of Montreal had aligned him with the separatist course so many of his friends and colleagues were now pursuing were erased, though no one who had read his work in *Cité Libre* could ever have harboured such thoughts. Instead, Trudeau sought to strengthen Quebec's role in Confederation, to accelerate the progress reflected and supported by Lester Pearson's sweeping "Bi and Bi" commission, and to bring about a truly bilingual country. Among the first major pieces of legislation the new government brought in was the Official Languages Act, which entrenched bilingualism, as it said, "where numbers warrant." Trudeau was determined to attract some of the brightest young Québécois to Ottawa, as he himself had come in to work, however briefly, with the Privy Council nearly twenty years earlier.

In Quebec itself, however, the forces loosed by the Quiet Revolution continued to swirl. Everything was changing: the authority of the Church, the traditional role of women, the education system, the power of unions — virtually every facet of daily life. *"Maîtres chez nous,"* the slogan of Jean Lesage's Liberal government, was taking on new meaning. Separatism, whose popularity had stood at just thirteen per cent in my days with *Maclean's*, grew steadily stronger, measuring now closer to twenty per cent. Not long after Trudeau's ascent to power in Ottawa, René Lévesque, one of the principal architects of change and one of the most popular politicians in the province, stepped down from the Lesage cabinet to work with the movement that would soon become the Parti Québécois.

And then came October 1970. For some time, there'd been evidence of a group that called itself the Front de liberation du Quebec that was willing to work outside the law for the separatist cause — most seriously by planting bombs in the mailboxes of English Montreal. But, with the kidnapping of the British trade commissioner, James Cross, on October 5, high drama began to unfold. The rebels' demands included the release of the few of their members who were in jail, the reading of their "manifesto" on Radio-Canada, and safe passage out of the country for the kidnappers. Just as the Quebec government seemed ready to accede to at least some of the conditions — the manifesto had already been read — another hostage was abducted: Pierre Laporte, a minister of the Quebec government. Quebec asked for help from Ottawa, and, on October 16, 1970, the Trudeau government, citing an "apprehended insurrection," brought in the War Measures Act, suspending many liberties and giving the authorities, among other powers, the right to haul people off to jail without charge.

This was a Pierre Trudeau we had not seen before; as ruthless in the suppression of civil rights as he had been steadfast in his defences of them. In the broadest terms, his decisiveness did nothing to hurt his popularity. The War Measures Act passed the Commons with near unanimity, and the first surveys of public opinion found an astonishing eighty-three per cent support — reinforced, no doubt, by the discovery of the body of Pierre Laporte, strangled and stuffed in a car trunk, the day after the act came down. Still, there were those who were troubled, not only by the sight of armed troops on the streets of Montreal, but by the draconian measures the prime minister had taken. In spite of my earlier infatuation with Trudeau, I was among them. I'd moved back to Toronto by this time, and was working at CBC Radio, where the powers of the government to limit free discussion of the act or its consequences were keenly felt. Also, as the list of people who'd been rounded up in the middle of the night and held without bail or recourse to lawyers grew longer, it included far too many people whose arrests seemed simply too bizarre to accept: the chanteuse Pauline Julien, the poet and later PQ cabinet minster Gerald Godin, the writer and bon-vivant Nick Auf der Maur, among others. I don't know if I thought of it then, but I have since wondered what would have happened if, instead of the gruesome murder of Pierre Laporte, the handful of people who turned out to be behind the "apprehended insurrection" had just released their hostages in their underwear and let them run down Ste.-Catherine Street. They might have demonstrated how out of proportion to the real threat to peace the government's — and Trudeau's — reaction had been, and thereby served their cause more effectively. But the murder destroyed any chance for that.

In the fall of 1974, I had a chance to raise the matter of the War Measures Act with Trudeau. I suggested to him that if the act had been brought down in the years when I first wrote about him, he, too, might have been among those rounded up in the midnight raids.

"Perhaps you're right," he said, "I had Karl Marx in my library and perhaps I would have been arrested and gone to jail. [But] I don't think I would have bitched about it. I would have bitched against the guys who created the climate in which the state, the elected representatives of the people, in order to defend the authority of the state, had to use strong measures."

He never did lose an argument.

That conversation, which took place in a radio studio in Toronto, was the last time I saw him in person until well after the next election. Much was to happen to him in the years that followed. In 1971, he married Margaret Sinclair (and broke a million hearts). In 1972, he fought the ineffectual "The Land Is Strong" election campaign that resulted in a Liberal minority government and taught Trudeau the political realities of trying to stay in power. He also continued his world travels, though as statesman now, not as the vagabond of his youth. The magic of Trudeaumania was ebbing, but he was still playing in a league of his own.

Occasionally, we saw the aloofness and contempt in which he held what he perceived to be wilful ignorance or simple stupidity. "Mange de la merge," he told grain farmers; "fuddle-duddle" (or something similar), he said in the House of Commons. "Just watch me," he crowed to a reporter who questioned his actions in the October Crisis.

I think now, looking back at those years, that he got a few things wrong. He never did come to understand the West, and there are still people in Alberta who have not forgiven him for his National Energy Policy. Curiously, for he knew Quebec and its principal players so well, his course of action to thwart the growth of separatism may have missed a seminal point: it was not a bilingual Canada the sovereigntists were after; it was a unilingual Quebec.

But there never was anyone like him, was there? And perhaps there never will be again.

• • •

I continued to see him occasionally over the decades that followed. Once, in the nineties, in his law offices in Montreal, I had a few moments away from the microphone with him. I asked him if by any chance he recalled our first meeting at his mother's house.

"I thought it was in my apartment," he said, "but, yes, I do."

I reminded him of the drink he had poured me and confessed to my own embarrassment. "I sure thought you Montreal intellectuals were a pretty fast-living bunch," I said.

He smiled that enigmatic smile. "And I," he said, "thought all you Toronto journalists were alcoholics."

Racism on the Prairies

Maclean's, *July 6, 1963*

This piece ran in Maclean's *in 1963 under the somewhat melo-dramatic title "This Is Our Alabama," and caused more than a little stir in the area in which it is set. Nearly forty years later, I'm still not sure I was wrong.*

Sometime after midnight, on May 11 this year, a slight young Salteaux Indian named Allan Thomas was killed in the village of Glaslyn, Saskatchewan, when a party of white men raided the encampment in which he was living, pulled down two tents and, apparently, fought with the Indians. The next day, a Sunday, nine white men from the Glaslyn district were arrested and charged with non-capital murder. These men were not, as one might have expected, young toughs out for a brawl. Most were farmers or businessmen. Five of their names are among the forty-seven listed in the local telephone directory for Glaslyn, and, with a significant fraction of its respected heads-of-household under charge of murder, Glaslyn was, in the days after Thomas's death, a shocked, puzzled town. "I just can't imagine what would cause a thing like that," said a pleasant, plump widow who keeps a boarding house at the edge of the town. A grim member of the RCMP's two-man contingent said to a reporter only that "there are deep, bitter feelings here. I don't want to add to them by commenting."

The surrounding area echoed the village's shock. Glaslyn is one of perhaps two dozen smaller communities that spread out around North Battleford, a friendly, mildly prosperous Prairie city of twelve thousand people about a hundred miles west-northwest of Saskatoon. Through the North Battleford area are laced ten Indian reserves, home for about thirty-eight hundred Indians. An equal number of Métis, or mixed-breeds, live at the fringes of both the reserves and the white population centres.

This is Canada's Alabama. In the next few years, we may have there, on a lesser scale, what the U.S. has had in the past few years in the South. One essential difference between our situation and the South's may save us the South's violence and heartache: virtually no legislation condemns the Canadian Indian to a second-class role, as legislation in many states does condemn the American Negro. But the other pressures exerted on the southern Negro — social, economic and just plain discrimination — are exerted at least as strongly on the Saskatchewan Indian. Indeed, in some ways our problems may be worse. Where the Southern Negro has the same language, the same religion and, in most respects, the same culture as his oppressor, many Canadian Indians still speak neither English nor French as their mother tongue, still practise a pagan religion and still follow a scale of moral and cultural values utterly different from ours. If the Canadian Indian is going to join the twentieth-century way of North American life — and there are almost no alternatives for him — the wrench he will suffer in the process will be far stronger than whatever an American Negro child may suffer when he moves to an integrated school. And *our* acceptance of *him* as an equal could well be an even more difficult decision than the Southerner's acceptance of the black man.

Canada's Alabama is not set apart from the rest of the country by any inherent quality of its citizens. Its Indian problem is worse than that of, say, Owen Sound, Ontario, simply because it has more Indians than Owen Sound: its prejudices are different only because they have had a chance to come out. Saskatchewan's Indians are only now beginning to enter the mainstream of its life. In some other parts of Canada, many Indians have already come to terms with the white man's way of life. In other parts, the Indian does not yet live close enough to the white man to precipitate the problem. Many parts of Canada have no Indian problem because they have no Indians. But North Battleford and Glaslyn and the towns around them have, and their problems are ours.

I went to Saskatchewan shortly after the death of the young Salteaux Allan Thomas. My purpose was not so much to dig into Thomas's killing — which was and is still before the courts — as to see what a stranger could learn just from talking to the people of Canada's Alabama. There *is* race prejudice in North Battleford, and it is an ugly and in some ways frightening thing to behold. But it is, if this is possible, the race prejudice of gentle, friendly people. I do not mean by this that "some of their best friends are Indians." For one thing, none of their best friends are Indians; practically no white citizen of North Battleford even knows an Indian to talk to. But these are not, at least from the result of my very brief investigation, the kind of people one thinks of as racists, or members of secret, murderous societies. The truly frightening thing here is that, in the opinion of many people who have written about the American South, neither were the American Southerners such obvious villains a decade or more ago. And I myself have heard enough white American Southerners talk about "Nigras" to recognize the same bewildered, paternal, hurt cast of mind in white Canadian westerners.

No racists? Well, not quite. A few days after the Glaslyn incident, Mrs. Gladys Johnston, a handsome Cree housewife who also works as a stenographer for the Saskatchewan Department of Social Welfare, was having lunch, as she does most working days, in the North Battleford bus-station restaurant. A group of men at a nearby table were talking about Thomas's death. Mrs. Johnston heard one of them say: "They ought to have killed about ninety of the bastards when they were at it." A white woman who devotes much of her time to working with Indians told me she has been called an

"Indian-lover" in the tone of voice Southerners use for "Nigger-lover." This woman is Mrs. Eileen Berryman, a young grandmother and businesswoman who runs a hobby shop on the main street of North Battleford. In recent years, her shop has been devoted more and more to Indian handicraft — she supplies some raw materials to the Indians and sells the finished goods — and has also become a place where Indians often drop in just to pass the time of day. As one result, Mrs. Berryman has become a moving force in the recently formed Battleford Indian-Métis Friendship Council, of which Gladys Johnston is the president. As another, she has had such experiences as, while sitting with some Indians in a local hotel beer parlour — something one simply does not *do* in North Battleford — having a man at the next table break into the recently popular song, "Don't Go Near the Indians."

But most of the prejudice in the North Battleford area is less overt. Very few Indians actually live in the city. No one keeps a record, but the guess I heard most frequently was about a hundred families out of twelve thousand people. The Indians the townsfolk see are more likely to be casual visitors from the nearby reserves, and these visitors are kept, by unwritten but very real rules, huddled in a small quarter of the older end of town. Mostly they hang around the corner of Railway Avenue and 101st Street — or King, as it is known locally. In one late evening interview I had with a lawyer I was told that if I left his office and walked around Railway and King I would be certain to see twenty or thirty drunken Indians. (He was wrong that evening, as it happened — it was raining — but right on another night I checked.) On my first day in town, I was taken on a short walking tour by the editor of the local paper. One of the sights he showed me was a vacant lot just off Railway and King where, he said, the Indians liked to take their beer to drink after the beverage rooms closed. Hard by this corner are two of the city's four beer parlours, and a poolroom. While none of these places is considered the exclusive demesne of Indians, all have a large Indian clientele. In at least one of these beer parlours, one of the largest I have ever seen, there is a sort of indoor Indian reserve: the Indians quietly take up the tables farthest from the bar, and when the room is not full there is usually space between their tables and where the white people sit. The same sort of voluntary segregation, apparently, affects the buses that run from outlying points into North Battleford. Gladys Johnston told me sadly that in her lunch hours at the bus station she often sees buses pull in front from the district. Invariably, she has noticed, the white people sit in the front and get off first.

The vocabulary of Canada's Alabama even contains the phrase, strange to hear in Canada, "integrated schools." For years, Indian children have been pretty well restricted to federally run schools on the reserves, and not even the most ardent apologist for Canada's treatment of the Indian has maintained that these schools have been as good as those in the regular provincial system. Attitudes have been changing, though, and the Indian Affairs Branch has been moving students — slowly, but with what the U.S. might call "all deliberate speed" — into provincial schools. In all Saskatchewan, which has an Indian population of some twenty-six thousand, seven thousand Indian children now attend one sort of school or another. Roughly five thousand are still in segregated schools. Of the ten bands scattered around the North Battleford area, only ninety-five children are in non-Indian schools. Two Indians from the North Battleford area now attend university.

North Battleford has even had its own version of a sit-in. In the fall of 1961, a daughter of Eileen Berryman went to work as a wait-ress at the café of a hotel called the Auditorium, one of the two near Railway and King which sell quite a lot of their beer to Indians. On her first day on the job, she was told not to serve Indians. If anyone asked her any questions, she was to tell them to see the manager. Bothered by these instructions, the girl went to get her mother. Mrs. Berryman got in touch with Ray Woollam, a Saskatchewan gov-ernment employee who is in charge of the province's Committee for Minority Groups. With Woollam's coaching, two Indian men and three women, all neatly dressed, entered the Auditorium café a few days later. They quietly took a booth and waited for service. No one came to their table. They waited a little longer, and finally one of the group got up and caught a waitress' attention. Gladys Johnston, who was one of the women, says the dialogue that followed was pretty close to this:

"I'm sorry. I can't serve you people."

"Why not?"

"I'm just not allowed to serve you. You'll have to see the manager."

"Where is he?"

"Well, he's not in just now."

"Whom may we see then?"

"You'd better see the girl at the cash register."

Eventually the group got an admission that the reason they weren't being served was that they were Indians. They laid a charge under Saskatchewan's antidiscrimination laws; the Auditorium was convicted and fined twenty-five dollars.

"We don't go there even now," Mrs. Johnston says. "But I think we made our point."

One man who is making a lot of points in and around North Battleford is the Reverend Ahab Spence, an archdeacon of the Anglican Church in Canada and a Cree. Nearly everyone I talked to about Indians said I must see Spence. They used him, in fact, as a sort of answer to any charge of discrimination they might infer from my questions. "Look at him," they would say in effect. "He is our equal, and treated equally. Why, he even talks about being an Indian." Time after time I heard how Spence makes jokes about his children being tired of playing cowboys and Indians — they always lose; or how he points to his nearly bald head and laughs, because Indians aren't supposed to go bald. All of which, to be perfectly frank, made me a little reluctant to see him, since I do not ordinarily seek out self-consciously one-of-the-boys clergymen. But when we finally got together the Reverend Spence turned out to be, under his jollity, a very serious and articulate spokesman for his people. He told me that he is concerned by, among other things, the contempt in which the Indian women are held by Saskatchewan whites. He spoke of white men prowling the reserves, knocking on doors, waving bottles of wine and shouting, "We want women." He told me of an incident that happened only a couple of weeks before my arrival in North Battleford. A couple of young white men had picked up an Indian girl near Railway and King and offered to drive her home. Following what Spence sadly assured me was usual practice, they drove her the three miles across the North Saskatchewan river to the smaller settlement of Battleford, and produced a bottle of wine. The girl, who was an abstainer, refused. Then they tried to kiss her and fondle her. When she objected they casually drove her a few more miles into the country and dropped her off in a field of grain, to get home as best she could.

As well as degradation, the Indians around North Battleford often face economic exploitation. Social welfare workers of the province told me of a market gardener north of town who hires "fifteen or twenty Indians for the summer" and "all he gives them is room and board and a little money for tobacco." "Even our local welfare officer," they went on, "can't get him to say how much — if anything — he pays them. It's not much better than slave labour."

The strongest force exerted against the Indian, however, is a subtler one: the all-pervasive atmosphere of unwelcome; the fact, of which he so quickly becomes aware, that the white man does not want him around. For several months, up to and including the time I was in North Battleford, the Indian-Métis Friendship Council had been trying to find a place where it could set up rooms as a referral centre and meeting place for Indians from out of town. To the people of the council this seems a vital part of their program, if for no other reason than that it would give visiting Indians some alternative to the beer parlours as a place to rest and talk. They have had some success in organizing individual functions — the local branch of the Canadian Legion has been "wonderful," renting them its hall for half price, among other things — but they have found it almost impossible to rent anything on a permanent basis. "Everyone we talk to seems certain that property values would go down," says Mrs. Berryman, "and some people have even told us flatly that 'they wouldn't have anything to do with Indians.' The only real offer we've had was a place right beside the beer parlours, and we didn't want that." In my own interviews in North Battleford, I found the same attitude towards Indians that is implied by the landlords' reluctance to rent to them. "I had a delegation in here last month," one professional man told me in the course of a conversation about something else, "and it took me a week to air the place out." "Oh, we don't refuse to serve Indians," said a hotelman, "but we sure as hell watch them closely when they come to the door." A businessman said: "Liquor will take the veneer of civilization off an Indian as quickly as it will take the polish off this desk."

What North Battleford fears, Glaslyn has already experienced. The Salteaux are a small, proud band of Ojibwa origin that numbered, before the death of Allan Thomas, two hundred and sixty-three. Mostly from a strong distrust of the white man, they did not sign a treaty with Canada until 1954, with the result that, although they had a reserve of their own near Cochin, about twenty miles north of North Battleford, none of the Salteaux who are now adults have ever been to school. Huddled between the plains and the bush Cree, the Salteaux speak a dialect of the Cree language, but they more closely resemble the independent Algonkins of the east than the peaceful, agricultural Cree. For centuries, they have been a nomadic people, living off what they can shoot or catch or pick. In the late 1950s, the merchants of North Battleford, many of whom had recently organized themselves to promote tourism in their area, began to covet part of the Salteaux reservation that touches Jackfish Lake, a holiday area around Cochin. North Battleford, the businessmen felt, should have a provincial park; the Salteaux land, occupying the last unsettled beach on the lake, was the ideal place for it. The negotiations stretched out for many months, and the eventual solution, which was reached in 1960, was stained by politics. The Salteaux agreed to accept what seemed to be a generous offer by the government. In return for two hundred and sixty-one acres of their reserve at Cochin, they would accept twenty thousand dollars in cash and five thousand acres of Crown land north of Glaslyn. The catch was that a number of farmers in the Glaslyn area had been taking hay from these acres of Crown land, at the nominal cost of fifty cents a ton. Through their local MLA, a Liberal member named Franklin Foley, the farmers lobbied against the exchange of lands. Although Foley won his next election, he lost his campaign against the park, and about half the Salteaux band moved north of Glaslyn.

Now distributed nearly equally on both sides of Glaslyn, the Salteaux began gathering in and near the village. Also in 1960, Saskatchewan, under a fairly complex section of the federal Indian Act, began to allow its Indians free access to beer parlours and, since Indians are still not allowed to drink on their reserves without a vote of the band (a vote that no band in Saskatchewan has yet passed), the Glaslyn Hotel beer parlour became the favourite meeting place of the Salteaux. Often they would pitch their tents near or even in the village, and on most nights there would be one or two tents on the Glaslyn sports ground, an untended grassy field on the edge of town. Glaslyn's problem was simply too many drunken Indians too often, and since drunken Indians lurching around a Prairie village are no more pleasant than drunken French Canadians or Jews or magazine editors, Glaslyn became a fairly unpleasant place to be after the pubs closed. It is still impossible to say how directly this unpleasantness affected the events of the night of May 11, but even if the death of Allan Thomas was a completely isolated event, which one can doubt, the warnings are obvious. In the words of an official of the Indian Affairs Branch, reported indirectly to me: "What happened in Glaslyn could have happened in any one of about nine little places where the Indians congregate."

Hostility between Indians and whites will almost certainly flare up elsewhere in Canada. For the first time, the Canadian Indian population is now back where historians figure it was when Jacques Cartier arrived here, around two hundred thousand. With the onslaught of the white man and his diseases, the Indians had dwindled to around *one* hundred thousand at the turn of the century, but they have been increasing since then at an ever-accelerating rate. Today, with vastly increased welfare and medical services, the Saskatchewan Indian population is growing at a rate of four and a half per cent a year — more than double the rate of increase for all Canada. It won't be long until there just isn't room on the reserves for all the Indians, and many of those who would rather stay will have to move to the cities. Furthermore, as Indians become more and more exposed to the comforts of civilization as we know them, they are going to be more and more dissatisfied with the squalor in which many of them now live.

On most Canadian reserves, the day of the noble Indian has long since passed. In spite of welfare allowances and relief and treaty money, most Indians live in conditions that would appal most civilized Canadians. They are undernourished, poorly clothed, rudely housed.

Perhaps a single example will serve better than any catalogue of misery. On one of the days I was in Saskatchewan, I arranged to be taken along with a Cree interpreter to meet the Salteaux people around Glaslyn. After meeting a Salteaux chief who was our entrée, we passed through the village, turned up a farmer's road and followed a scarcely defined wagon trail past a few thickets for about a mile. We came upon the camp of two Salteaux families, and I was introduced to the man of one of the tents, Bill Gopher. Gopher is a big, husky man in his late twenties, with a few black straws of beard on his chin and shaggy black hair. Wearing a faded checkered shirt, tan pants and work boots, he came out from the tent and greeted our party near his wagon, a sturdy vehicle he made himself and uses for both family transportation and work. His two horses grazed in a nearby field. He offered me a surprisingly soft handshake. Through most of our conversation his eyes were cast downward and he shuffled awkwardly from one foot to the other, thumbing back and forth — although, like the other adult Salteaux, he is illiterate — through a ragged comic book. He spoke some English, but to give more than a one-word answer he frequently changed to the soft gutturals of Cree, and our interpreter translated for me.

Gopher was obviously both hurt and baffled by Thomas's death; when he spoke of the dead youth, who had, Gopher told me, spent two of his twenty years in a TB san, his dark, downcast eyes welled with tears. He interrupted our talk once to ask if I thought the accused men would be let out on bail (they later were) and to express his fear that there would be more trouble. He told me he got along well with nearly all the people in Glaslyn as a rule and that he was frequently given credit by the merchants. He has a house on the new northern reserve, where he spends his winters, but in summer he travels with his family in the tent. He makes most of his living cutting pickets (slim fence-posts) and doing occasional odd jobs for farmers. With welfare and relief, his income last year was about eight hundred dollars, and he spent most of it in Glaslyn, on clothes and flour and tea and beer.

As we spoke, my gaze wandered over the ashes of the Gophers' campfire, with a tin can converted into a cooking utensil lying beside them, and back beyond that into the opening of the tent. On some ragged blankets spread on the bare ground the Gopher family — wife, grandmother and children — huddled together in what looked to me like a picture of poverty and despair.

Yet treating the Gophers and the scores of thousands of Indians like them as innocent, exploited victims of the white men's cruelty would be as wrong, or at least as oversimplified, as seeing blatant racism in all the prejudices of the people of North Battleford. Both those concepts are right, but both are wrong, too. Part of this complex and uncomfortable story is that the Indian is a second-class citizen of Canada not only because we have made him one, but because, by nearly any standards one cares to apply — hygiene, North American morality, ambition — the Canadian reserve Indian fails to measure up to what *our* world demands. Much as I may admire the skill with which Bill Gopher can build a cart with his hands, I would not myself — and please do not begin your letter to the editor until I have finished this paragraph — like to have him for a drinking companion, or, I suppose if I ask myself frankly, for a neighbour. But the other half of this concept is at least equally important. By *Bill Gopher's* standards — and who am I to say his are less valid? — I am a second-class person. Much as he may envy my ability to read the comic book he thumbed as we talked, what good would I be out hunting rabbit? If I cannot understand why he would take his whole month's relief allotment and blow it on beer, leaving himself and his family literally not knowing where their next meal is coming from, neither can he understand why I must lock my door in Toronto every night. I have told him that my religion preaches generosity and brotherly love — he already *knows* his does; he would share his last piece of bannock with anyone who was hungry — yet he has seen how I treat my neighbour in the city. He knows that I try to keep my front lawn trimmed, and that if he were my neighbour I would expect him to do the same. Why? Does it keep him warmer? Does it fill his stomach? As John McGilp, the knowledgeable and dedicated supervisor of Indian Agencies for Saskatchewan, put it at the end of a full afternoon's conversation about the plight of the Indian in his province: "They've seen through us."

The reserve itself exerts strong pressure on the Indian to stay out of our way of life. The reserves are not a Canadian system of apartheid, as some critics have charged. No Indian is forced by legislation to stay on one. But the reserve is the Indian's one guarantee against anonymity, the one remainder of his heritage and his one bulwark against the discrimination he will feel in the city. While no one will get rich on a reserve, no one will starve, either. Strong ties of tradition hold him there, too. A welfare officer in North Battleford told me of one boy who was taken from his home on the reserve at the age of five for a lengthy series of stomach operations. He was treated first in the Indian hospital at North Battleford, a hospital the Indians have insisted on keeping separate, and later and more extensively at the University Hospital in Saskatoon. When he got home, he had become so "Europeanized" that he could speak no Cree. Worse, in his family's eyes, he could no longer digest the Indian diet of bannock and rabbit. His father beat him brutally as punishment.

"We don't realize how different their culture is," said the welfare officer who told me this story. "Often we take children home after as much as a year's absence. The parents show no affection at all. It's just not their way. We'll have to learn that. At other times we've had kids who are brought to the most comfortable boarding homes in the city so they can go to high school, and they'll be so ill at ease they'll go out and sleep on the river bank, even in winter. They just can't get along in our ways without education."

And there is the terrible dilemma of Canada's Alabama. Unless the Indian will change his ways completely — change his values, his language, even his religion — he can hardly hope to be accepted into our world. But have we the right to make our values his? Or can we afford not to force him into our mould?

Gordie

Maclean's, *December 14, 1963*

Gordie Howe, thirty-five, now in his eighteenth season with the Detroit Red Wings and generally regarded as the finest hockey player there has ever been, is a hero of our time, but he doesn't look very heroic. A six-footer, Howe weighs almost exactly two hundred pounds when he's in playing shape, which is most of the time. This makes him the seventh-heaviest man in the National Hockey League, but hardly a giant in the measurements of modern sports. In street clothes, he looks quite slim, an impression heightened by his long arms, rather long neck and narrow face. His most outstanding physical characteristic is the slope of his shoulders; his trapezius muscles — the muscle you feel if you stretch your arm out to one side — rise into his neck at an angle not far from forty-five degrees, while his deltoids, at the top of the arm, look scarcely better developed than the average dentist's. The enormous strength he displays in hockey flows from him, rather than exploding, and the easy grace with which he moves on the ice, and which has given so many hockey fans pleasure over the years, is also evident in his loose, almost lazy walk.

Howe goes through life much as he goes through a hockey game. He's a quiet man, at once relaxed and in control, very cool. His success has sprung from both his great natural gifts and his dedication to his job, and he seems to take it as his due, and to exploit it, but not to be overwhelmed by it.

A while ago he was talking about an experience he had had on the highway going to the Detroit suburb where he lives with his wife, Colleen, and their four young children in a $60,000 house. "A police car pulled me over, and the guy said I'd made an illegal pass. I said I had not, but he said I'd gone past a truck on the right a few miles back. Well, everybody does that, eh? I told him I'd been doing it for twenty years. But he just started to write me up. I said I guessed *he'd* be pretty popular around the station. I've been giving about five days a year to that police department kids' work, at their picnics and that, and I said he could tell the gang that he was the fellow who stopped *that*. A ten-dollar ticket would just run them about two dollars a day for getting rid of me. But he just wrote me up, and I drove over to the station to pay it right then."

Howe told this anecdote mostly as a joke on himself and on his inability to buffalo the cop. He quite patently was *not* going to stop helping with the boys' work. But at the same time a listener could sense that he really *had* expected to be recognized, and, because he is Gordie Howe, to be let off a traffic ticket. He is at the top, a man who is known and admired. This role affects him as a man, and it should also affect the people he encounters. (In one of its more interesting experiments, the CTV program *Telepoll* recently flashed on its screen the names and pictures of a dozen famous Canadians. Then its researchers asked a thousand people who had watched the show which of the dozen they could identify by occupation. Howe came in second, being recognized by eighty-eight per cent, behind Lester Pearson's ninety-six, but ahead of such figures as Georges Vanier, Charlotte Whitton and Jean Lesage.)

A couple of days after Howe told the traffic-cop story, he drove across from Detroit to Windsor to catch a plane for Toronto. The rest of the Red Wings had gone the day before, but Howe was nursing a minor injury and had stayed on at home for extra treatment. Howe was driving, and in the car with him were the team doctor, the Red Wings' publicity man, and I. Our examination at the border consisted solely of a customs officer saying, "Are you going to play tonight, Gordie?" Gordie — as nearly everyone in the world seems to call him — said he was, and we went on through. Someone in the car said, "Next time you're coming across I've got a little white powder I'd like you to take with you." Howe was not amused. Being recognized and let through is part of being The Best. Howe could no more imagine using his exalted position to smuggle something across the border than he could really fink out on some kids because a policeman didn't know who he was.

• • •

Hockey players — like most professional athletes, I suppose — live in a world of their own. They are boy-men, many of whom have never done an honest day's work in their lives, and because they play a game for a living they often seem to make all life into a game. They joke mercilessly and incessantly among themselves but they close ranks against outsiders, and they are often quick to express their contempt for people who are not "in the game." It is difficult to blame them for this tendency. Much of their contact with the public comes through sportswriters, men who hang around the outside of their world, having to report every day about a game that few of them have played. In between game-days a writer facing a deadline has to think of *something* he can say, and many sports-page stories cover some of the most striking non-events of all time. And although hockey players do make fatuous remarks about "only playing one game at a time," and such things, they do not confine their conversations solely to such remarks, as anyone reading most sports pages would believe they do. And the result is that not many players hold writers — i.e. the fans — in very much respect. Howe, however, is something of an exception to this rule. Although he is in on all his team's bantering, his jokes, unlike those of most of his colleagues, are almost never directed at someone's person. He is as close to being utterly unassuming as it is possible, after seventeen years in a steadily increasing limelight, to be. He seems willing to answer the most banal questions as seriously and fully as he can, and he presents a shy and grateful attitude to the many fans who approach him nearly everywhere he goes. Although he is still a boy-man, in that he still plays a boy's game for a living, he is a mature one.

There is, in fact, very little about Gordie Howe that isn't admirable. His off-ice personality is something that might have been designed by Lord Baden-Powell. He swears, of course. Listening to a hockey player talk without swear words would be like watching him play without his stick. He has been known to consume an entire can of beer in an evening, and to smoke a whole cigar between seasons, but he is not what is usually described as a rake. His most serious sin seems to lie in the wicked number of crossword puzzles he goes through. In Detroit, he is almost more popular than hockey; it is not the game that seems to sell tickets there so much as Howe's domination of it. He gets roughly three times as much mail as the rest of the team combined (typically, he tries to answer all of it himself, and even enlists his wife's help on occasion) and, although Detroit newspapers don't take hockey seriously enough to send their own men on every road trip, as papers in Montreal and Toronto do for their teams, a minor skate cut he suffered this fall was a daily story, with pictures of his foot and lengthy bulletins from the medical department.

For all his fame, Howe is still astonishingly shy. The nervous blinking of both his eyes that is apparent when he is being interviewed on television is much less evident in private moments, and when he is relaxing in a pinochle game with teammates it all but disappears. Part of his shyness he covers with his warm, disarming wit, and it is evident that all the people who are in frequent contact with him, from his bosses at the Red Wings to his partners in business to his neighbours' children, whom he sometimes smuggles into the Olympia to go skating, like him as much as they respect his ability to play hockey.

On the ice, though, Howe can be as cruel and vicious as he is personable and generous off it. He is not the most penalized player in the NHL — although only seven men had more penalties last year

— but he is the acknowledged leader at getting away with things that would draw penalties if the referees saw them. His illegalities are as controlled as his play. He seems able to deal out punishment and pain with a complete lack of passion. In one game a couple of years ago, Howe and Carl Brewer of the Toronto Maple Leafs fell together in a tangle behind the Toronto goal just as play was stopped. Brewer was on top. "Okay, okay, Carl," said Howe. "Play's over." Brewer resisted the temptation to give Howe a last one in the clinch, and rose. In the next period, the same two ended another play in another tangle. This time Howe was on top. When the whistle blew, Brewer, thinking a standard of gentlemanliness had been established for the evening, relaxed. Pow! Howe gave him one in the ribs.

"He's always at the outer edge of the rule-book anyway," says Eric Nesterenko of the Chicago Black Hawks, a veteran who has played frequently against Howe man-on-man. "You never know when he's going to slip over into what's dirty." Ted Lindsay, who was Howe's linemate with Detroit for a dozen years and his opponent with Chicago for three more, says, "Gordie gets away with more than anyone else in hockey." Andy Bathgate, the New York Ranger star who was fined by the league in 1960 for writing an article called "Atrocities on Ice" for *True* magazine, has accused Howe of deliberately inflicting head cuts, of deliberately cauliflowering at least one ear and of deliberately raising the puck at other people's heads. About the only crimes Howe is not generally accused of are the heinous ones of "spearing" — the art of jabbing the business end of a hockey stick into an onrushing opponent's unpadded belly — and "butt ending," another manoeuvre with a stick that takes place in flurries around the goal mouth or in the corners. He is a recognized master of "high sticking," an action that is almost impossible for the fans or even the referees to separate from an accident, and which has carved his signature on a good many faces around the league.

To the players who suffer most from its effects, Howe's cruelty is a thing to be admired rather than disliked. It is, simply, part of his superiority at their game: violence and intimidation are a facet of hockey, and Howe is good at *all* facets of the game. Furthermore, Howe has to be dirty. Because he is so much the outstanding performer on his team, he is — or would be if he allowed it — the most closely checked player in the league: stop Howe and you have stopped Detroit. But a man who holds Howe or clutches him or chips away at him for an evening's play is not likely to come out of that game unscathed. "Sure you're a little scared," says Nesterenko, one of the few frank players in the league. "But you admire him for the way he can keep you off. It's your job to stay with him and keep him under control, but unless you keep thinking about it all the time, you're inclined to stay a step or so away from him."

Still another aspect of Howe's cruelty, of course, is his strength and ability to fight. Red Storey, the former all-around athlete who watched Howe from a referee's vantage point for nine years, has said that if Howe had wanted to he could have been the heavyweight champion of the world. He is without doubt the heavyweight champion of the NHL. When Howe first broke into the league in the 1940s, Ted Lindsay recalled not long ago, "he seemed to think he had to beat up everyone one at a time." But Jack Adams, then the Red Wings' general manager, took him aside and told him to take it easy. In recent years, Howe hasn't fought very often. He hasn't had to, since not many people want to take him on. But in 1959 he made it clear that he had not relinquished his title by default. Throughout the 1958-59 season, New York Ranger coach Phil Watson had assigned Eddie Shack, then a bumptious rookie, to stick with Howe when the Rangers played Detroit, and for the first several games Shack did a remarkably fine job. In New York one night, though, the predictable occurred. Shack emerged from a skirmish with Howe with a face cut that needed three stitches to close. Lou Fontinato, who was then the Rangers' "policeman" — the man charged with retaliating for any indignities his teammates might suffer at the hands of opposing bullies — drew a bead on Howe at the first opportunity and smashed him into the boards. Both Howe and Fontinato dropped their gloves. Fontinato went low, for Howe's body. Howe grabbed him by the sweater with his left hand and, with his right, administered the most famous single punch in NHL history, shattering Fontinato's nose. That week, *Life* magazine ran one full-page photo of Fontinato in the hospital, his nose a wreck and his eyes swollen and bruised, and another of Howe in the dressing room, with his shirt off and his muscles rippling. In a nice summary of the importance of a man playing a body-collision sport like hockey not only *being* tougher than his opponent but *appearing* to be tougher, the Rangers' coach Watson said later that the heart went out of his team not when Howe threw his mighty punch but when the two contrasting photos appeared for the world to see: the Red Wings' cool Goliath had made a patsy out of their champion. The Rangers finished a bad last that year.

But even Fontinato, a likeable ruffian who has unfortunately been lost to hockey through a serious injury, couldn't hold Howe's victory over him as a *personal* grudge. Scott Young, then writing his excellent sports column for the Toronto *Globe and Mail*, happened to be present when Howe and Fontinato met for the first time off the ice after their match. "I guess you know Gordie Howe," Young said to Fontinato. "I guess so, but I'm not sure I should lower my hands to shake with him," Fontinato said, and then smiled and did so.

"Baseball," goes one of the most common clichés in sports, "is a game of inches." So is hockey. But in hockey the inches, since they are covered a lot more quickly, are not so evident to the casual observer. All the men who play in the NHL — the best hundred and twenty or so of the hundreds of thousands of Canadian boys who play hockey in every generation — have completely mastered the fundamentals of their game. By the time one of them has reached that plateau, he can skate, shoot, pass and check nearly as well as he is ever going to, so that the only things that separate those who are going to remain journeymen from those who will rise to stardom are such natural qualities as physique, desire and what might be called hockey sense. Howe has all three in abundance, and in various combinations they have given him a tiny but real advantage over virtually every player in the NHL at virtually every department of the game.

He is so well co-ordinated that he could almost certainly play with the best at any sport he chose to take up. A few years ago, in fact, he became friends with a few of the professional baseball players who live in Detroit and, mostly for conditioning, he worked out with the Detroit Tigers occasionally. Bucky Harris, then manager of the Tigers, saw him in the batting cage one day, pounding balls out into the bleachers with the strongest of Detroit's long-ball hitters, and was heard to remark that it would take only a few months to turn Howe into a regular in the big leagues. And Howe has been seen at a Red Wing practice standing beside the goal, holding his hockey stick like a baseball bat and knocking back many of the hardest shots his teammates tried to force past him.

Howe's co-ordination, however remarkable, probably does not set him so far apart from the average professional hockey player as his strength does. He can shoot a puck from near one goal and make it rise into the seats at the other end of the rink — an impossible feat for nearly anyone else in the league. One man whose shot comes close in speed to Howe's, which has been measured at a little better than a hundred and twenty miles an hour, is Bobby Hull, the glamorous and exceedingly talented star of the Chicago Black Hawks and the man who may some day succeed to Howe's mantle. (Significantly, Hull this year began wearing number 9 on his sweater, after having been 7 for his first six seasons; 9 is Howe's number, and was also worn by Maurice Richard of Montreal, when Richard was the biggest name in hockey.) But for Hull to take his fastest shot he has to raise his stick three or four feet and slap the puck. Howe can move his stick only a foot or so and actually *flick* the puck away at close to his maximum speed. Another curious similarity between Howe, the old bull, and Hull, the young one, is that Howe has for years been the only man in the league who can change the position of his hands on the stick from his natural grip, right-handed, to his unnatural one, left, and still retain most of his power, and now Hull appears to be the second one — although Howe's wrong-side shot is still stronger than Hull's. This technique of switch-hitting, as it were, gives Howe an advantage of an inch or more over anyone who is trying to check him. When he first broke into the league, in 1946, he played against Dit Clapper, who had stayed in the NHL for twenty years, a record Howe is almost certain to match. For all his age, Clapper still had surprising speed, and he was able to stay with most of the young forwards who came scooting in on him. One of the first times Clapper checked the young Howe, though, Howe changed his hands on his stick, thus putting his body between Clapper and the puck, and getting a clear shot on the Boston goal. "I think that's when Dit decided he'd quit hockey," Ted Lindsay says.

Except for his exceptional shot, Howe doesn't move *quickly* on the ice. His motions are graceful and economical: he never seems to waste energy. As one result, he has not only played more NHL games than any other player in history (more than eleven hundred) but he has frequently been able to put in as much as forty-five minutes in a single game. Most forwards average perhaps twenty-five. Howe often comes off the ice exhausted, and he can lose as much as six pounds in a single game, but anyone watching him on the bench will notice that no matter how he droops when he first hits his seat, he always seems to be the first resting player to recuperate. In about half a minute, it seems, his head is up and he is studying the play as if thinking about what he can do during his next shift. Unfortunately for medical science, no one has yet tried to measure the source of Howe's remarkable endurance. His counterpart in basketball, Bob Cousy of the Boston Celtics, now retired, was once discovered by some Massachusetts scientists to discharge ten times as much of an adrenal hormone called epinephrine as any other basketball player they tested. It would be fascinating to see if Howe has similar characteristics, or if he secretes an exceptional amount of another adrenal hormone, norepinephrine, which is associated with "aggression, anger and competitiveness," and is sometimes called the hockey player's hormone.

Physical gifts aside, Howe brings to hockey a fierce pride and dedication that would probably have made him excel at whatever line of work he'd chosen. As it is, he applies it to bowling and golf, at both of which he can best any of the people he plays with. Whatever he does, he *must* win, and in hockey he's been willing to work long hours to achieve his near-perfection. In the early years, for instance, Howe and his linemate Lindsay used to stay at practice well after lesser luminaries of the Detroit team had gone to the showers, and work on special plays. Once they discovered that if the puck were shot into the other team's corner at a certain angle it could be made to bounce out in front of the goal, but out of the goalie's reach. Howe and Lindsay worked on this play for hours, until they were able to use it in games, and for a season or two Lindsay received dozens of apparently fluke breakaways by going straight at the goal while Howe shot the puck into the corner. Now, of course, every team in the league executes this play (usually most effectively on home ice, since all boards react differently).

Howe's third talent seems, to some, almost supernatural. He appears to anticipate the puck — or his opponents — almost as if play gravitated towards him by some natural force. In fact, it is a result of many qualities: a thorough knowledge of the game, his ability to remain always in control of himself, and his high sense of timing. Hockey at the NHL level is not so much a matter of how you make your move — since so little separates the good players from the mediocre in their ability to make it — but *when*. With his graceful control, Howe can appear to the man checking him to be relaxed, but if that man gives him so much as half a step, Howe will seize on the instant to send or receive a pass or get away a shot. In the same way, he can sense a play developing, and without giving away his plan to the man on his back, move towards the place he knows the puck must come, or shake his check for the brief instant that he will be in the clear. Situations form and disintegrate so rapidly when a hockey game is flowing back and forth at full tilt that a split second's advantage — an "inch" of ice — is all a player of Howe's certainty needs to appear to be all by himself. (Another reason Howe gets the puck a lot, of course, is that his teammates give it to him as often as they can, as who would not?)

In the opinion of the people who ought to be able to judge best, Howe is now not quite as fast a skater as he was a few years ago (he never was as fast a breakaway skater as Maurice Richard), although he can still move pretty rapidly when he gets loose. If he's lost anything in speed, though, he has more than made up for it in guile. Last season, when Howe led the league in scoring for the first time in five years (he did it five times in the fifties), and led Detroit into a surprisingly close Stanley Cup final, Dave Keon, the young Toronto Maple Leaf star, remarked: "There are four strong teams in this league and two weak ones. The weak ones are Boston and New York and the strong ones are Toronto, Chicago, Montreal and Gordie Howe."

Howe began to skate at about the age of five. He was the fifth of nine children of a family that had been farming in the district of Floral, Saskatchewan, in 1928 when Gordon was born. The family had moved to a two-storey clapboard house on Avenue L North, in Saskatoon, when he was an infant. From the time he got his first pair of skates, he recalls, he spent most of his winters on ice, skating across a series of sloughs to get to school or playing hockey outdoors. As a boy, he played goal, and he recalls that one teacher told him "if I ever moved out from between the pipes I'd never get anywhere in hockey." (Howe thinks his season and a half as a goalie, holding his stick with one hand, has something to do with his ability to switch-hit as a pro.)

In the summers, young Gordie worked on farms around Saskatoon, putting in twelve-hour days, and, he says, eating five big meals a day. His father was nearly as strong as Gordie is today. Gordie remembers straining to hold up one end of a giant boulder they were lifting together, and his father muttering, "Come on, boy, don't let me down." He weighed two hundred pounds at sixteen. But talent bird-dogs from the professional hockey clubs had sniffed him out even before that. Fred McCrorry, a scout for the New York Rangers, talked him into going to the Rangers' training camp at Winnipeg the summer he was fifteen.

The camp was a miserable experience for him. On the first day of practice, the boy who had been assigned as his roommate was injured and Howe was forced to spend the remaining weeks by himself. He was too shy to join in the general scramble at mealtime, and occasionally missed eating. Homesick, he went back to Saskatoon.

The next year, though, a Detroit scout named Fred Pinckney was able to talk him into trying the Red Wings' camp at Windsor, Ontario, and Jack Adams signed him to a contract to play with the Red Wings' Junior A farm team in Galt, Ontario. This was an "illegal" transfer, taking a western boy to an eastern team, and Howe was forced to spend his first year away from home as a pariah, allowed on the ice only in practice or exhibition games. (He did, in fact, play one league game, which the Galt Red Wings won but had to forfeit because of his participation.) His shyness affected his life in Galt, too. The Red Wings had enrolled him at the Galt Collegiate Institute and Vocational School. But, never a good student, he "took one look at the size of the campus and all those kids and decided not to go." Instead, he got a job at Galt Metal Industries, and suffered through his lonely winter.

The next year, 1945, the Red Wings sent him to their U.S. Hockey League team in Omaha, Nebraska, where he scored twenty-two goals and convinced his bosses that he would be ready for the big team at eighteen.

In Omaha, Howe had been so shy that he used to leave the arena by the dressing-room window rather than face the ardent fans outside the door — particularly a very ardent girl fan the Omaha players called Spaghetti Legs. The Red Wings hit on a good antidote. They gave him, as a roommate, Ted Lindsay, a cocky, aggressive youngster from Kirkland Lake, Ontario, who went on to become the game's third leading goal scorer, behind only Howe and Richard. These two vastly different personalities quickly became good friends and earnest allies in the Detroit cause, and to this day are mutual admirers.

Howe was slow to start in the NHL, although he scored a goal in his first game, and before his first season was over had won a fight with Maurice Richard and lost his front teeth. In his first three years in the NHL, he scored only thirty-five goals, but he hit his stride quickly after that, matching his total of thirty-five in his fourth season alone. Since then he has failed to score thirty goals only three times, and for one of those seasons he was named the most valuable player in the league anyway. For the last fourteen years, he has completely dominated the statistics of the NHL, never being worse than sixth in league scoring, making eight first and five second all-star teams, being judged the most valuable player to his team six times. When he finally scored his five hundred and forty-fifth goal in league play this year and passed Maurice Richard's lifetime total, he completed a clean sweep of all the significant scoring records: most goals, most assists and, naturally, most points. Since he intends to play at least two more seasons after this one, he will undoubtedly run his record totals well out beyond the reach of anyone now in sight.

Hockey has been immensely good to Howe — almost as good as he has been to it. Through the years, he has suffered far fewer than his share of injuries. (Although he has had serious ones. In the Stanley Cup finals in 1950 he hit the boards after a check by Toronto's Ted Kennedy and slumped unconscious to the ice. For two days he was close to death, and an operation was needed to relieve the pressure on his brain. In the season of 1952-53, he broke his right wrist around Christmas time. But he had a cast put on, played the next game and went on to win the scoring championship. In eighteen seasons, he's missed only forty-one games.) He is now being paid thirty-five thousand dollars a year by the Red Wings, and his outside activities may well bring him nearly as much again. He is a partner in a commercial rink in Detroit called Gordie Howe's Hockeyland, and in another firm that sells ice-cream machines. He is known as a cool negotiator. He endorses a cornucopia of products from milk to shirts. This year, Campbell's Soup has brought out a little hard-cover book called *Hockey . . . Here's Howe*, written by Howe and the Toronto writer Bob Hesketh, from which young players who have a dollar and two soup carton fronts can learn the fundamentals. Howe also has a column in the *Toronto Star*.

Howe will likely stay in hockey when his playing days are over. The Red Wings have already named him an assistant coach, and it does not seem impossible that he will take over all the coaching when he retires, so that Sid Abel, now handling both that job and the general manager's, can concentrate on being manager.

There is some light on the horizon for the fans who will miss Howe's power and grace. At least one of his three sons — to avoid family jealousy no one is supposed to say publicly which one — has all the makings of a hockey player. He's big for his age, skates with long, strong strides and has a powerful shot. But I suppose it would be too much to hope for another Gordie Howe.

A Hockey Writer's Last Stand at *Maclean's*

The Canadian Forum, *October 1964*

One time when I was managing editor of *Maclean's* magazine I wrote that sixteen Toronto Maple Leaf hockey players had each been paid $50 by Schick without even all having to shave with one blade. This event became known as the time the Schick hit the fan, I being the fan. The advertising agency — Walsh — that had signed the contract with Maple Leaf Gardens about the Leafs shaving was annoyed. Gillette, someone told someone else, was arming its salesmen with copies of my article. Our advertising manager reported that Schick had been on the verge of signing a contract with *Maclean's*. (We were often on the verge of getting new accounts in those years.) I started getting phone calls from the office. I was working on another story in Montreal, where luckily, the Leafs were playing a game. I went down to the lobby of the Mount Royal and found two of the players who had originally told me that no, they couldn't recall being asked to use a special blade. They confirmed what they'd said before. After my article had been written the Leafs had traded two players to the New York Rangers for Andy Bathgate and Don McKenney, and pictures of Bathgate and McKenney had immediately appeared in the Schick-Leaf ad, pasted over the heads of the men they'd replaced. In Montreal I asked Bathgate if, when he'd come to the Leafs, someone had come running up to him and said,

"Here, you're number 9, and will you shave with this blade we've been saving for six months in case someone got traded?" He said no one had.

In the same article I included a passage that contained some conversation with George Imlach, the Leafs' coach and general manager. Imlach swears a lot. He swears more, in fact, than the hero of the joke that ends, "They were having sexual intercourse." I wrote his favourite word this way: "——ing." Ken Lefolii, then the editor of *Maclean's*, passed it, and the article was set in type, proofed and pasted up in dummy pages. Then someone at the plant, a foreman or something, read my piece in metal, and was offended. He called the publisher. The publisher talked to me and to Lefolii. What was wrong? "It means 'fucking,' doesn't it?" Yes. "Well, we shouldn't put that in *Maclean's*." "We're not. We're putting in '——ing.' "Well, everyone who reads it will say, you know, 'fucking' to himself." Not if they don't know the word. "Well, some people will find it offensive. How about just two dashes or something?" Do you know what that could mean? "I think we should put it in anyway." We replated four pages (I told you Imlach swears a lot). The whole thing, Lefolii said, was a ——ing fuck-up.

Lefolii is one of my best friends, and I am nearly as embarrassed at discussing his ability in public as he will be to have me do so. But too many people who don't know what happened have explained why we all walked out of *Maclean's* recently, and I thought someone who was there might be able to cast some light on what was, I believe most people agree, a fairly sad event in the history of Canadian journalism. One of the facts no one brought out is that Lefolii is a very gifted editor. Only people who have worked closely with him will know how gifted he is, and how much his particular ability stamped *Maclean's* over the past few years. Canada has been very lucky about *Maclean's*, really. In recent years its English-language circulation has been held fairly deliberately around 550,000. In our English-language population of, say, 14 million that's equivalent to the 7 million sold in the U.S. by *Life*, *Look* or the *Saturday Evening Post*. Can anyone imagine any of those three magazines with a regular column by the equivalent of Robert Fulford? With frequent articles by Mordecai Richler? With Harry Bruce writing about the press, or Wendy Michener about movies? Or with the let-the-chips-fall medical and social reporting of Sidney Katz? Or some of Barbara Moon's better pieces? Or Peter C. Newman at his dogged best? I certainly can't. There may be an awful lot of better magazines than *Maclean's* in the world, but there aren't many tougher, or more honest, *general* ones, and I think Canada has been a better place to live because of the guts *Maclean's* has shown.

One of the most remarkable things about Lefolii's tenure at *Maclean's* was that the people who worked for him did so for fees or salaries about a third of those of, say, the *Post*. The wordage output of many of *Maclean's* staff-writers over the past few years would leave most American writers dizzy. And most *Maclean's* writers did other jobs as well. Harry Bruce, as just one example, rewrote to the authors' satisfaction nearly every "For the Sake of Argument" that appeared. Yet most people, excepting always J. K. Lamb of the Orillia *Packet and Times* (O give us back the *Packet and Times* we knew before Roy Thomson bought it!) seemed to think *Maclean's* was enjoying its best years, editorially, in the early 1960s. Its news-stand sales, a good yardstick, were at their highest; they rose thirty per cent in Lefolii's first year as editor. Its subscription sales, when we left, were very close to showing a profit — a remarkable accomplishment for a general magazine; only oddities like *Playboy* or *TV Guide* take in more than it costs them to sell their subscriptions. *Maclean's* whole editorial budget wouldn't produce eight one-hour TV documentaries at the going rate in Canada, and while the magazine showed steady editorial improvement under Lefolii, its budgets were going down at a rate slightly better than ten per cent a year.

Lefolii did not invent editorial ability at *Maclean's*. Arthur Irwin ('45-'50) was willing to be just as controversial, and it was Irwin who banned advertising salesmen from the editorial floor. Ralph Allen ('50-'60), among so many other things — he was and is surely one of the most talented editors in North America — built the kind of magazine that attracted most of the people whose names appear above, including Lefolii. And Blair Fraser ('60-'61) let no one down. But Lefolii was an editor for the sixties, brash, rational and cool, and no matter how browned off I eventually became with the Maclean-Hunter Publishing Co., I'll never be able to ignore the fact that its owners gave him, in his early thirties, control of their most important property and for more than two years they let him run it as he saw fit.

I began this account with two frivolous anecdotes because they happen to be two that I was involved in that, to me, typify the reasons Lefolii *et al.* don't want to work at *Maclean's* any more. Trivial as they are, they show the change in the situation that affected more important (to us) issues. No matter how successful *Maclean's* has been editorially, there is no doubt it's been a financial catastrophe since about 1956, and Maclean-Hunter, while anxious to keep *Maclean's* as a sort a flagship for its publishing fleet, isn't, as the chairman of the board said during our terminal conversations, running a Canada Council. The attitude Lefolii brought to editing wasn't one to win the unadulterated support of advertisers. This is something the publishers knew, or ought to have known, when they appointed him. Indeed, just before Lefolii was named editor he wrote a piece himself that, through an unforgivable careless error, cost the magazine something like $50,000 in ads, and I think it is a great mark in Maclean-Hunter's favour that they named him anyway. Nevertheless, they are businessmen. And when not enough advertisers appeared ready to buy the audience we were attracting without having some control over what we were saying to it the owners began to get edgy. I might have been edgy too, if it had been my money. Too, our — meaning Lefolii's — approach to things was drawing a few libel suits. I think we were near the nine-million-dollar mark at one time. In none of these cases — this is worth emphasizing, I think, *none* of them — did any court find *Maclean's* guilty of libel. But (1) Maclean-Hunter's lawyers belong to the apologize-first, argue-later school of fighting libel and (2) even nuisance suits, which we were attracting, cost money to fight. *Maclean's* was making a lot of people angry, and while this may be good journalism — at least *I* think it's good journalism — it doesn't show up on the old balance sheet. The owners, we may assume, began to wonder if maybe the people we were making angry, a group that often included the owners themselves, were right, and Lefolii wrong. (I can't help adding that one of the letters written by management during our last arguments explained that a piece killed over Lefolii's head had been "unfair to both sides," which is what I went into journalism to be.)

Anyway, the owners began taking the cutting edge off Lefolii's editorial control. The appointment of R. A. MacEachern as executive vice-president in charge of magazines was the beginning of the end. (Peter Newman quit almost as soon as it happened.) MacEachern had had a marvellously successful career, first as editor, and then as editor and publisher, with the *Financial Post*, and anyone who would have expected him to keep his hands off the editorial direction of *Maclean's* would have been out of his mind. When the interference grew steadily more evident, Lefolii felt there was implicit mistrust of his judgement. He resigned over the killing of one specific story that is not important here. Five others, Fulford, Bruce, Barbara Moon, David Lewis Stein and I, went with him.

Since each of our decisions to quit was an individual one, I can't here explain all our reasoning. *Time* called it college-paper loyalty. In many ways I suppose it was. My own reason for quitting was simply that if they no longer wanted the kind of magazine Lefolii had been editing — in the tradition of Irwin, Allen and Fraser — then they no longer wanted the kind I wanted to help to edit. As an individual, I still want to write for *Maclean's*, and I hope other people who have been writing for it will make the same decision; it's still a place where some things can be said more effectively than they can be said anywhere else in Canada — unless the new regime changes even that. But, like most of the people who left *Maclean's* this year, I worked harder there than I ever hope to work at anything again. Quite a lot of it was bull-work: rewrites or cutlines or worrying about why the Thermofax machine wouldn't work. It was the other things — the opportunities to get the most interesting writers to look at the toughest subjects; the willingness of the editor to try new ideas; the chance to make honesty and literacy the main editorial criteria — that made any amount of drudgery worth it, and from my experience, those are the things that were being eroded away.

No Canadians were luckier to have *Maclean's* exist than the people who worked there. For as long as most journalists can remember it's been the best place in Canadian journalism to work. Probably still is. And probably our six resignations will help to make it a little better for a while than it might have been. But it can't be as good as when they let the editors do the editing.

Why *Maclean's* Still Matters

Globe and Mail, *March 31, 2001*

Unlike most of the people who've been giving Anthony Wilson-Smith free advice this week on what he should do now that's he the editor of *Maclean's*, I've actually had the job myself. I wasn't very good at it, and I kept it about as long as it took me to find the executive parking garage, but I know what kind of pressures Tony Wilson-Smith is facing.

People — at least people of a certain age, and there are still enough of us around to matter — *care* about *Maclean's*, and in the world of print journalism editing it is the equivalent of lighting a barbecue, hosting a talk show or mixing an extra-dry Martini — everyone thinks they can do it better than the incumbent.

As editor, I came between eras. Ralph Allen, the storied "Man from Oxbow," an elementary-school drop-out who'd been a sportswriter, a war correspondent and an astonishingly erudite radio panellist before he became editor, had hired me in 1958; I walked in the door the same week Pierre Berton, who'd been the managing editor, left to start his career as columnist and author. Like everyone who worked for Ralph (as even the most callow among us called him), I regarded him with an equal mixture of fear and worship. He took the magazine and its writers seriously, but never himself, and he asked — nay, demanded — the best of us. I remember riding down the elevator with him after my first manuscript had come back with perhaps fifty marginal notes — some of them mercilessly rude.

"Pretty tough, eh?" he said. When I tried to smile bravely in response, he said, "I had 123 on my first piece."

Building on the foundation laid by Arthur Irwin, who had brought Maclean's out of the colonial age (and who later went on to be commissioner of the National Film Board and a successful diplomat), Ralph Allen assembled a stable of contributors that included not only the best periodical journalists of the day but many of the emerging tribe of novelists and short-story writers, from Morley Callaghan to Hugh MacLennan, with W. O. Mitchell, who published his Jake and the Kid stories in Maclean's, as a sometime fiction editor.

The first article I ever worked on as an editor was a piece by Farley Mowat, messily typed, full of inconsistent spellings but unforgettable in its power. We called it "The Two Ordeals of Kikkik" (I, ahem, wrote the title) and it became part of the book *The Desperate People*, which, along with *People of the Deer*, had so much to do with awakening southern Canadians to the fate of the Inuit in the 1950s.

Ralph Allen left in 1960, needing a change. For a couple of years, Blair Fraser, the great Ottawa reporter, took over until Ken Lefolii, a brilliant and uncompromising journalist still in his early thirties was deemed to be ready, and we all worked to try to maintain the traditions of the magazine that had meant so much to us. But in 1964, Ken Lefolii was on a collision course with management. He resigned, and five of us — Robert Fulford, Harry Bruce, David Lewis Stein, Barbara Moon and I went with him.

It was a long time before I ever wrote for Maclean's again — and then, since the editors seemed to want my prose but not my by-line, it was usually under a pseudonym. The era of Arthur Irwin and Ralph Allen was over.

Going back — it was 1969 when I sought and was given a chance to run things on my own — was a mistake. I wasn't tough enough to clean house or sure enough of what I wanted to do after I cleaned it. Management lived up to its promise to give me my head, but there was no money to make any kind of drastic changes without a driving vision, which I didn't have.

But Peter C. Newman, it turned out, did. I'd scarcely finished typing my second resignation letter in less than ten years when Peter, whom I'd known since we'd worked together in the Allen days, emerged with a plan and a mandate for change.

At first I hated what he and his team were doing. The very heart of what *Maclean's* had always been — a writer's magazine — had been ripped out in favour of an Americanized format: *Newsweek* with Allan Fotheringham on the back page. I tried to write for it and couldn't cut it.

Slowly, however, the new magazine grew on me. Either my discomfort with the homogenization was wearing down or its mannerisms were becoming less pronounced. More and more voices were coming through: Barbara Amiel (I often wish the people I agree with could write as engagingly as the bad guys), Charles Gordon (who can), Peter C. Newman himself, the apparently ageless Foth. And, on politics, the obviously knowledgeable and resourceful Anthony Wilson-Smith. It may never have quite had the magic of the *Maclean's* that used to be, but to Peter Newman's undying credit and the credit of Kevin Doyle and Robert Lewis who succeeded him, they saved a Canadian institution.

And now, we're reading, even from Peter Newman, the man who brought it to Canada, that the newsmagazine itself has run its course.

So my advice to Tony Wilson-Smith? Bring on the writers: there must be a hundred times as many of them now as there were then, from a hundred more different backgrounds. Give them the time and the resources to produce the kind of graceful notes that set magazines apart from newspapers or the Internet and always will.

Forget trying to be newsy — except in the events that really touch people's lives. Be as bold in reshaping the publication Peter Newman built as he was in reshaping the one he inherited.

And above all: Be more Canadian than ever. The answer to the globalization of practically everything isn't to join it. It's to declare ownership of your own corner.

Even in its greatest days, *Maclean's* was never a general magazine. It was and is a specialty publication — about Canada. May it live a thousand years.

In the Days of the Seven-Day Hour

The Nation, *"Television," July 11, 1966*

An American friend of mine once spent part of a trip to Canada asking Canadians, who devote a lot of time to worrying about their independence from the United States, just what it was they were trying so hard to preserve. "Well, there's the CBC," he reported most of them as saying, "and . . . well, there's certainly the CBC, and the . . . I don't know, I guess the CBC sort of sums it up."

The CBC, the Canadian Broadcasting Corporation, does fulfill a unique and important function — at least as far as Canadians are concerned. Films, magazines, newspapers, records, books and, of course, radio and television signals flow virtually unhampered across the border from the United States into Canada. In most of their tastes, people who live in Vancouver are more like people who live in Seattle than they're like people who live in Montreal; what's hip in New York this month will be hip in Toronto next month, just as certainly as it will be hip in Cleveland. But there are still differences, and the CBC, a Crown corporation that requires about $100 million of federal government money to make up its annual deficit from advertising, helps to preserve them. It forms a kind of East-West counterforce to the natural North-South pull of American geography.

Because of its relative freedom from the dictates of advertising, the CBC is also, as I imagine most readers of *The Nation* know, probably the best big television network — in terms of not being afraid sometimes to appeal to minority tastes, even in prime time — on the Continent. That doesn't mean it's as good as I understand many Americans who aren't able to watch it believe. But it is good. Here is a breakdown of a reasonably typical week on my own local channel, in Toronto: twenty-five hours of straight American imports (*Bonanza, Hogan's Heroes*, Ed Sullivan and so on); nineteen hours, forty-five minutes of Canadian entertainment shows, generally no better, if no worse, than their American counterparts (although this list does include a ninety-minute production of *A Doll's House* at 9:30 Wednesday evening); twelve and a half hours of movies, nearly all of them American; ten and a half hours of children's programs, nearly all of them Canadian; ten hours of sports (this was the last week of the Stanley Cup playoffs); three hours of educational and two and a half hours of religious programs; one and a half hours of material imported from England; and seventeen hours and fifteen minutes of news and public affairs.

It's that last category that makes the difference. The CBC News, which is, of course, unsponsored, is a national institution. Lorne Greene learned how to sound like *everyone's* daddy by reading it on the radio during the war and, on television, it now provides the one truly Canadian medium of communication. But in recent years the Public Affairs Department has become even more important. Which is why tremors that have shaken the Public Affairs Department of the CBC this spring have made a lot of Canadians worry about whether the really excellent parts of the corporation can continue to survive.

For the last two seasons, the heart of public affairs broadcasting on the CBC has been an hour-long program with the Zen-like name, *This Hour Has Seven Days. Seven Days* runs — or has been running — in the primest of times, at ten on Sunday evening. It has what television people call a magazine format; it deals with as many as a dozen topics a week. In fifty shows, those topics have included LSD, teenage prostitution, political corruption, automobile safety, French-Canadian separatism, the American Negro, thalidomide, labour bosses, spies, stock manipulation — almost everything that is noticeable on American television by its absence. *Seven Days* has broadcast interviews with perhaps half the Canadian cabinet and a wide assortment of other important, interesting or controversial Canadians. There have been interviews also with Collie LeRoy Wilkins, George Lincoln Rockwell, Robert Kennedy, Arthur Schlesinger, Buckminster Fuller, Pete Seeger, Cassius Clay, Ralph Nader, Bertrand Russell, Edith Sitwell, Susan Sontag, Julian Huxley, Jules Feiffer, I. F. Stone, Herman Kahn, McGeorge and William Bundy, Orson Welles, Robert Morley and Carol Doda, the topless dancer from California, of whose act we Sunday evening viewers got a slightly edited version on film.

Seven Days edits everything ruthlessly. Its producers, some of whom are among the world's leading disciples of Marshall McLuhan, seem to have grasped the idea that public affairs broadcasting is not so much journalism — no matter how journalistic the subject — but *television*. Rather than explain stories or ideas, it has exposed them; it has given its viewers not a complete picture of the people it has interviewed but a genuine experience of them.

And even when it has dealt with subjects like the birth control pill, the influence of Tony Richardson and Jean-Luc Godard has been more evident than the influence of Fred J. Cook or even Edward R. Murrow. And it has worked. In spite of some frequently sophomoric satirical pieces and some ventures into what even its ardent fans have felt is questionable taste (should George Lincoln Rockwell be on television at all?), *Seven Days* has been enormously successful. Next to hockey, which is the real national bond in Canada, *Seven Days* has been the most popular Canadian show on the air this season. In a nation with a population of twenty million, roughly five million of whom speak French first, it has achieved an audience of more than three million — right up there with *Bonanza*.

In mid-April, with *Seven Days* still having three editions left to put on the air, a vice-president of the CBC went over the heads of the show's executive producer, a soft-spoken former newspaper man, Douglas Leiterman, and informed the two on-air hosts, Patrick Watson and Laurier LaPierre, that their contracts wouldn't be renewed next season. The vice-president's reasons, as they've come out, were cloudy. He questioned the "loyalty" of both Watson and LaPierre to CBC management. (Watson, who along with Leiterman, founded *Seven Days* in 1964 and emerged as an on-camera personality only this season, was the president of the CBC producers' association last year, and signed a brief to the Fowler Royal Commission on Broadcasting, whose report turned out to be highly critical of the CBC management. LaPierre, a professor of French-Canadian studies at McGill University in Montreal, who has been commuting to his weekly job with *Seven Days* in Toronto, had made some speeches in which he didn't exactly butter up his part-time bosses.)

The crucial question, however, as most people on both sides of the dispute have seen it, was really the matter of *Seven Days*' excellence, and particularly its predilection for controversy. Through the past winter in particular, there has scarcely been a Monday morning when the newspapers haven't been forced to carry some report of what *Seven Days* has done the night before, and usually it has been a front-page report. Quite a few toes got stepped on. And, instead of taking the bold and direct action of firing Leiterman, it seemed, the CBC's management had tried to de-fang the show by taking away the two hosts and, by implication, some of Leiterman's independence.

It was, as Judy LaMarsh said, only the top to the iceberg. Miss LaMarsh is the Secretary of State. As such, she answers to Parliament for the CBC. And, while one could have wished for a fresher figure of speech — there must be *some* other way to get that idea across — Miss LaMarsh seemed to be right. The CBC has been divided into two factions for years: on the one hand, the people who make radio and television programs; on the other, the civil servants who administer the Crown corporation. Each faction has had a different idea about whether boats ought to be rocked, and neither has always believed the other acted in constant good faith. "It's totally impossible to carry on a sensible conversation with the principal officers of this corporation," said Reeves Haggan, the corporation's supervisor of public affairs, English-language division, and the owner of another head that had been gone over in the firing of Watson and LaPierre. (In his turn, Alphonse Ouimet, the CBC's president, said later that Haggan hadn't been given a raise last year because "his supervisor performance had not been up to expectations.")

The creative people — the producers — quickly closed ranks over the *Seven Days* firings. Unless there was a satisfactory solution, the producers' association announced, not only to the Watson-LaPierre affair but to the whole running battle, they would "withdraw" their "services." (Since the producers don't negotiate as a body on any other question, they've been very careful to avoid the word "strike.") They were riding a remarkable wave of public support. On the evening of the first edition of *Seven Days* to go on the air after the announcement of the firings, pickets surrounded the CBC's Toronto studios. Most of them were students — WE LOVE YOU LAURIER, GIVE US FOOD FOR THOUGHT, and so on — but they obviously represented a strong body of public opinion. The CBC got more than eleven thousand phone calls protesting the firings.

A citizen's committee to "save *Seven Days* and restore the integrity of the CBC" sprang up around a group of professors and journalists in Toronto. People who in the past have worked hard to prevent political interference with the CBC wired their Members of Parliament to have the decision reversed. The Parliamentary Committee on Broadcasting, chaired by Gérard Pelletier, a tough-minded former labour journalist and editor of the Montreal daily *La Presse*, held hearings on the issue. At the last moment, Prime Minister Lester Pearson, who once won a Nobel Peace Prize for his international diplomacy, announced the appointment of a mediator, Stuart Keate, a newspaper publisher from British Columbia. The "withdrawal of services" was averted. *Seven Days* completed its season, with Watson and LaPierre in their usual chairs, although their futures, and the show's, are still in doubt.

And F— as a Dirty Word

Saturday Night, *May 1969*

The April issue of *Esquire* has a piece by Ethel Grodzins Romm called "—— Is No Longer a Dirty Word." It's a good piece, too, and I agree with it. God knows you hear —— (the word!) blathered about with the most incredible casualness in all sorts of company these days, and Ethel Grodzins Romm gives us a little bibliography of recent usage that ranges from *The New Republic* to the *National Review* and even includes (December 14, 1968) the *Saturday Evening Post*, if you remember what that magazine used to stand for when it stood at all.

Ethel Godzins Romm doesn't print the word herself, although she makes it pretty ——ing clear what she's talking about. The closest she ever comes is f—k. When a *Saturday Night* researcher called *Esquire* to enquire about this decision not to use a word that they were pronouncing not dirty, she was told *Esquire* felt that since it had no shock value any more it wasn't worth it. I agree with that. I've had my jollies out of getting it into print anyway (*The Canadian Forum*, 1964). Besides, it's more fun to type out —— than the real letters. One of the great things about bleeps on television and —s in print is that you allow the reader or viewer to let his own imagination go to work. Think of the possibilities.

"Where have all the f —ers gone?"

"Jack and Jill went up the hill
"To f—— a pail of water."

"Mary had a little ——."

And so on. In any case, I intend to follow the example of Mrs. Romm and *Esquire* except for one instance, which follows now. It concerns life, or in this case *Life*, imitating art. After that, back to the —s. (If looking at the word itself still really bugs you, read the next paragraph with your eyes closed.)

Art: Sometime around 1965 Anthony Boucher, a New York reviewer who specializes in mystery stories, solemnly told Paul Krassner, the editor of *The Realist* (and America's leading authority on all things ludicrous about obscenity) he'd come across a book that used the word m—— fucker. Krassner never actually saw the word, but the idea broke him up, and for the next several weeks he delighted in telling everyone he met about it. Then he sort of forgot about it.

Life: The December 6, 1968, issue of *Life* magazine carried a lengthy summary of Rights in Conflict, the report prepared by the Chicago Crime Commission on the events — now *there* was what I would call obscenity — surrounding last summer's Democratic Party convention. Not unnaturally, the report had included detailed and exact quotations of phrases used by police and others during those events. In summarizing the report, *Life* chose to print the epithet I've indicated above this way:

m —— f——

What has happened, in other words, is something beyond even Ethel Grodzins Romm's keen observations. While the big F has lost its power as a dirty word — has, that is, if you'll agree with Mrs. Romm and me — the big M, mother, has become one.

Mother, for crying out loud!

"*M is for the million things she t-o-l-d me . . .*"

"Hey, wait a minute, you can't sing that in here."

"But it's Mother's *day*. I mean the florists and everything . . ."

"Listen, buddy, this is a decent place. So get the f— out of here, you can't . . ."

Impossible? Listen, as part of the research for this article, I tried to find out when, if ever, was the first time anyone had ever broken through the —— barrier at the CBC. One radio producer I already knew used to sneak it onto taped shows by snipping out the offending bit of tape and putting it in again backwards, which tickled him immensely, although it might have confused his listeners. But that didn't count. The first recorded instance I could find — and man, was *it* recorded, on the memories of the people involved — was on that excellent FM program, *Ideas*. It occurred in 1967. The program was a tape Canadian writer Austin Clarke had made from a series of conversations with black American writer Piri Thomas about life in Spanish Harlem. The opening sequence had Thomas reading from the preface of his book, *Down These Mean Streets*, against a background of Harlem street noises. A very moving bit of radio it was, too, except for — well, *not* except for — the fact that the preface happened to contain a version of the word that *Life* won't print.

Just to finish the story off: One listener — from the west — complained, and the CBC brass came down heavily on the producer (then new to the CBC and to BBG regulations) who'd prepared the tape. The fact that several people, ignoring the word in question, called or wrote to *Ideas* to compliment the producers on a superb piece of programming probably has more bearing on Mrs. Romm's point than on mine. *My* point is that Thomas, the speaker of the first big F I've been able to track down on a CBC network, neither wrote nor read aloud the word "mother . . ." etc. In his book, it appears as "*mudder* ——" (—s mine). In other words, even in the hands of a sensitive writer trying to capture the sounds of black America, the word that is dirty is not ——, but ———. And if you're still not convinced, I can tell you that the producer who put the Clarke-Thomas interview on the air certainly is. In the course of our conversation about the 1967 crisis he told me about a similar one he'd had — this time with himself as censor — concerning an *Ideas* program just this winter. This second incident concerned a talk in which a professor from Yale was attempting a psychiatric explanation of the Oedipal connotations of the word we've been talking about. The events he was basing his analysis on were the Columbia riots of this fall, during which, of course, a predominant student motto was "Up against the wall, you ————ers." Like most men trying to analyse a phrase, the professor *used* it, and the producer was left with this problem of the tape. "The first thing I did," he told me, "was snip out the 'f' sound. Well, you should have heard that! It sounded like mother-*uck*ers. I mean, really dirty. Worse than the original. So I finally took out a little bit here and blurred a bit there and what went out on the air was something like 'muhrerers.' It did the job and I hadn't broken any regulations. We didn't get any complaints, either. I learned my lesson the first time round."

All of this would be silly, I suppose, if it weren't so . . . if it weren't so *really* silly. Mother as a dirty word, indeed! It's just that we've got to have *something*. But what bothers me about Mrs. Romm's observations is not so much that she hasn't taken them any farther — hasn't worried about what is supposed to replace —— as *the* dirty word — as that she is so utterly right. —— *isn't* a dirty word any more, and its impotence has weakened us all. All us men, anyway. We've shot off the ultimate weapon and found that it was just that: ultimate. There is nothing left. How you gonna keep 'em down on the farm after they've said —— you? It's not just a sexual thing, although certainly there is, or used to be, something horny about hearing a girl say ——. (In spite of the fact that any Canadian who's reasonably adept at cursing uses —— about ten times as often in the abstract sense, of —— you, or —— off, whatever that may mean, as he does in its literal sense.) I can remember my first time. I was about fourteen. A bunch of us were trying to pick up some girls. We sidled up to a car full of them at a drive-in hamburger place, and began making eyes at them and doing whatever else it was we used to do when we were fourteen.

"Do you guys —— ?" one of them asked.

"Well, uh . . . well," I said, as various things started to happen to various of my glands. (Actually I didn't, but I had a lot of *ideas*.)

"Well, —— off," she said, breaking up the rest of her party.

And now: nothing. Today hearing a girl say —— is about as exciting as hearing her ask you to pass the salt. And it's changed so quickly. Not us but the times, the climate. Paul Krassner can even remember the first —— in *The Realist* (Issue No. 16, in 1960, in an interview with Albert Ellis.) But to younger magazine editors — and Krassner isn't forty yet — the decision to print —— depends only on whether it's necessary to make the point the writer is aiming at. Even *Esquire*, which started me on this whole thing, stuck it right in there in Norman Mailer's *An American Dream* four years ago. Then, presumably, it had shock value. Kenneth Tynan stammered it out on BBC television, and if no one's quite said it on a North American channel they're getting closer every day. My own favourite elegant variation occurred on a night-time talk show in March, when one comedian told another to "in the biblical sense, go ye forth and multiply."

Yet the media, bless them, are only reflections of us all. It may not be true in Winnipeg yet (I can remember being pretty wide-eyed in New York just a few years ago when everyone I talked to sounded like a very articulate B.C. lumberjack) but it's certainly true in Toronto: —— in its various forms has become as common on the cocktail circuit as gin, and at least in the generation under forty, the generation now assuming corporate power, the impact of a good solid "go —— yourself" is about as potent in the skirmishes of office politics as "I'm afraid I just don't think your idea is viable." I'm *serious*. You're reading the words of a man who has been told by his own secretary that she wished a certain third party would just —— off and stop pestering her.

What to do? ——ed if I know. According to Farmer and Henley's *Slang and its Analogues*, as quoted by Wayland Young in his authoritative book *Eros Denied*, early versions of —— used to pop up quite frequently in normal literature until about 1660. After that, "it begins to be written f—k and f—. It was during the first and shorter of the two hegemonies which Puritanism has enjoyed in England that the word fell into disfavour, that is, at a time when the action it describes came to be regarded with special alarm."

And there, presumably, it lay, confined to barracks and barrooms and barbershops until whatever it is that's happened in the last several years. After three centuries of lying underground, —— has burst into life like a volcano. As late as 1953, Olympia Press published it only in Paris, from where daring tourists would smuggle the works of such writers as Henry Miller and de Sade. Norman Mailer, the linguistic pace-setter of us all, kept it down to "fug" in *The Naked and the Dead* in 1948, and then became the butt of a Tallulah Bankhead quip that hovered around the cocktail circuit for years: "Ah yes," Miss Bankhead is reported to have said, on being introduced to Mailer, "you're the young man who can't spell ——."

But now there is no rolling back of the stone that has for so long covered the cave of ——. Our word — *the* word — is in the public domain. My own efforts to unearth a new set of dirty words have gained little. Paul Krassner can suggest only "Negro" — now that one is obliged to say "black" — but what fun is that? Ralph Ginzburg was scarcely more useful when I called him for guidance. Ginzburg, I'd have thought, would have a greater stake in changing the ground rules than anyone since Lennie Bruce; his efforts in *Eros* magazine, after all, have already got him in trouble with the courts. But he seemed as baffled as I. "I know what you mean," he said. "I don't even notice it when someone says ——. My wife and I have been looking around for an alternative, and all we've been able to come up with is 'swive'. It means the same, but . . . you know."

Yeah, I know. Hell, it wouldn't even be any good in Scrabble — you'd have "wives" just as easily. You're just out of luck if it don't sound like ——.

How CBC Radio Made Me a Canadian

from The Private Voice, *1988*

Like everyone else who was born in English Canada when I was, or who came here as a child, I was schooled to be British. I sang for God to save the King in the morning and studied his ancestry in the afternoon. Galt was Scottish, as it happened, home of the Highland Light Infantry, but there were touches of England everywhere too: Manchester School, Victoria Park, the fish and chips store near the corner of Main and Water streets — the corner itself marked by four staid banks — or the overcooked mutton that even my mother prepared at home. I went to Cubs in the basement of the Church of England and studied the gospel of Baden-Powell. At Christmas, if I was lucky, I got *Chums* or *The Boy's Own Annual.* My first war hero was Dave Dawson of the RAF, fighting for King and country with his side-kick Freddy Farmer. I went from the *Just So Stories* of Kipling to the novels of Dickens and Scott, from the verse of A. A. Milne to the poems of Wordsworth, both of which I can — and do — still quote. There were exceptions, of course — "Along the line of smoky hills" — but they were oddities; the only Canadian writer I saw in the flesh was William Drummond, who came one afternoon to Galt Collegiate when I was in grade nine, to spout his racist doggerel to our assembly.

But if I was being schooled to be a young Englishman, I was being acculturized to be an American: Abbott and Costello at the Grand, the *Saturday Evening Post* in our mailbox, Glenn Miller, when I was at last allowed to go, at Teen Canteen. Gradually, as I grew older, the extracurricular influences grew stronger; the residue of my academic brainwashing and childhood reading weaker. The red of Empire receded in the landscape of my mind, and the Stars and Stripes marched in. Their principal route was the radio. The movies were Saturday afternoons, the big bands were Friday evenings and the magazines were for grown-ups. But the radio was everywhere, all the time. American radio. On Mondays, while she ironed, my mother listened to *Lux Radio Theatre* (or *Theater*, as I'm sure they spelled it) with Cecil B. DeMille. On Sunday evenings, prime time, we gathered around the pulsing green eye of our living-room console to listen to Jack Benny, Fred Allen and Charlie McCarthy, from Lucky Strike to Maxwell House, LSMFT to Good to the Last Drop. I heard Bob Hope and *Fibber McGee & Molly*, *Amos 'n' Andy*, *The Thin Man*, *The Whistler* (I can still whistle the theme), *The Lone Ranger*, *The Shadow*, *Dragnet*, *The Green Hornet* and *Mr. Keene, Tracer of Lost Persons*. On Saturday mornings, where I lived, it was *Uncle Ben's Club*, from WBEN in Buffalo; I joined. When I was sick, and allowed to take the kitchen radio to bed, I could catch up on *Ma Perkins* and *Pepper Young's Family*, *Big Sister* and — a touch of England here, to make me feel at home — *Our Gal Sunday*. Eighty per cent of the programs that were broadcast in Canada when I was a kid were American, I read somewhere not long ago, but at the time I would have told you all of them were, except of course for *Hockey Night in Canada*, with Foster Hewitt from the gondola, broadcasting to hockey fans in Canada, the United States and Newfoundland, but most of all to me.

Hockey aside, I was American too — an American kid who knew some British history and said "out of the house" differently from Uncle Ben, who did Hirohito imitations and scribbled Kilroy Was Here in his notebooks (while the father he scarcely remembered slogged through the mud of Italy, saving, as I believed, the Empire), who thought Bing Crosby was the greatest singer in the world, had a crush on Jeanne Crain and wanted to grow up to be Tyrone Power. I knew the words to "The Maple Leaf Forever" but sang "The Marine Hymn" to myself. The HLI was in Europe, distinguishing itself in battle, a regiment of neighbours, but, as I pictured them in my mind, I saw the kid from Brooklyn who would die in the second reel and the white southerner who would at last make friends with, as I learned to call him, the Negro. In Galt, Ontario, I read the same comics, sang the same songs, laughed at the same jokes and worshipped the same heroes as any kid in Akron, Ohio, or Corpus Christi, Texas.

Then, slowly, slowly, something else began to creep in to the culture that enveloped me. Right between Benny and Allen ("You were expecting maybe Tallulah Bankhead?") on Sunday evenings came *L for Lanky*, which turned out to be, if you listened closely, about the RCAF. At noon, if my mother had the day off from the library, there would be on the kitchen radio "Knock, knock." "Who's there?" — *The Happy Gang*, which came from, of all places, Toronto, where my grandparents lived. If I lingered, I could hear the homey conversations of a farm family called the Craigs, whose adventures lacked the high drama of *Our Gal Sunday* — "Can a girl from Wyoming find happiness in the stately homes of England?" — but who sounded curiously like the people we bought tomatoes from, over on the Blair Road. Sometimes, at night, my mother would swirl to the strains of Mart Kenney and His Western Gentlemen, from Vancouver. And for news, as the war wore on, she seemed to turn more and more to the sepulchral tones of Lorne Greene and the vivid front-line reports of Matthew Halton, coming to us from CBL Toronto, on the Dominion Network of the Canadian Broadcasting Corporation.

Preoccupied with growing up, I scarcely noticed.

I went away to Ridley, spent summers on construction sites beyond the reach of radio. Television came when I didn't live at home, and flickered on the edge of my life: Ed Sullivan, *Your Show of Shows*, *Life With Elizabeth*, *I Led Three Lives*. I didn't pay much attention. Radio faded too, the Hit Parade in the background. I can't even tell you what stations I listened to.

And then, in Timmins, I found *Stage 54*, bearing, as the series did, the number of its year, 1954.

Sitting here now, with a landslide of galley proofs already piling up at *Morningside* for the launch of their authors' fall tours, with this year's Berton nearly in the stores, this year's Mowat on its way, with last year's Davies and last year's Atwood still perking from their solid run at the Booker Prize, with Gallant and Newman and Richler and Hood all nearing completion of new projects, with Laurence and Engel (Marian) sadly gone but Munro still here and in her prime, and with Sandra Birdsell and Sharon Bhutala and Heather Robertson and Isabel Huggan and Susan Kerslake and Audrey Thomas and Joy Kogawa and Katherine Govier and Bharati Mukherjee and Jane Rule and a host of others all following in their footsteps, and with Findley travelling, Rooke spieling, Hodgins residing, Mitchell teaching, Kinsella talking baseball on the radio, but all busily writing too, with MacLennan resting on his laurels for a while but Callaghan still churning it out and Matt Cohen and David Adams Richards and Austin Clarke and John Metcalf and Scott Symons and W. D. Valgardson and Andreas Schroeder and Edward Phillips and Michael Ondaatje and Lesley Choyce and Graeme Gibson and David Lewis Stein and Ray Smith and Robert Kroetsch and Clark Blaise and another host of others all hot on their heels. . . .

It's hard to remember how rare a creature the Canadian writer was then. MacLennan had published *Barometer Rising* in 1941, and, seven years after that, Mitchell had brought out *Who Has Seen the Wind*. I'd heard about them in 1954, but mostly as curiosities. I couldn't believe they were any good. They were, for heaven's sake, Canadian. I'd relished Leacock, knew Frederick Philip Grove's name, and as a kid had browsed through the Glengarry novels of Ralph Connor and gobbled up the lore of Ernest Thompson Seton — had played, in fact, *Two Little Savages* in our duplex apartment's living-room. Other than that, and if you didn't count Robert Service, the words "Canadian" and "writer" didn't seem to belong in the same sentence.

Yet there, on the radio, *Stage 54* was putting on plays, some of them classics (and wonderful productions they were), but a great many of them written by Canadian writers — Canadian writers! — performed by Canadian actors and telling Canadian stories.

By 1954, the *Stage* series was ten years old. It had started in 1944, under the direction of Andrew Allan, and was to run, virtually every week, for another seven years after I left Timmins, until 1961. In that time, Allan, and the equally important Esse W. Ljungh — it was nearly twenty years before I learned his name was not Young — put on six thousand radio plays, almost exactly half of them Canadian originals. The writers whose works were produced included Lister Sinclair, Joseph Schull, Mavor Moore, Fletcher Markle, Tommy Tweed and Len Peterson, and the actors who appeared in them included, among many scores of others, Lloyd Bochner, Budd Knapp, Don Harron, Jane Mallett and the incomparable John Drainie, whose work even now can raise the hair on the back of my neck. Before I met the cast of the Canadian Players' *Saint Joan*, who played Timmins, I had probably heard all of them on the radio.

The *Stage* series was not the first radio drama in Canada; Rupert Caplan had produced some plays on the old CNR station in Montreal in the early 1930s (Tyrone Guthrie directed a number of them), and there was drama on CKUA in Edmonton. But it was the best, and it was heard everywhere. In Timmins, some of the young reporters with whom I was working used to make a weekly pilgrimage to the listening-room of CKCL, a CBC affiliate in the second storey of the *Daily Press*'s comfortable art deco building. They would light cigarettes and drink coffee out of cardboard cups while they sprawled on stuffed green-leather couches to listen to the magic from Toronto. They initiated me into the ritual. I was entranced.

It is possible to make too much out of this memory, I know, as if it were Keats discovering Chapman's *Homer*. And, to be sure, there was no moment — or I can recall none — at which I leaped from the green leather and snapped my fingers in epiphany. But it was a revelation for me, a signal that people could make drama and literature out of the same experiences that had formed me, that Canadians had something to say that was worth listening to, and I began to wonder if there wasn't something more I could write about than forest fires or service clubs. I wouldn't have said it then and have some difficulty with its pretentious overtones now, but I was beginning to think of myself as a Canadian. And the instrument through which the discovery arrived was CBC Radio.

And How Being Canadian Helped
Make *This Country*

from Peter Gzowski's Book About This
Country in the Morning, *1974*

When I grow up I want to be Paul Hiebert. Paul Hiebert, of course, is the creator and biographer of Sarah Binks, the Sweet Songstress of Saskatchewan, and the winner of the first Stephen Leacock Award. I say "of course" because that's all I knew about him before I got to meet him through the CBC Radio program I worked on for three years, *This Country in the Morning*. One day a bunch of us from the program were talking about how much we enjoyed the deliberately bad poetry Professor Hiebert had written years before, and wondering what had become of him. We found him in Carman, Manitoba, where he retired after a long career of teaching chemistry at the University of Manitoba. We called him and I talked to him on the air, about Sarah and other things. He told me that he'd started to write bad poetry because, as a young academic, he'd found that he didn't have the right kind of small talk for faculty parties. So he created Sarah, and started quoting her — deadpan — to his colleagues. Sarah grew on him, and eventually he put together a "critical" book about her and her works. The manuscript made the rounds of a few publishers (being rejected by, among other people, a New York editor who wasn't quite sure whether Sarah — this mythical writer of hilariously lousy poetry of the Canadian prairies — was quite "major" enough to be the subject of a full-length book), until Oxford University Press finally saw the point and brought out his small Canadian masterpiece.

I kind of fell in love with Professor Hiebert in my first conversation with him, but it wasn't until later that someone told me he had written another book as well. That book is called *Tower in Siloam*, and it is a religious work. It is the study of a man in search of God, and — I don't know why, on reflection, this should have come as a surprise — in reading it I found that the man I had known as a satirist, whom his students had known as a chemist, was also one of the wisest and most gentle-minded men I have ever read. I talked to him about that too, on the radio, and later, when we were winding up our second season, we asked Professor Hiebert to fly to Toronto and to sit in a studio with three other people who had become important to the program, as we, I hope, had become important to them: Bob Ruzicka, an Edmonton dentist who is, I think, the best song writer in Canada today; Sneezy Waters, an Ottawa street-singer who is just fun to have around, and Edith Butler, a tall, shy, graceful Acadian who may have the most beautiful eyes in Canada — she certainly writes and sings some of the most beautiful songs. The singers sang and Dr. Hiebert read bad poetry, and we all glowed. The party carried on after the program ended, and Professor Hiebert, the satirist, scientist and philosopher, who is, I'd guess, about sixty years her senior, made twinkly-eyed, flirtatious remarks to Edith.

On my way to becoming Paul Hiebert, I'd like to be W. O. Mitchell. Bill Mitchell is — and this really is an "of course" — the creator of Jake and the Kid, the author of, most recently, *The Vanishing Point*, and before that the book that I think is the best ever written about the Canadian prairies, *Who Has Seen the Wind*. But he chews cigarettes. Well, he used to chew them. Now he sniffs snuff. He also chews up phonies. I remember one morning when he came in to visit the program; he'd seen something on CBC television the night before that had annoyed him, and he used a phrase that has stuck permanently in my mind. The program he'd seen had been one of those CBC attempts to describe things Cultural. It had been, said Bill Mitchell, "rarefied nightingale piss." There is no RNP about Bill Mitchell. Bill Mitchell, like Paul Hiebert who was Bill Mitchell's chemistry teacher at the University of Manitoba, knows who he is. That's why they're heroes of mine.

There are a lot of other people I got to know because of *This Country in the Morning*. There is no way I can capture everything that program meant to me or to the people who made it, who included not only its staff and its contributors but its listeners, too. There is no way, for example, I can transcribe Jean-Claude Germain's belly laugh from Montreal, or Adrian Hope's five dialects of Cree from Edmonton, or the nervousness of the young girl bagpiper who was to open our program from Sydney, and who could show that nervousness only by wailing away on her pipes for fifteen minutes before the show while Kenzie McNeill, the gentle young genius who wrote "Johnstown Boogie," and some fiddlers and other musicians with whom we'd partied the night before tried to tune up their own instruments for the music we wanted to broadcast live. Nor can I properly convey such moments as the time I was talking to two nice old men in Fredericton about the lore of the fiddlehead fern and I asked them how high a fiddlehead could grow. The man to whom I'd directed the question said . . . well, he didn't say anything. He looked me straight in the eye and he held his hand about a foot above the studio table. He knew how high they grew, but did the listener? I loved it.

I think, now, if I were asked why *This Country* worked, my answer would be about as eloquent as the man who knew the height of fiddleheads. It worked because a lot of people, some of whom hated each other and some of whom loved each other (and the permutations were not always constant), cared about it. People in other units around the CBC used to call us "the family" and, although the nickname was not born in a flattering way — it originated, I think, about the time of the Manson murders — it was a hard one to dispute. What drew us together was the program. In contrast to some other places I've worked with a tight sense of common purpose, we spent virtually no time together away from the office. I think, actually, that the fact that a lot of us got on each other's nerves created some of the energy that made the program what it was. I guess I haven't even got the right to say "a lot of us." All I know is that a lot of the people who inspired me, drove me, supported me and teased me sometimes got on my nerves.

I know too that we had no model. I think that was one of the reasons for our success. We weren't the Canadian *Esquire* or the Canadian *Merv Griffin Show*. We weren't the Canadian *Goon Show* or the Canadian *Pravda*. We were *This Country in the Morning* — a radio program of conversation, puzzles, games, essays, recipes, advice, music, nostalgia, contests, skits, arguments and emotions. Were we trying to keep the country together? People kept asking me that. The best answer I could think of was no. But Alex Frame, the executive producer, once said that if you wanted to do that, a rope would be better than a radio program. We were, I think, a daily event. Our mood could be changed by anything from an interoffice argument to the weather. Furthermore, we were live — or at least what broadcasters call "live on tape." Wherever we were coming from — and in three years we originated from nearly three dozen places from St. John's to Tuktoyaktuk — we had to be on the network at 9:13 Atlantic time — or 9:43 in Newfoundland, which is an exception to everything. (The world will end at midnight tonight; 12:30 in Newfoundland.) What I said live to the Maritimes was recorded in Toronto and rebroadcast an hour later, then recorded in Winnipeg and so on, so that everyone, so to speak, heard the same thing at the same hour.

• • •

One of the things that has always surprised me about, for example, men who have been to war, is the way their good memories are able to blot out the bad ones, and in thinking back over the three years I spent on *This Country*, I am almost overwhelmed by a sense of . . .

I don't know, pleasure, adventure, joy. During the strike of early 1972 that kept us off the air for fourteen weeks, a few of us went to Vancouver Island, to record some leisurely interviews and have a look around. Vicki Meacham, whose son had won one of our earliest contests, along with her husband, John, drove us from downtown Victoria to their home in Milne's Landing, and on the way we stopped to pick up some fresh oysters. Vicki cooked them up for us, and we washed them down with a bottle of their homemade pear wine. On the way back to the city we stopped and turned the car lights out and the radio off, and it was as dark as it has ever been, and as beautiful.

On Cape Breton, Kenzie McNeill and a friend of his drove us down to Fortress Louisbourg; Kenzie had been smoking some dope on the way and was singing "The Rocky Road to Dublin," and my heart was with him, and then we threw stones into the Atlantic and Kenzie told us that the sound they made was called "cutting the devil's throat." I tried the same thing later, on the shore of Hudson's Bay, but I got too close to the water and I had to rush to the Churchill airport with my pants wet. In Montreal one time, Pauline Julien, trying to explain her feelings about going to jail for what she had sung about, reached across the studio table and clutched both my hands; her English was almost indecipherable, but what she was saying, I'm sure, came over on the air. After I got home from the Arctic trip, the phone rang late one Sunday night and Denis Ryan of Ryan's Fancy said the sun was going down in St. John's, as it had never gone down in the Mackenzie Delta, and he wanted to sing me a song. After we taped our Christmas show in Happy Valley, Labrador, the manager of the CBC station there wanted me to go to the Goose Bay officers' mess, but I was tired and not in the mood for officers, and all of us who had made the program went back to our hotel and drank drinks and sang songs . . . just as we had done in Montreal after our last hour there once, when Michel Garneau, a poet, had sung a raunchy drinking song called "Prends un verre de bière, mon Minou" as if it were a love ballad, and all of us realized once and for all that Quebec had what Canada was only beginning to have — a sense of itself — or as we'd done in Thunder Bay where, instead of partying to wind ourselves down, a bunch of us went for one of the world's great saunas.

This sounds sloppy, doesn't it? Parties, new friends, meeting some of the famous people of the country (some of whom, confidentially, are dorks), roaming around the landscape and generally having a good time. The trouble is, it *was* a good time, the best and most exhilarating time I've ever had in my life. But it had its terrible moments too. I imagine most of the people who listened to the program know about Andrew Allan. Each Friday morning, *This Country* used to begin with an essay by Andrew.

Because he had led such a full life, I think all of us at *This Country* were able to cope with Andrew's death, of a stroke, early in 1974. What we were not able to cope with — what I am still barely able to cope with — was the death of Sheilah White. Sheilah had been one of the first people Alex Frame hired when he was putting *This Country* together. I used to call her "Perfect Sheilah" because she was, as well as being remarkably physically attractive, calm and funny and lacking in any pretence. She got on no one's nerves. During the middle of our second season she went into hospital for major surgery, from which she apparently recovered. I remember that I called her on a Sunday morning, the weekend I had been given an award by ACTRA. I called her because I knew that she had nominated me for that award. She sounded terrific; she'd soon be back at work. When we finished doing the Monday show, Alex told us that Sheilah had died. We didn't know how to honour her. Someone mentioned how much she had loved the song "Amazing Grace." I wrote something that afternoon, a dedication of the hymn. I can remember how we recorded it, because I know I could not have done it live on the air. To read it, I had to turn my back to the control room. There was no producer there, only Ron Grant, the technician who worked with us the whole three years. Ron is a tough, squat guy who used to be a wrestler and a truck driver. Our office name for him was "Archie Bunker." To do Sheilah's obituary, we had to have our backs turned to one another, because when I finished trying to say what all of us felt, I broke down completely. Ron did too. Sheilah was twenty-six when she died. We never played "Amazing Grace" on the radio again.

• • •

I don't think I'll ever be Paul Hiebert or W. O. Mitchell. I've started too late. But I do know that the time I spent on *This Country in the Morning* changed me. I don't mean in the magazine-article sense of "How Pot Saved My Marriage" or "How I Found God by Growing Tomatoes," but both publicly and privately I am not the same person Alex Frame hired to host the CBC's new three-hour morning radio show in 1971. I have certainly changed in my attitudes towards my profession, my country and myself.

In the three years I spent working on *This Country* I met more people who are better and smarter than I am than I ever dreamed existed. As a consequence I have learned about my profession that it is not "them" against "us." It's not a group of people who have "paid their dues" writing to and for a group of people who haven't. It's everyone trying to communicate with everyone else. I wouldn't have known that without *This Country*. So that one of the things I learned about myself and my profession was that in no way was I one of the élite. There are more literate, wise, even brilliant Canadians who have never been paid a cent for what they've written than there are copies of books sold by some people I once considered in a class by themselves.

The Rules of Hopscotch

from Peter Gzowski's Book About This
Country in the Morning, *1974*

It's clouding over in Toronto today, and apparently cooling off, but yesterday was one of those March days that could make even Victoria jealous. The newspapers had their obligatory pictures of girls in short skirts — I'm not knocking those pictures, you understand, just pointing out that they're obligatory, just like the pictures of kids throwing their books in the air on the last day of school. There were people out in parks, on driving ranges, and just ankling around the sidewalks. It even smelled nice, and you could see green where a week before there had been mud or snow or bare branches.

And some of us, I suppose, went a little silly. My own car has been in hospital for a few days and when I got home from work about five o'clock it was by taxi — the old harried businessman trick. In the driveway of our house was a game of mixed singles hopscotch, and I put down my homework and settled in to watch it for a while. The players were a nine-year-old boy named John and a twelve-year-old girl named Maria. John was ahead, throwing a set of keys that he'd found somewhere (stones bounce on pavement and don't make good markers) at the seven, which was on the left of the second arm of the hopscotch pattern. I don't know if there are regional variations on this, or temporal ones, because for the life of me I cannot remember the details of how we used to play hopscotch, but the Toronto rules are as follows.

On the ground you mark off this pattern: three single squares in a row, then a double, which consists of squares number four and five, another single, a double — seven and eight — and at the far end a semi-circle which is space number nine. You throw your objects — John's keys, for example (Maria was using a chain bracelet she wears, which has terrific stopping powers on the pavement) — into, first, square number one, and then you hop over that into square two, three and so on, using one foot only except on the doubles — you may straddle four and five — and so on up to the other end and back. Then you throw into square two and repeat, and you keep on with this operation until you fail either to hit your object square with your talisman or to hop cleanly through the prescribed pattern. There is no butterflying, which is balancing on the ball of your foot and wiggling the heel to achieve balance, and no touching the lines. You may — and this surprised me — touch the ground with your hand while reaching over to retrieve your object while you are balanced in the square with the next highest number.

There is one other rule which was unfamiliar to me. After the first player has successfully got through nine and, so to speak, come out the other end, he or she begins at the top and works backwards to number one. *But* — and how about this, sports fans — that player may pick one "lucky number" and chalk it in. From then on, he or she may land on that square in any way that seems fitting — two-footed, wiggling or anything else. It is sanctuary for him, or her, but it is also forbidden territory for the other player or players. This means, for example, that in a three-handed game, after two of the players have each made nine and are working their way back, a third player is given some incredible feats to perform.

By now, you will have guessed that the game in our driveway last night did have a third player, a thirty-nine-year-old, slightly over-weight cigarette-smoker who had arrived home in a taxi, and who was using for his throwing piece a quarter which, dammit, bounced too much until I got the hang of it. John blocked off square number six, the one between the two doubles. Maria took three. This meant that at one point, when each of them had a talisman on one arm of the first double — and you cannot land on a square where your opponent's man is — I had to go bippity, boppity (that's one and two) and then hurl myself Nureyev-like towards the farthest flung double. I almost did it once, but kids draw squares for kid-sized feet and I was just about to try it one more time when. . . .

Well, we have this fairly stuffy neighbour who lives down the street a way. I do not know his name, but I do know he has no children, and he does have a front yard that is bowling-green clean, and that whenever our dog chooses to relieve herself illegally she aims at his hedge, and that whenever a road-hockey ball goes out of bounds it seems to end up on his lawn, and whenever . . . well, no one can do anything wrong without it somehow affecting him. And there he was, standing at the end of our driveway, watching me bicker with a nine-year-old over whether the nine-year-old had linesies or not.

I wish there were a Gregory Clark ending for this or something. I wish the old coot had come and joined in the game too, and I could report that to you. But he didn't and I can't. I just stood there feeling sheepish, and scratching my hair, and feeling as if I were nine years old with my hand in the cookie jar. And then I thought, you know, on a day like today I *am* nine years old, and I wish I had a worm and a roller-skate key in my pocket, and the biggest problem I would be facing over the weekend was a soaker. And I liked that quite a lot, quite a lot indeed. So up yours, neighbour, I said to myself, and we finished the game. John first, Maria second, me trying to hit the damn eight.

I went inside to join my wife for a predinner drink, and the real kids stayed on. But after dinner, when I was stretched out with a book, Maria came in and said, "Hey, Dad, do you want to play hide and seek?"

Why Summer Never Lasts Long Enough

Canadian Living *magazine, August 2000*

Operas, speeches, movies, meetings, sermons, monologues, dinner parties, car trips, airport waits, supermarket checkout lines, hockey playoffs, answering-machine messages, TV series, bad books, tax forms, instruction manuals, apologies, farewells and, in fact, all too many conversations. Everything in life, I have come to conclude, is about fifteen minutes too long.

Except for summer. In Canada at least, summer never begins early enough and always ends too soon. The dates vary according to where you are, but also by the stage in life you've reached. For really little kids everywhere, the change is gradual and almost un-noticed, though it's sure nice to get out of your snow gear and into what my mother used to call a play-suit. But when the opening day of summer began to matter was at school. Summer began dramatically on the magical magic last day. "No more classes, no more books/ No more teacher's dirty looks," and off we would go for all those weeks of lethargy and play, of hikes through the countryside, pickup games of baseball, experiments with fishing and pretences of learning to swim.

I spent a couple of childhood summers at camp, one of those places that the young novelist Andrew Pyper recently described as being named after "trees and Indian tribes that no longer exist."

(It's interesting that so much of the literature of our wintry land, from Stephen Leacock's classic *Sunshine Sketches of a Little Town* to David Macfarlane's magical new *Summer Gone*, is set in the warmest months of the year.) My times at camp were scarcely idyllic. I seemed to be better at catching poison ivy or having my bed apple-pied than at roughing it in the bush. But I did learn to paddle, to portage and to gunwale a canoe — although if, as Pierre Berton is reported to have said, a Canadian is someone who can make love in a canoe, I'm afraid I'd never qualify.

Later, at various cottages (they'd have been cabins in much of the west, or camps in some of the east), I added to my store of summer images: blueberries on the mossy rocks, moonlight swims in the crystal waters, lakeside picnics with iced tea (or icier beer when my grandparents weren't looking), the patter of rain on a shingled roof (I still can't play bridge when the sun is out), misty evenings with the dreams and heartaches of teenage love.

By university, where classes ended earlier, I began to venture afield. I spent two summers in frontier (as it was then) construction camps, one in the endless bush of the Labrador, the next among the foggy mountains of coastal B.C. From each I watched foraging black bears and spawning salmon (the former sometimes in patient pursuit of the latter) and came to realize that a more unifying emblem for all of Canada than the maple leaf (ever seen a maple in Alberta, for instance?) is the blackfly, which, along with its evil cousins the mosquito, the deer fly and the lyrically named no-see-um, brings us all together, from sea to sea to bug-lined sea.

And wherever I spent it, I never wanted summer to end.

On the train that took me from university to my first real newspaper job in Moose Jaw, I sat next to a brooding English immigrant. As we rolled across the prairie, I asked him what he thought of the view. "It is," he said, "the biggest expanse of bugger-all I've ever seen." In the months that followed, I was to learn how wrong he was. The Saskatchewan summer turned out to be a myriad of ever-changing green, of air sweetened by wildflowers and swept by the awesome power of the wind, blessed by the song of the meadowlark.

Ah, summer. Wherever I travelled it cast its spell.

In Nova Scotia once, the sky went dark with the smoke of forest fires from Quebec. In P.E.I., I was directed to a beach where no (other) tourist had ever appeared to tread. In Tuktoyaktuk, the temperature reached thirty degrees Celsius — that's *plus* thirty on the edge of the Beaufort Sea — and the Inuvialuit with whom I was working couldn't figure out why I was sweating.

But summer in Canada is more than just the landscape. Many of our cities — the most dramatic examples being Vancouver, where people seem to live outdoors, and Montreal, which is one long festival of street life from June to September — find new vigour in the gentler climes. And everywhere, people just slow down, read more, cook differently (viva la barbecue), travel farther, turn browner and smile more frequently.

Now, if only we could make it last a little longer. Even fifteen more minutes would be okay with me.

But Winter Can Still Happily Surprise Us

from Peter Gzowski's Book About This
Country in the Morning, *1974*

This may sound pretty dumb to those of you who live in less temperate parts of Canada than I do — temperate in climate, that is — but the highlight of this Canadian winter for me, in an outdoor sense, has been the one time it really snowed here in Toronto. It was the Thursday between Christmas and New Year's. It had started to snow during the night and just refused to stop. By noon the streets were jammed; that evening, a lot of people who commute by car were making arrangements to stay in town overnight; it took me over an hour to drive home, a trip that usually consumes only about twenty minutes. We got something like eight inches of snow — good, heavy wet stuff that really drifted and hung the way honest Canadian snow should.

What on earth could a normally sane — I like to think — man find to like in that kind of mess? Well, first of all there was the driving itself. Like most people who take the same route to work and back every day of their lives, I am bored by driving. It is one of the times I am most grateful for radio. And the chance to turn it back into an adventure — even though that adventure was only one of skidding and sliding and slipping and getting stuck — the chance to make it an adventure was one I enjoyed seizing. That's the key word, really: adventure. There was a kind of anarchy in the air that day, a hint of the same feeling that people remember from such other real emergencies as a power failure or a crucial strike. For once in our too-routine lives — too routine physically, I mean — we had to find a way to cope; to rely more on each other. We shared our difficulties and our discomforts and out of our common problems arose an accompanying sense of common friendliness. The driving may have been arduous, but the drivers were a heck of a lot nicer than they usually are.

Like almost everyone who grew up in Canada, a great many of my childhood memories involve the winter and being out of doors. A big dog that wouldn't stop chasing my sled. Soakers from a winter creek. Making angels in the snow. The way the snow matted in your hair and around the edge of your parka. Just being cold, the exquisite pain of nearly frozen toes and fingers, and the equally exquisite relief from a warming fire. Hot chocolate and sleigh rides, snowball fights and skating across the fields, endless hockey games and a whole fantasy life about the Arctic — some of the imaginary adventures I had on my way home from school made Duncan Pryde's stories sound like girl guide hikes. Later on, trying to get a goodnight kiss when it was fifty below and then walking home across a Northern Ontario town because the buses had all stopped running . . . cold, clear nights, and brilliant days. Most of my memories, as I say, are physical, related to the elements, and there are days now when I would just like to run out and make angels, but have instead to go to work or to a meeting that cannot be missed.

Canadian winters are not getting milder or shorter; but to those of us who live in cities they seem less — winterish. The snow is more often grey than white; the chances to go out and romp with kids and dogs, with sleighs and toboggans are increasingly rare. Although there always is enough snow to shovel or scrape — or so it seems — there is never enough for a snowman. It is possible, of course, to *go* to winter. But somehow there is something wrong with climbing into a car and driving fifty miles or so just to find an open field — not wrong, exactly, and I know a lot of people enjoy doing just that —

but it is at least artificial. The reality of outdoors in winter is still the children rushing out to taste the cold of the year's first snow; still a six-year-old coming home an hour and a half late from school, his clothing invisible under a solid layer of snow. He looks as if he rolled home, as well he may have done, but his cheeks are red and his eyes are shining. Now, that's winter. And if the only way we can get back to those elementary experiences requires an unexpected blizzard — well then, let all us city folk pray for more unexpected blizzards.

Why All My Teenage Romances
Ended in December

from Peter Gzowski's Book About This
Country in the Morning, *1974*

This is the time of year I used to break up with girls. A little earlier than December 21, I guess, but around now, just before Christmas. This was not, I hasten to point out, any part of the Christmas blues, or any of those other psychological phenomena that social scientists have recently come to associate with Christmas. It was because I could never figure out what kind of present to give my girlfriend. And what was worse, it was easier to give than to receive: I used to live in terrible fear of getting from someone I liked something I did not, or what might have been even worse, something I did like, but which would be a lot better than whatever it was I would have given her, because I never could, as I say, figure out what to give them.

I'm talking now about being — what? — about thirteen, or maybe through most of my (and those girls') early and middle teens, so I'm talking about *serious* love, real *crushes*, as opposed to the kind of love that leads to deeper love and, in my own case at least, to marriage. The only girl I ever gave a real Christmas present to, in fact, was Jenny Lissaman, and I married her before the next Christmas came round, although I don't think — I really am quite sure — that

that was one of the reasons. But the girls I had gone steady with in high school — and come to think of it, this lasted through university too — I used to break up with as diplomatically as I could about four o'clock on the afternoon of December 18. "It's not that I don't like you any more, Jane . . . it's just that, well, I think we each ought to go our own way for a while."

I realize I'm leaving the impression that I was some kind of Holden B. Lothario or something. I wasn't. It wasn't very often I was able to get close enough to girls to be able to break up with them, and more often, when I did get closer, it was they who broke up with me. "It isn't that I don't like you any more, Peter . . . it's just that . . ." and so on. There weren't that many of them, either. I think, in fact, that I broke up with the same girl on December 18, 1947, as I did on December 18, 1949. And I think the reason I broke up with her in '47 was that in '46 she'd given me this wallet for Christmas and I, well, I hadn't been able to think of anything to give her, and I had this awful moment at home on Christmas morning, when my mother asked who the wallet was from and I blushed and shuffled my feet and hemmed and hawed and finally told her, and she asked what I'd given the girl and I said that I, ah, that I had, well, actually I hadn't given her anything. And then my mother made me phone her to say thanks. And that was really fine, I'll tell you, phoning this girl while your mother listened to make sure you were polite.

I mean, what was there to give? A charm bracelet? They already had a charm bracelet. Who'd go out with a girl who didn't have a charm bracelet? A sweater? What size? You couldn't ask. I know this sounds easy, but you just think about being thirteen years old in 1947 and trying to figure out what size sweater your girlfriend wore. Parents were no help either. "Why don't you get her a nice book, dear?" A book, for God's sake. You might as well have given her mittens. That was another thing, I suppose. Gloves. Once I even got up to the glove counter in one of the big department stores in Galt, Ontario, but three guys I used to play basketball with came by and I had to fake to the right, pivot and pretend I was picking out a pair for myself. Earrings? She'd have looked silly in earrings.

Barrettes? Skate guards? One of my first loves was the greatest figure skater in the GCI & VS and, in my view, in the world — but you still couldn't give skate guards to someone at Christmas time. That was the whole problem. If it was useful enough — "why don't you give her a nice warm scarf, dear?" — it just wasn't the sort of thing Humphrey Bogart would have given Lauren Bacall, and if it was that sort of thing it was too soppy to give to anyone in case someone else found out. So I used to break up with the girls in late December. This left me with problems for New Year's Eve, of course, but somehow they seemed to get solved. "Jane? Hi. I know we're not going steady any more, but listen, next Friday night is . . . and, well, you know, Rhonda's having this party and, well, if you're not going with anyone . . ."

I've got a couple of daughters now, and the oldest one at least is exactly the kind of girl I used to break up with. As a father, I'm still having difficulty trying to figure out what to give her — the boys are easy. I'll solve it, of course, and I promise her, if she's listening today, that it won't be mittens. But I can't help wondering if somewhere there isn't some young guy sneaking around the glove department and hoping like mad no one from his basketball team shows up.

The Complete Works of Pete Gzowski, Lyricist, as Recorded by Ian and Sylvia, the Chad Mitchell Trio and — Seriously — Bob Dylan

"Song for Canada," 1965

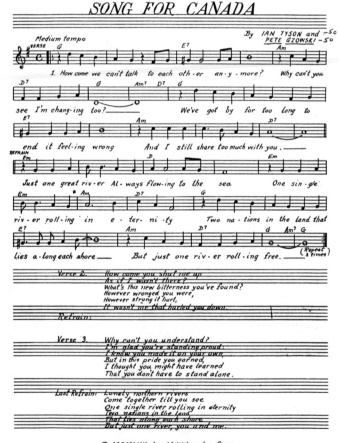

How come we can't talk to each other any more?
Why can't you see I'm changing too?
We've got by for too long to end it feeling wrong
And I still share too much with you.

(refrain)
Just one great river
Always flowing to the sea
One single river rolling in eternity
Two nations in the land that lies along each shore.
But just one river rolling free.

How come you shut me up
As if I wasn't there?
What's this new bitterness you've found?
However wronged you were,
However strong it hurt,
It wasn't me that hurled you down.

(refrain)

Why can't you understand?
I'm glad you're standing proud:
I know you made it on your own.
But in this pride you earned,
I thought you might have learned
That you don't have to stand alone.

(last refrain)
Lonely northern rivers
Come together till you see
One single river rolling in eternity
Two nations in the land
That lies along each shore
But just one river, you and me.

The Abbreviated Memoirs of an Abbreviated
Talk-Show Career

Toronto Life, *October 1978*

The key guest on the first national edition of *90 Minutes Live*, from my point of view anyway, was Tom Berger. This was in Vancouver, in the spring of 1976, and Berger — Mr. Justice Thomas R. Berger — had pretty well wrapped up his hearings on what a pipeline would do to the Mackenzie Valley. His report wasn't out yet, but I happened to know he'd already formed some pretty strong opinions. We'd talked one time in Yellowknife, privately, and while I didn't expect him to be quite as blunt on television as he'd been over a few Scotches, I thought what he had to say was dramatic and important and I wanted him to say some of it on our first program.

By then, having done some regional shows in Halifax, we'd learned a few things. What the CBC calls "public affairs," for example, doesn't mix with the kind of pizzazz we hoped to sprinkle Canadian late-night television with. We thought we could put heavy material on the same show as the frivolous stuff, but we figured we'd have to give it a special place. Tom Berger knew that, too. The night before our debut, I went over to his house, along with Alex Frame, the executive producer of the show. We said we hoped he'd speak his mind, and he laid down the conditions under which he'd come on at all. He would not, he said, sit between "some blonde singer and the head of the local Mafia." We said that was okay. We couldn't have accommodated his fears anyway; we did have Patsy Gallant, but even our bookers couldn't get anyone from the mob. He asked me to call him Judge, or Mr. Justice, instead of Tom, and I said that was fine, too; getting him at all seemed something of a coup. Frame and I left, excited.

On the air, Mr. Justice Berger turned out to be terrible. Not as a man, or as a judge, but as that curious creature called a talk-show guest. However colourful he'd been in private, on the air he was grey, judicial, dull. I was worse. The more guarded Berger became the more panic-stricken I got until, trying to elicit some flavour of the man I admired (and still do), I must have sounded like the worst kind of peewee-hockey mother. I cudgelled and cajoled until, to anyone who'd never heard us talk in private — which would be, I'd guess, about one hundred per cent of the audience — I must have sounded like the judge's (and common sense's) worst enemy.

The critics, of course, beat me up, and my own confidence began a slide that didn't really reverse itself until the spring of this year, when I told the CBC I didn't want to host that show any more.

All of which, of course, is an oversimplification. Tom Berger wasn't that bad, and not all the critics savaged us. I went on to do some things of which I'm enormously proud and, as I said when I finally left *90 Minutes Live* in May, I wouldn't have missed the experience for the world. We did put on two years of late-night television in Canada, and that in itself is no mean accomplishment. Frequently, we got the centre of gravity out of Toronto and, in doing so, brought new life to the shows we put on here. We presented aspects of a number of people — from the giddy show-biz side of Patrick Watson or the warmth of Adrienne Clarkson to the genuine wisdom of my hero — W. O. Mitchell — that viewers might not otherwise have seen. And, in a country famished for them, we helped towards the creation of some stars: James Barber, John Kastner, Patsy Gallant, Yvon Deschamps (in English), and quite a few others. But the truth remains: The show — and I — started haltingly in Vancouver and never really hit our stride until I said I was quitting.

After that, I think, it got quite good. I'd argue there was cause and effect there. With nothing at stake, I suddenly started to enjoy both the guests and myself, and that enjoyment showed. Even those critics who'd been toughest on us at the beginning — and to whom I sometimes secretly wished I could send copies of their own first columns to see if they'd like to be judged on those early tries alone — even they came to recognize we had something going. By the end, I think, I was treated a little like the Robert Stanfield of television, more honoured in retirement than in office. I guess I even do some of that filtering of the past myself; looking back on those years from this side of the screen, I think we did . . . well, not badly, and the agonies of the daily, draining grind, and the constant smartass bickering from the press, fade into a not unpleasant glow.

I write all this — and in doing so break a promise to myself to let those years, and my own feelings about *90 Minutes Live*, become history — with a purpose. I'd like to write about television and about other forms of communication occasionally; I don't think the world will be hurt by hearing the view of someone who's actually been there, and I do have some things to say. Whatever, though, my opinions are probably suspect. If I'm critical of the CBC, sour grapes; laudatory, I'm sucking. So I'd like to get some things out of the way first. I do have prejudices. I think television is the least understood by its critics of all the things that are written about critically — although I'm sure anyone who paints, writes or performs music, dances, acts or cooks omelettes would disagree with me — and I think the carping, and frequently stupid, attitudes of the television critics in this city are dangerous to the future of something that matters very much to me. I mean it: dangerous. There is quite a bright and dedicated group of men in charge of the CBC these days (I'm generalizing) and I think it's fair to say they no longer wait up, as their predecessors are reported to have done, to read in the papers whether or not they'd enjoyed their own shows. But a constantly bitchy press, which, by and large, sets a higher standard for Canadian productions than imported ones (it would be interesting to see Merv Griffin held up to their scrutiny), can wreak a lot of self-fulfilling damage on an industry's morale. To an astonishing degree, the real judges of television — the viewers — seem to do exactly what the CBC brass of yore was reputed to do: see by the papers whether or not they've liked a show. I cannot count the number of people who have stopped me on the street to say they liked the show and were sorry it wasn't working. They forget — and so, eventually, do a lot of those who work in television — that the people who hold the critical chairs in Toronto have no more credentials for those posts than membership in a newspaper guild, an editor's whim and an ability to type.

I was a television critic once myself — for *Maclean's*, back in the early sixties. I know how easy it is to judge. I know a lot of things now I didn't know then, in fact, and the principal one is this: Doing television is hard, very hard indeed. What tends to get written about — *vide* even my casual reference above to Merv Griffin — is not so much what you do, but who you are. Like a beauty contest. And that's wrong. *Being*, on television, is doing. Looking natural, with the hot light glistening off your glasses, and a pound and a half of allergy-tested, fragrance-free, Clinique foundation in honey beige covering your cheeks, with a couple of hundred clamorous people who've wandered off Yonge Street into the dripping warmth of Studio 4 of a winter evening . . . looking natural then is an unnatural act, as unnatural, and as much in need of learning, as hitting a golf ball or dancing on point. Speaking fervently into a glass lens with a red light (sometimes) staring back at you just isn't the way God meant us to talk to each other. It can become the way we communicate — just as holding a piece of wired plastic to our ears and mouths has become easy for us — but it isn't in the old genes.

It's a learned skill. The best analogy I can think of is musical. No one without training would think of walking up to a good jazz group and asking if they could sit in for the pianist or the horn-player. But they do think they can sit in for the drummer. Because it looks easy, everyone thinks he can do it. And so with television.

There are some people, of course, who don't know — or care — how hard what they're doing is. But the real masters, or the people I like to watch as much as I like to see Rod Carew hit a baseball or

Dennis Burton draw a line, are the students of their craft, and we have far too few of them in Canada — yet.

The most difficult test of the skill — or art, if you will — is what we still unfortunately call the "talk show." Unfortunately, because it is really so many other things: circus, platform, arena. Talk, in the sense that one "talks" to one's mate, friends, boss, is one of the least important elements. So, in fact, is the "interview" — the means by which one person obtains information from another. Tell me, if you can, just one thing you can remember someone actually saying on a talk show. You remember who was there, what they did, how they looked, how they sounded, what you thought of them. What they said is essentially irrelevant. The "talk show" is the ultimate television *event*. People who are good at talk shows may be good at virtually nothing else; people who master them, unfortunately, aren't really prepared for anything else. What does Steve Allen do now? Jack Paar? Hugh Downs? Or, for that matter, Rick Campbell, who hosted a talk show years ago in Toronto. The only place for a talk-show host is on a talk show, as Johnny Carson may well be forever.

To anyone who's tried to emulate them, Carson's skills are awesome. Interviews? Who cares? He doesn't *do* interviews; he does *pieces* in which his guests are either — when they're not too good — secondary players, or — when they are — superbly supported. With someone who clicks with him — Burt Reynolds, McLean Stevenson, Don Rickles — Carson is matchless. But try to re-create his best turns for someone who didn't see them the night before and you realize what they are: the definitive you-had-to-be-there jokes, because, in fact, you did have to be there, to watch him in action.

And so, the final question: Do we want Johnny Carson on the CBC? I'd say no. He's already on television and, while there are many nights when, tired or cranky, I'd rather watch him than anyone I can think of, there are many other nights when I'd like to watch someone who has a little more to do with me, who uses the same vocabulary as I do, someone mastering the skills Carson demonstrates so wonderfully every night, but doing so in Canadian.

Meeting Rhonda

Toronto Star, *18 and 19 December, 1987*

After I stepped down from talk-show television, I tried my hand at a daily newspaper column. That career didn't last long, either, but I met some memorable people, perhaps the most memorable the young woman about whom I wrote these two pieces.

I

"I can't hear you very well," said Rhonda Tepper on the telephone to Israel, "but I can hear you say my name, and I can hear you say Happy Hanukkah, and that's all I wanted."

Rhonda was crying, kind of — with happiness, and so I imagine was the man she was talking to, Eitan Nesher, who lives on Kibbutz–Shar Hamakim near Haifa.

My eyes weren't exactly dry, either.

Rhonda is the winner of the little contest I started in the *Star* last month, the fantasy game about how people would spend a day if it were the last day of their lives.

Rhonda, twenty, is a second-year student at the University of Toronto.

Eitan Nesher is the man she calls her "kibbutz father." She met him the summer before last when she stayed in Israel for three months. They became very close. She has never known her natural father. Her parents split up the year she was born.

Placing the call to him was part of Rhonda's fantasy — what she'd do if she had a day dedicated totally to spoiling herself, when she didn't have to worry about money.

The reason she had trouble hearing his words is a very moving one. Rhonda is almost deaf. She has only fifteen per cent of normal hearing. At her university lectures she sits in the front row and reads lips. She is an Ontario Scholar, which means her grade thirteen marks were over eighty per cent.

But I didn't know that when I chose her as the winner of my contest. She doesn't make a big thing out of it. And that is all I'm going to say about her handicap, and how she handles it, today.

I chose her because I liked her letter. While there were more profound entries, and more wildly imaginative schemes, it seemed to me that of all the couple of hundred people who played the game she understood it best.

Here is what she wrote:

> Hello:
>
> If I knew tomorrow were the last day of my life I would go down early to Kensington and loiter at the Global Cheese Shop for a good half-hour sampling to my heart's content . . . pretending I was planning to buy.
>
> I would go to the top of Commerce Court and view my city . . . call up my favourite school teacher and recall some of our favourite lessons. Go to Mars Bakery at College and Bathurst to enjoy a grand bran muffin and a real cup of coffee.
>
> I'd read a few chapters of my favourite book (A Tree Grows In Brooklyn, by Betty Smith), wear my favourite white blouse and most comfortable shoes . . . call up my kibbutz father and say shalom . . . rent a roller coaster for a full fifteen minutes . . . sneak into a Robertson Davies lecture at U of T and introduce

myself afterwards . . . go swimming, borrow someone's dog, kiss a child, take a hot shower and not feel guilty for twenty minutes.

I'd read a whole newspaper, work on my scrapbooks, think of a real funny joke to grab my brother at the supper table . . . listen to Lady by England Dan and John Ford Coley, and Everybody Has A Dream by Billy Joel . . . sing a song of my own . . . dance cheek-to-cheek across the living room with my big brother, and clean my bird (John's) cage.

Rhonda Tepper

P.S. . . . Boy, was this ever fun!

It was fun reading it too, and even more fun hurtling around the city with her on Friday, trying to see how many of her fantasies we could make come true.

The people at Conklin shows broke out their roller coaster for her. She couldn't ride all the way around it — it's been taken apart for the winter and the power is cut off — but two men drove in from Brantford, spent six hours setting a car up far her and then pushed her around as many curves as they could.

When her mini-ride was over we went into the office to say thanks to the Conklin people. They said they'd enjoyed doing it and gave her a season's pass for the summer.

We arrived — unannounced — at Mars Bakery just as a fresh batch of bran muffins was coming from the oven, and Sam the manager gave her a box to take with her, and I found out, by eating one, why she'd go there on her last, or any other, day. She has good taste, this young woman I was beginning to think of as my Rhonda.

She has good taste in authors too.

Robertson Davies doesn't give lectures over the holiday break, but when I called him he quickly invited Rhonda up for what he laughingly called "an audience." He met her with warmth and graciousness in his study in the master's quarters at Massey College, and he and Rhonda chatted about literature for a while before he signed a copy of his latest book, *One Half of Robertson Davies*, for her.

Then it was back to the *Star* to make the phone call, and for her to let the emotions of the whole event, and of talking to Eitan Nesher, come out.

"He couldn't believe it was me," she said when the tears had dried. "He must have thought I was in Haifa or something, and I was going to ask when the bus would come. I can't get over it. I could hear his voice. It was him."

"Come on, Rhonda," I said. "I'm supposed to be a cynical old newspaper guy, and you've got me all wrapped up in this thing too."

What I didn't tell her then, but I think she knew, is that I'd also had just as good a time as she did.

"I'd better go home," she said. "Can you call my grandmother and tell her I'm on my way for supper?"

Okay, I said, but she had to promise to dance with her brother that night.

"If he's not working," she said. "He waits on tables on weekends, you know."

Her brother, incidentally, who goes to York University, also has a hearing handicap. Their mother, who is a supervisor at Chargex, is totally deaf. Tomorrow, I'll tell you about how this remarkable family copes.

In the meantime . . . oh, forget it.

Happy Hanukkah, Rhonda Tepper.

II

Rhonda Tepper, the bright and attractive university student who won my fantasy contest, and about whom I wrote yesterday, took a chemistry course last year.

Like a lot of students who have taken this course, she found it very difficult. After one particularly knotty lecture, she approached the instructor.

"Excuse me," she said, "could you repeat that last section on . . ."

"What's the matter?" he said. "Are you deaf!?"

Rhonda is deaf, as it happens — or nearly so. Her lack of hearing plays a major part in her life. But she has put her handicap into such perspective that her first thoughts, after her chemistry teacher's potentially embarrassing outburst, were for him.

"I didn't want him to feel bad," she says. "So I didn't say anything about it. Besides, my hearing had nothing to do with why I couldn't understand him. The lecture was just too complicated."

Rhonda, twenty, has about fifteen per cent of normal hearing. She wears an aid behind each ear. She can't hear a phone ring or a door close. If you turn away from her when you're talking, she can't understand you. She reads lips. At the college she goes to — Victoria, at the University of Toronto — front seats are reserved for her in lecture halls.

As I said yesterday, I didn't know about her hearing problem when I picked her letter from all the entries in the contest I ran — how you'd spend tomorrow if it were the last day of your life.

My first inkling came when I tracked her down to arrange for her to spend at least part of the day she'd outlined. Rather than chat on the phone, she arranged to come down to see me.

Talking on the phone is difficult for her. She has an amplified receiver, but the words she hears are not clear.

"My speech is funny, too, isn't it?" she said when we met for the first time. When you know the reason, you can hear differences, but the variations from "normal" speech are no greater than in, say, a regional Canadian accent.

"I'll tell you something funny," she said. "Because I can't hear myself, I'm not always sure when to stop. The worst are words that end in 's.' I'll say, 'And when he brought me home he gave me a kiss,' but it comes out 'kisssss.' It's weird."

I am giving the wrong impression here if Rhonda is coming across as some kind of comedienne. She isn't. She is an intelligent, spirited, pleasant young woman for whom reduced hearing is a fact of life, and she would be embarrassed and probably even annoyed if I held her up as any kind of inspiration.

But I am setting down some of the things I learned about her as I got to know her a bit because . . . Well, just because I like them, and I think they're worth sharing.

Rhonda's mother is totally deaf. She holds a supervisory job at Chargex, and she is, her bosses say, very good at it. Rhonda's only sibling — an older brother named Bill — also has limited hearing (the handicap is hereditary).

"He goes to York," she says of Bill. "He's a waiter on weekends, and sometimes he gets the same thing as I got from the chemistry teacher. He has to lean right down to read lips, and one time a customer asked if he was deaf. He said he was, and pointed to his hearing aid. Those people left him a $2.50 tip. Now, he says, he wishes more people would ask him!"

I wondered about one of the fantasies she'd mentioned in her letter to me — the dance cheek to cheek with her brother.

"We can hear the beat," she said. "And one of the great things about a lot of the new records is they print the lyrics so you can follow along."

What about the nuances she must miss in everyday speech?

"Are you kidding? When you have to look right at someone to know what they're saying you probably get more real meaning than people who just hear the words. I'm a hard person to lie to."

We talked a lot, Rhonda and I, as we tried to set up her fantasy day. One story has stayed with me. I had asked her how she's got to know her "kibbutz father," the man she wanted to telephone in Israel and did.

"Because of his son," she said. "I was visiting at the kibbutz — I spent three month there altogether — and I noticed this little boy who was deaf. I asked who his parents were, because I thought I could tell him some things.

"So I met the father, and we became good friends. It was like a new family for me. And when I left, the father said to me that he'd been worried about his boy, but that after talking to me he wasn't worried any more."

Neither, I told her, would I be.

Postscript:
My friendship with Rhonda lasted well beyond her appearance in my column. I had the honour of speaking at her wedding, taking care to trim my moustache and face her so she could read my lips. And we have remained close to each other ever since, even though she still hasn't heard me on the radio.

Life in the Big Leagues I: Behind the Bench

from The Game of Our Lives, *1981*

The Forum, Montreal, Monday, January 12: The game has two different dimensions from the perspective of the team's bench. The first is the tension. You can *feel* it down here. It started well before the game. Fogolin was the first man in the dressing room, arriving shortly after 4:30, three and a half hours before game time, changing to his underwear and beginning his ritual of stick-taping and checking his equipment. Peter Millar worked for a while on one of Fogie's leg muscles, which has been cramping. Brack was next, working out on his push-up blocks even before the game. Then Mark Messier, still suffering from a groin that was pulled in Toronto last week. Messier put on a special girdle Millar has given him, then spent much of the pre-game time limbering up in the outer dressing room practising sprinter's starts, hoping he looked better than he felt. There is such animal grace to him, even when he's hurt. Several of the others had made a trip to one of the league's most popular tailors. Doug Hicks reported he'd had a dozen pairs of trousers altered to fit the season's new style, and Kevin Lowe was sporting a snappy new tweed jacket. But the sartorial stand-out was Semenko, who appeared in a purple jacket, white shirt and black tie, ready to conquer Crescent Street.

At first, conversation was light and bantering. Linda Ronstadt's picture was on the front page of the *Gazette* this morning, and the players were making much sport of the weight she had gained. "I see the trouble," said Don Murdoch. "It's in her right hand." In the picture she was holding a fork.

The first ripple of tension hit about 5:30, when everyone was at the rink and it was time to start suiting up. It washed over the room, stopping the banter and turning faces grim. It receded, then rose again, receded and came again, faster each time, like waves on a rising tide. By 7:30, when it was time for the pre-game skate, no one was saying anything. Breaking sweat out on the ice failed to help. Not speaking, they clumped back up the aisle to the dressing room. Millar, in what must be the worst of all his unpleasant chores, had the assignment of telling Semenko he would be sitting out tonight. In front of his silent teammates, big Dave stripped off his uniform, had an unnecessary shower and made his way past their drooping heads, the purple splendour of his attire now looking somehow ridiculous.

The other dimension that changes from behind the bench is the speed and violence of the game. Here, you get an extraordinary sense of how fast the players on the ice are moving and how hard they are hitting each other. Early in the first period, Bob Gainey, the Canadiens' stalwart defensive forward, ran Stan Weir into the boards right at the bench. Weir's face was clenched in pain and concentration. The collision was as hard as if a car had run into the boards; I was sure I could hear bones crunch. Yet for Weir and Gainey the crash was part of the routine. Eighty nights a year they do this, all of them, thrashing their bodies about at inhuman speeds, trying to focus on a bouncing puck while some of the best and toughest athletes in the world hack and pound away at them, and they, in turn, hack and pound back. Perched above the action, the fans view it from an angle that slows it to a comprehensible speed. But down here, the speed and the force spill over the boards. Eyes bulge, throats sweat, mouths suck for wind.

There is an awesome, rushing beauty to this game. Even from this perspective, patterns emerge, fade, shift, change, fade and form again. A rhythm sets in, as the play flows back and forth, eases off, gets broken and picks up. For an immeasurable instant, a gap appears, a pathway down the ice, and suddenly a player moves into it, or sends a pass skittering down its length, and other openings appear around it. Then they close. The play stops, hangs in balance as one man controls the puck, feints. Then the action pulses again. Fresh bodies leap over the boards.

Combining so many skills, played at such speeds, hockey is, surely, the most difficult of games, and the men who play it are the finest athletes now playing any sport in the world. They are fast, strong, balanced, brave and quick. And unlike the other men who play fast and violent games for a living — notably football and basketball — hockey players are men of normal physical proportions, selected not for their eccentric physiques, but for their skills and talent. It is possible to think of any of them playing golf, or baseball, or even fighting for a living — and, indeed, Gordie Howe came close to doing all of those — but it is impossible to think of Jack Nicklaus or Johnny Bench or Muhammad Ali playing hockey.

Tonight, the Canadiens are roaring up and down the ice in the fire-wagon style that has characterized Montreal teams since Morenz's day, whipping crisp, short passes to one another, blazing past the defence. They pour in on Mio as if he were alone, blasting thirteen shots at him in the first period alone and scoring on three of them, while holding the Oilers to four shots and no goals. At the intermission, Sather has little to say, allowing the players to sit in silence for nearly all of the fifteen minutes. From the inner room, I hear a few shouts of encouragement — "Come on, guys, it's not over yet" — but on the bench, as the second period begins, the feeling is that it is over. The Canadiens simply keep coming at them, and in response the Oilers appear flat and over-awed. It is 4-0 before the period ends.

In the third period, disaster strikes. A blistering shot by Rejean Houle hits Mio flush on the mask, and Eddie goes down as if injected with curare. Before he even hits the ice, it seems, Peter

Millar is over the boards, and shortly after there is a call for a doctor. Finally, a stretcher is wheeled out, and Mio is whisked away through a gate at the opposite side of the ice. Spared the sight of their fallen comrade, the Oilers are nevertheless shaken.

As Andy Moog skates out to replace Mio — his first day in Montreal and, aged twenty, about to face the guns of hockey's greatest dynasty — word passes along the bench to try to give him extra protection. For a few minutes they seem able to. But, almost inevitably, the Canadiens score on Moog, and the game ends 5-0.

There are no jokes in the dressing room afterwards. Peter Millar is still at the hospital with Mio. As unobtrusively as possible, I help Kelly Pruden pick up the towels and dry the skate blades. "God *damn*," says Sather despondently, "were they ever flying tonight."

For some time after the others leave, Andy Moog sits quietly by himself. In spite of the goal he allowed, which was scored on a power play, he played steadily. He is pleased with himself. I ask him if he found a difference between the NHL game and the game he has been playing in Wichita. He cocks an eye at me to see if there is anything behind the question. "It's still hockey," he says. "They just go a little faster here."

Life in the Big Leagues II:
How Gretzky Does It

from The Game of Our Lives, *1981*

Northlands Coliseum: The Oilers are playing St. Louis, who are still in first place, and have lost only three of their last twenty-seven games. Tonight could be another showdown between Liut and the Kid. In the first period, Gretzky is concentrating on setting other people up. At 2:25, he takes a pass from Paul Coffey in the middle of the St. Louis zone, fakes a shot and sends a backhand pass to Callighen, who makes a smart move to score. At 12:30, on a power play, he is an intermediary again, this time between Siltanen and Kurri, who pops his twenty-first of the year. With Pat Price off for his usual first-period penalty, Bernie Federko scores for St. Louis; a minute later, Wayne Babych adds another, and the period ends 2-2.

Wayne did not arrive early at the rink, but when he did, he went right to the video machine, my tape recorder in hand, and sat down to work. This morning we chose one of the goals he had scored in the 9-1 romp over Montreal. This afternoon he played it through once at regular speed and once at slow-motion, recording his comments. When Sather arrived in the coaches' room, where the video machine sits, he found Wayne still in street clothes. "We have a hockey game tonight," he said.

At 4:44 of the second period, he sets up Brackenbury, who is out to create some action. Brackenbury shoots, Liut saves, and Wayne pokes in the rebound. 3-2. At 7:03, Mark Messier, who is playing with the abandon we have expected from him all along, combines with Glenn Anderson to make it 4-2.

Stan Weir wins the opening face-off of the third period, and passes to B. J. MacDonald. B. J. drops it back for Paul Coffey. Coffey carries it to the blueline, feints twice, appears indecisive and then swerves to his backhand to beat Liut again. 5-2.

And then the deluge starts. At 5:49, with Pat Price and Perry Turnbull off for roughing, Gretzky picks up a loose puck, cuts to his left and drifts a shot along the ice back across in front of Liut and into the furthermost corner of the net. Bill Tuele, the Oilers' publicity man, begins an announcement in the press box that this is Gretzky's thirteenth goal and thirty-eighth scoring point in the last sixteen games, when . . .

He does it again. Nine seconds after the unassisted goal, he takes a pass from Coffey and moves in alone towards the goal. Liut comes out. Gretzky moves to his left again and shoots with the same motion as for his last goal, but this time aims it instead for the closest corner, and Liut misses.

The crowd gives Gretzky a standing ovation.

With the hat trick, Liut publicly acknowledges his loss of tonight's showdown, and takes himself out of the game. In his place comes Ed Staniowski, who has been doing yeoman service all year as his more celebrated colleague's back-up.

At 8:17, with the Oilers short-handed, Gretzky scores again. Stealing the puck, he cuts yet again to his left, and this time, as Staniowski tries to outguess him, he repeats the low, short, cross-corner shot that first beat Liut. There is no power to these shots that are going in, but they are as accurate as a surgeon's needle, and there is something about their timing that is keeping the goalies off-balance.

The press box is buzzing. The three consecutive goals are among the fastest ever scored by one player, although Jean Beliveau once got three in forty-four seconds. The crowd stands again, this time mixing their applause with merriment. The Oilers are whipping the first-place Blues 8-2. Tuele is chattering statistics into the press box PA.

And then Gretzky does it again. He is standing in the attacking zone when Doug Hicks, taking a pass at the blueline from Siltanen, rips an apparently harmless slapshot in the vague direction of the goal. As the puck is about to whistle by Gretzky, he flicks his stick in the air and directs it into an open corner of the goal.

Are these the fastest four goals ever scored? No one in the press box knows. But the record he has tied — four in one period — goes back to 1934, when Busher Jackson did it for Toronto against a team called the St. Louis Eagles. And what about Gretzky's five goals in one game? In all the NHL's history, only seven men have scored five goals in one game; one was Maurice Richard, one was Howie Morenz, and five of them were Joe Malone.

• • •

There is an unhurried grace to everything Gretzky does on the ice. Winding up for a slapshot, he will stop for an almost imperceptible moment at the top of his arc, like a golfer with a rhythmic swing. Often the difference between what Wayne does with the puck and what a less accomplished player would have done with it is simply a pause, as if, as time freezes, he is enjoying an extra handful of milliseconds. Time seems to slow down for him, and indeed, it may actually do so. Dr. Adrian R. M. Upton, the head neurologist at McMaster University in Hamilton, Ontario, has done some fascinating experiments with élite sprinters that suggest (the reservations about the work are that it is very hard to get a sufficiently large sample to test) that their motor neurons fire faster than those of mere mortals; the quicker their reaction times were to even simple tap tests, the faster they were liable to run. If this is true, it may account for much of what we see among the champions of a lot of sports. When Bjorn Borg, playing tennis as fast as any human can play it, appears to have the same control the rest of us would have in a casual Sunday morning knock-up, it may well be that for him the pace is slower; his neurological motor is running with such efficiency that his response to his opponent's actions is as deliberate as ours would be at a more turgid pace. Dr. Upton, who has published several technical papers about his work with athletes, compares the difference between the neurological systems of the superstars and those of the rest of us to the difference between a highly tuned sports car and the family sedan. The sports car is simply capable of firing faster. When George Brett claims that he can see the stitches on a baseball spinning towards his hitting zone, he may be telling us something about his motoneurological capacity. Wayne, too, if Dr. Upton's suppositions are correct (and from neurological evidence alone he was able to predict the 1976 Olympic sprint victory of Hasely Crawford of Trinidad), is reacting to the situations of the games he plays as if it were being played for him in slow-motion film.

In the fall of 1980, John Jerome, a former editor of *Skiing* magazine, brought out a book called *The Sweet Spot in Time*, in which he examined much of the most recent exploration of athletic anatomy. His title was an echo of one of his central observations, that just as there is a physical "sweet spot" on a tennis racquet or a baseball bat, so is there, for the exceptional athlete, an almost immeasurably brief moment in time that is precisely right for performing his action. In explaining this thesis, Jerome cited a musical analogy. He wrote:

> *I happened to hear violinist Isaac Stern discuss his art one night, and a jazz musician (whose name escapes me) the next. Both of these immensely talented individuals would sing wordless snatches — "dum dum ti dum," and so on — to illustrate points about their very different forms of music. I am not a musician, and could barely catch the significant differences they were demonstrating so effortlessly. I could discern, but I'm sure I did not fully comprehend, these differences — in emphasis and tone, but mostly just in timing. Each man would illustrate one way to play a phrase, then an alternate, varying the timing of the notes subtly without violating the form, changing in major ways the emotional*

content of the music without changing a note. I suddenly realized
that for musicians — and for athletes — there must be a great
deal more room, in effect, in the flow of time than there is for the
rest of us.

Gretzky uses this room to insert an extra beat into his actions. In
front of the net, eyeball to eyeball with the goaltender, he will . . .
hold the puck one . . . extra instant, upsetting the anticipated rhythm
of the game, extending his moment, as he did against Liut and
Staniowski, the way a ballet dancer extends the time of his leap. He
distorts time, and not always by slowing it down. Sometimes he will
release the puck before he appears to be ready, threading a pass
through a maze of players precisely to the blade of a teammate's stick,
or finding a chink in a goaltender's armour and slipping the puck
into it before the goaltender is ready to react. Because of hockey's
speed, the differences between his actions and those of anyone else
are invisible from the stands (as they often are, for that matter, from
a position next to him on the ice). If he did not repeat their results
so many times it would be possible to dismiss many of them as luck.
If there is such a thing as sleight of body, he performs it.

On top of his neurological advantages, Gretzky seems to bring
certain special qualities of metabolism to the game. With Gordie
Howe, he shares an exceptional capacity to renew his energy
resources quickly. Even when Howe had been out on the ice longer
than any of his teammates he would be the first man on the bench
to lift his head. Similarly with Gretzky, who often, as against
St. Louis, has his best moments in the third period. When Dave
Smith, a University of Alberta exercise physiologist who tested all
the Oilers in the spring of 1980, first saw the results of Gretzky's test
of recuperative abilities, he thought the machine had broken.

In the simplest terms, Gretzky is an exceptional pure athlete.
Bearing out Dr. Upton's suppositions, he is a runner fast enough to
compete at respectable levels. (His sister, Kim, was a provincial
champion.) In baseball, he batted .492 for the Brantford CKCP
Braves in the summer of 1980, and he was offered — seriously — a

contract by the Toronto Blue Jays. But he is hardly a superman. Smith's tests also showed him to be the weakest of the Oilers. ("Am I stronger than my Mom?" he asked when he saw the results.)

His physical gifts, in any case, are not enough to account for Gretzky's supremacy. Each year in Canada alone, some hundred thousand boys totter out on the ice for their first game of organized hockey. By the time they reach puberty, about half of them will have dropped out. Some of those who leave will have done so for reasons that have little to do with ability: girls, school, their parents' unwillingness to continue the Saturday dawn drive to the rink, or simply because they don't like playing hockey. At about the age of twelve, however, those who are playing at the most competitive levels will include a high percentage of gifted and ambitious athletes. All that will keep most of them from professional hockey is that somehow they are not good enough. I asked various sports physiologists how many of, say, a hundred élite Canadian peewees they could eliminate from potential stardom in the NHL through physical measurement alone. The highest guess was twenty, which came at the University of Alberta; the lowest was none, which came at Waterloo, in Ontario. Given a certain minimum standard of size-for-age, in other words, and a general aptitude for sports, there is almost nothing in the human body — unless Dr. Upton's sophisticated tests are someday made universal — that can separate the potential million-dollar hockey player from the potential weekend racquetballer.

Much of the most interesting recent work in sports physiology has been done with muscle fibres. Researchers have taken painful biopsies of athletes to see what they could learn. While much of this work has been of value in understanding how muscles work — what fast-twitch fibres (the dark meat) do, as opposed to slow-twitch fibres — it has not been of much predictive use. "Little, if any, of the information has been of any value to the athletes studied," wrote the authors of an overview of their work in *The Physician and Sports Medicine* in January 1980. For an even more exhaustive view of "Physiological and anthropometric characteristics of élite Canadian ice hockey players" published in *The Journal of Sports*

Medicine and Physical Fitness, Drs. William Houston and Howard Green of the Waterloo department of kinesiology studied various characteristics of two teams of different levels. They concluded: "The absence of significant physiological differences emphasizes the fact that physiological criteria were not differentiating factors."

And yet by the time the hundred thousand boys who started hockey reach an eligible age, perhaps fifty of them — in a very good year — will win places in the NHL, making the odds against a young hockey player reaching the pinnacle of that profession higher than they are against a random student in grade one becoming a university teacher. What has winnowed them out, finally, is not their ability but the way they are able to apply it. As Drs. Houston and Green concluded: "In the absence of a fundamental understanding of the physiological systems involved, coaches tend to differentiate between hockey players on that aspect with which they are most familiar, skill."

Even skill, however, is not a sufficient standard by which to measure Gretzky's mastery. At many of the skating techniques the Oilers' scouts would rate, he would be, perhaps, seven out of nine; at shooting less. And yet scrawled across his reports are only the words "can't miss." What separates him from his peers in the end, the quality that has led him to the very point of the pyramid, may well have nothing to do with physical characteristics at all, but instead be a matter of perception, not so much of what he sees — he does not have exceptional vision — but of *how* he sees it and how he absorbs it. Here, some work in fields that at first glance seem a long way from hockey yield some enlightening clues.

Much of this work is recent, but it is an extension of experiments carried out in the late 1930s by the Dutch psychologist Adrian de Groot. De Groot worked with chess players, whom he divided into groups according to their level of play: grand masters, experts and club players. In one experiment he had each player look for a limited time at a number of chess pieces arranged on a board in a fairly complex middle-game position. Then he asked his subjects to reconstruct that position. Perhaps not surprisingly, the grand masters did much better than the experts, and the experts much better than the club players. Then, however, de Groot exposed all three groups to yet another set of positions, only this time the pieces were arranged not in game situations but at random. This time, there was no measurable difference in the participants' ability to recall the arrangement. What the better players had remembered, in other words, was not so much the positions of the chess pieces but the overall situations. Later experiments confirmed these findings; the more highly gifted the chess player was, the more likely he was to see on a board not individual pieces, but the combinations they formed, the forces in play. In the 1970s, Neil Charness, a professor of psychology at the University of Waterloo, himself a chess player who had carried on work in the de Groot tradition, extended these explorations to the field of bridge. Charness found — to oversimplify — that expert bridge players could remember bridge hands much better than beginners, but at remembering combinations of cards that had no relationship to bridge they were no better at all. And in a recent Ph.D. thesis, an Ontario psychologist named Lynne Beal showed that the same principle held for music: accomplished musicians could recall and repeat sets of chords better than nonaccomplished musicians could, but when notes were assembled in random clusters, the experts fared no better than their less well-trained partners in the experiment.

The more we are trained in a given field, then, the more we tend to understand that field in combinations of familiar information, or what the psychologists call "chunks." A chunk, to use one of Neil Charness's examples, might be a telephone number. If you are familiar with a telephone number — your own — you can summon it up at will. If you're learning a new one, you will stumble over it as you begin to dial. Given two new numbers at once, you will almost certainly get them confused. This is the difference between short-term memory and long-term memory. Short term is what you pick up and use instantly. Long term is what has become part of your bank account of information. When a *chunk* of information becomes part of your long-term memory, it can be summoned up as a single piece. The chess player can react to a combination he has seen before, and expert chess players carry around as many as fifty thousand combinations in their memory bank. A concert pianist tends to practise longer phrases from his musical repertoire, and recall them as longer phrases, than a Sunday thumper.

In the 1970s a sociologist named David Sudnow set out to teach himself to play jazz piano like a professional. When he had progressed to the state he was happy with, he wrote a book called *Ways of the Hand*. At the beginning of his experiments, Sudnow wrote: "I wrote down the names of the notes under each finger, then went home and duplicated the songs. I gained a little repertoire of tunes this way, but I didn't know what I was doing." At the end, he concluded, he had absorbed a new language. "I learned this language through five years of overhearing it spoken. I had come to learn it in a terrain . . . of hands and keyboard whose respective surfaces had become known as the respective surfaces of my tongue and teeth and palate are known to each other."

In 1965, the American journalist John McPhee set out to discover some of the secrets that at the time appeared to set the basketball player Bill Bradley (now a U.S. senator) as far apart from his peers as Gretzky now appears from his. McPhee found that Bradley, who, like Wayne, had an impressive ability to articulate his own performance, had an almost mystical sense of the shape and situation of the basketball court. McPhee wrote:

> *All shots in basketball are supposed to have names — the set, the hook, the layup, the jump shot, and so on — and one weekend last July, while Bradley was in Princeton working on his senior thesis and putting in some time in the Princeton gymnasium to keep himself in form for the Olympics, I asked him what he called his over-the-shoulder shot. He said he had never heard a name for it, but that he had seen Oscar Robertson, of the Cincinnati Royals, and Jerry West, of the Los Angeles Lakers, do it, and had worked it out for himself. He went on to say that it is a much simpler shot than it appears to be and, to illustrate, he tossed the ball over his shoulder and into the basket while he was talking*

*and looking me in the eye. I retrieved the ball and handed it back
to him. "When you have played basketball for a while, you don't
need to look at the basket for a while when you are in close like
this," he said, throwing it over his shoulder again and right
through the hoop. "You develop a sense of where you are."*

In 1980, Fran Allard, a colleague of Neil Charness's at Waterloo, did
some tests whose results seem to bring together both the conclusions
of the work done on chess, bridge and music, and the "court sense"
— a phrase Allard used in the publication of her work — that Bill
Bradley had exhibited for McPhee. First, Allard exposed basketball
players of various levels of accomplishment to photographs of basketball situations that were both structured and unstructured — real
game positions or arbitrary ones. As with the more exotic disciplines,
she found the better the basketball player the more likely he was to
be able to recall a real situation; with the unstructured positions there
was no difference. Elite basketball players, Allard and her fellows
wrote in *The Journal of Sports Psychology*, "as do chess and bridge
players, encode structured information more deeply."

With volleyball players, however, Allard at first seemed to have
found an exception. Exposed for a short time to slides of players
on a volleyball court, expert players seemed no better able than
non-players to answer questions about whether or not there was a
ball in the picture. Puzzled, Allard and her partner, Janet Starkes
of McMaster, began running the same test with a timer. Now, there
was a difference. The good players were able to figure out the situation more quickly than the rest of their group. The principle
had held.

Elite athletes, then, like chess masters or artists of the jazz piano,
may not so much think differently as perceive differently. Moreover,
because they can quickly recall chunks of information from their
long-term memories, they can react to those perceptions more effi-
ciently. What Gretzky perceives on a hockey rink is, in a curious
way, more simple than what a less accomplished player perceives. He
sees not so much a set of moving players as a number of situations

— chunks. Moving in on the Montreal blueline, as he was able to recall while he watched a videotape of himself, he was aware of the position of all the other players on the ice. The pattern they formed was, to him, one fact, and he reacted to that fact. When he sends a pass to what to the rest of us appears an empty space on the ice, and when a teammate magically appears in that space to collect the puck, he has in reality simply summoned up from his bank account of knowledge the fact that in a particular situation, someone is likely to be in a particular spot, and if he is not there now he will be there presently.

The corollary, of course, is that Gretzky has seen all these situations before, and that what we take to be creative genius is in fact a reaction to a situation that he has stored in his brain as deeply and firmly as his own telephone number. When I put this possibility to him, he agreed.

"Absolutely," he said. "That's a hundred per cent right. It's all practice. I got it from my dad. Nine out of ten people think it's instinct, and it isn't. Nobody would ever say a doctor had learned his profession by instinct; yet in my own way I've put in almost as much time studying hockey as a medical student puts in studying medicine."

• • •

Even before he got on skates, Wayne seemed to have an almost spiritual attraction to hockey. Once, when Walter and Phyllis were both working, Wayne, not yet two, was staying with his grandparents at their home on the Nith River. His grandmother had a Saturday afternoon hockey game on television. Wayne imitated the players, sliding back and forth on the linoleum. When the game was over, he cried, thinking his grandmother had turned it off to punish him.

He started skating before he was three years old; there are films of him on the ice, taken by his father, when he was two and a half. Walter built a rink in the back yard. He couldn't flood it with a hose; a hose might have made it too lumpy. He got out his lawn sprinkler, and laid on coat after coat. Every night, when he got home from his job as a technician with the telephone company, he would turn on the sprinkler and lay down another smooth coat. One year, the sprinkler broke, and Walter asked Phyllis to get him another one. When she got home from the store, she told him that was the last time for that. The clerks had thought she was crazy, buying a lawn sprinkler in February.

Walter had played Junior B himself, but he had been too small, they said, to make it to the pros. He was determined to give his children every chance. Wayne's first skates were single bladed, not the bob-skates so many kids wasted time on. When Walter couldn't find a hockey stick small enough for Wayne, he bought the lightest he could find, then shaved it down with a plane. Even today, the Titan stick Wayne uses is shaved thin.

Walter had a lot of ideas. He got some tin cans, and Wayne would skate patterns through them. He'd set sticks down on the ice and Wayne would hop over them while Walter sent him passes. There were balance drills and target shooting. Walter would put targets up on the net he had bought for the back-yard rink, and Wayne would fire at them for hours, going in for supper and coming back out again under the lights Walter strung, and practising again until bedtime. Walter put a picnic table on edge so that it blocked all but the outer edges of the net. Wayne would shoot for the corners.

"When the Russians came over here in 1972 and '73," Wayne once said, "people said, 'Wow, this is something incredible.' Not to me it wasn't. I'd been doing those drills since I was three years old. My dad was very smart."

When Wayne was five, Walter drove him all around the Brantford area, looking for an organized team that would take him. No one would let him play until he was six. Walter coached him anyway, and when Wayne was finally old enough, Walter took over his team.

"People say you can't teach anticipation," Walter says now. "I'm not so sure. I used to get them out on the ice and I'd shoot the puck down the boards towards a corner and I'd say, 'Chase that.' Well, they'd all go right into the end after it. Then I'd say, 'Wait, watch me.' I'd shoot it in again, and let it roll around the net. Instead of following it around the boards, I'd cut across to where it was rolling. 'There,' I'd say. 'You've got to know where it's *going* to go.'"

• • •

The concentration, the dedication, has never relaxed. From training camp on, none of the Oilers, not even the labouring Brackenbury, practised skills with more single-mindedness than Gretzky. At training camp, long after everyone else had headed for the showers, he would still be out on the ice. Sometimes, he would lay a stick down beside the net and take a bucket of pucks behind it, and practise flipping them just high enough to clear the stick and lie in the goal-crease. Often Glenn Anderson would work on this drill with him. But sometimes Wayne would just stand alone and shoot at a cross-bar or a goalpost. The trick he does in the 7-Up commercial — the one that he pretends to let his little brother, Keith, teach him — is one he does at practice all the time, hoisting a puck in the air with the blade of his stick and then bouncing it as long as he can. In the summers, when he cannot skate, he still works for hours in his driveway, honing his stickhandling skills or trying to figure out what he was doing wrong on breakaways.

The practice alone, of course, has not made him what he is, nor even the early beginnings. Although all the superstars whose boyhood stories we know, from Morenz to Orr, started skating at amazingly early ages, so did millions of other boys who never made it past peewee. It is a combination of things, the neurology, the metabolism, the father, the coaches, the kid's own determination to succeed, and the gift of mind he has. In various permutations, these elements have combined in modern hockey's brief history to give us all our superstars, and if Gretzky is unique in the pantheon it is in his knack of articulating his skills. Today, the ability he showed as a young teenager to re-create game situations has become uncanny. There is scarcely a goal he has scored, or a chance he has missed, which, if asked, he cannot recreate in detail, setting each teammate and opponent into place with the precision of a chess master replaying a game. The joy of it all is that we have found him, that the game is so much a part of our lives that when a Wayne Gretzky is born we will find him. The sorrow is that there may also be Wayne Gretzkys of the piano or the paint brush who, because we expose our young to hockey so much more than to the arts, we will never know about.

The World of the Racetrack I: The Fans

from The Private Voice, *1988*

～⊗～

Sunday, July 19, the cottage, 11 a.m.:
Queen's Plate day, and we have gathered our team of racing partners
for our excursion. Peter (my son) and Heather Black arrived last
night, all atingle. Peter and Heather, engineers who met at Queen's,
are ferocious racing fans. They discovered the sport while I was
researching my book about thoroughbreds. Peter has written a computer program to help his handicapping, but mostly they enjoy the
scene and the people, and today, the 126th running of everyone's
favourite race and spectacle (founded, as we like to remind ourselves,
by Sir Casimir Stanislaus Gzowski), is a highlight of their summer.
Heather has brought a hat to wear to the clubhouse this afternoon,
and they have, of course, brought *Racing Forms* for the whole party.
Their excitement is infectious.

Just as pleasantly for me, Lefolii has shown up, my friend now
for nearly thirty years — I must have given him the first cigar when
Peter was born.

11:30:
Everyone's raring to go. Gill, already behatted, leaves in her car to
join her family at their house near Woodbridge.

12 o'clock:

Peter and Heather, who have gone out to their car while Ken and I do some last-minute cleaning up, return with the annoying news that my BMW, parked in the driveway, sports a flat tire. We send the impatient kids off to the races and tell them not to worry: experience in these matters is more important than energy. Lefolii goes to put on the spare while I throw the last of the breakfast dishes into the dishwasher and add a cup of All.

12:10:

All isn't dishwasher detergent. All — Concentrates on Clean! — is for laundry. When you put laundry detergent into a dishwasher, it turns out, you make foam. A lot of foam. Now, while Lefolii, his hands covered in grime, tries to figure out how to stop the BMW's jack from sinking into the gravel driveway outside, I swab the pine floor, trying to keep up with the suds. I'm losing. The machine churns out bubbles the way the magic bowl in the fairy story churned out porridge.

12:12:

Lefolii appears at the doorway. He is about to seek my advice on jacking up cars when he sees me playing King Canute at the dishwasher.

"Wow," he says, helpfully.

"All isn't for dishes," I explain.

"Why don't you turn the dishwasher off?" he says.

"Why don't you call the bloody garage?" I reply.

We dissolve into helpless laughter. Another Gzowski-Lefolii production is under way.

Once, years ago, we bought a boat together. When we were sailing our new purchase across Toronto harbour, it sank. A lot of years after that, while I was researching my book on the racetrack, we bought a horse together, a shining yearling we paid $10,000 for. We called him Johnny Canuck, got Gill's brother Ian to train him, turned down $20,000 from someone who'd seen one of his brilliant workouts before he got to the track and then . . . well, in a way, Johnny Canuck sank, too. You could claim him now at Fort Erie, if you had $2,500 you wanted to invest in a good-looking gelding with no heart.

5:00 p.m., Woodbine Racetrack, Toronto:
Floor dry, tire changed, we have made it, scarcely missing a race on the card. I don't know what number Queen's Plate this is for Lefolii and me. We used to come with our wives in the *Maclean's* days, picnicking in the parking lot before we made our way up to the grandstand. Now, as then, we are caught up in the pageantry and the tradition, and we delight as much in the swirling crowd as in our fruitless attempts to out-handicap Nancy Howard. The sun shines, the wine flows, the women in their hats stroll by.

• • •

The route that led me to *Maclean's* and my friendship with Lefolii (along with so much else) took me first to Chatham, in south-western Ontario. The managing editor of the *Daily News* was Ray Munro, already (I learned later) a legend in the business. He'd been a decorated fighter pilot in the war, and had taken up peacetime newspapering in Vancouver with the same zeal he must have applied to gunning down the Luftwaffe. He had captured a rapist in Stanley Park after persuading a copy-boy to sit, in drag, in the front seat of his car. He had claimed to have been shot at in the *Vancouver Sun's* plane while he flew over a Japanese ship in the harbour and produced photos of the bullet holes to prove it. (It dismayed him not at all, apparently, that the bullets seemed to have been fired from inside the cockpit.) Still working on the *Sun*, he had uncovered (genuine) evidence of corruption in the Vancouver police department, and when the established papers refused to carry his material, he resigned and published it in the tabloid *Flash*.

That spring, Ray was elected Kent County's Man of the Year in a contest the *Daily News* sponsored with much flourish. But, inevitably, he came to a parting of the ways with the local Thomson management, and I succeeded him as managing editor. I was twenty-three, newly married and an expectant father.

Meanwhile, back in Toronto, *Maclean's* had launched a new department — eight pages of yellow stock wrapped inside the covers and carrying short, bright, topical material with a more immediate deadline than the major articles. Ralph Allen, who had noticed my work at *The Varsity*, called to ask if I'd be interested in a reporting job. I leaped at the chance. Though Thomson offered me a hundred and twenty dollars a week to stay on in Chatham, the nation's youngest managing editor quickly became its youngest ex-managing editor. On the day after Labour Day, 1958, I started my real education in journalism, as a bright-eyed, six-thousand-dollar-a-year assistant on Ralph Allen's *Maclean's*.

At University and Dundas, we all signed on for the course in what Pierre Berton once described as "a school of writing with Ralph Allen as the faculty." He was not gentle. "Oh, for Christ's sake," I can still remember one of his inky marginal comments chastising me, or, on another occasion, "This is bullshit." But he could encourage you, too. A little "nice touch" in the margin became, in the light of his immutable standards, more important than the Pulitzer Prize. Somehow, too, he managed to make it clear that his criticism was not of you but of your work; he was not so much angry as disappointed that you, of all people, could hand in such shoddy stuff. The editor, he used to say, is a referee between writer and reader.

After months and months of being convinced I could never learn the trade and that I would have to go back to Thomson again, homburg in hand, I began to write articles, at first mining the familiar territory of my family's past ("What it's like to have a famous but forgotten ancestor") or the undergraduate press, and then, gradually and tentatively, venturing into the unknown. I wrote about bridge, hockey, politics, women. After the copy desk, I took over the yellow pages, and masterminded, among other triumphs, a special section that welcomed the 1960s and featured drawings of domed cities and one-man helicopters and other developments we haven't quite seen yet. Mistakes and all, I was, as the hockey players might have said, turning pro.

The World of the Racetrack II: The Backstretch

from An Unbroken Line, *1983*

The backstretch at Woodbine is a special place to be on Queen's Plate morning, as all racetracks are said to be on all mornings, for mornings are a time of hope, and hope is at the heart of racing. No one ever committed suicide with an unraced two-year-old, the race-track saying goes, and on a summer morning, for that day at least, all two-year-olds are unraced, and all three- and four- and five- and six-year-olds, too. Sexy young fillies and placid geldings, studdy colts and stately mares; greys, bays, roans, browns, blacks and chest-nuts . . . they are all, by the morning light, potential stakes winners, champions, legends. The most fractious colt holds the promise of standing as a foundation sire. The most broken down of claimers, eyes red, belly drooping, hocks spavined, could still . . . *could*, still . . . finish on top that one afternoon and get someone a stake, walking-around money, something to start again.

Hope. The mornings are always full of hope.

The backstretch is a village. It is set apart from the real and swirling world by a moat of time and ritual. On one side, at Woodbine, a road lined with tall poplars stands between the village and the arena of its wares, the track itself. Beyond the track is the grandstand, which in the afternoons can hold — and will hold on Plate day — 35,000 roaring spectators, but in the morning light stands as empty as a Roman ruin. To make their way into the arena, the horses tiptoe across the road and into a tunnel through the banked grass wall of the Marshall turf course. At other points along the perimeter are two sandy training tracks and a chute that holds a starting gate, where young horses work at the fundamentals of their trade. A sales arena, empty all year except for the furious, dream-filled action of the annual yearling sales, stands at another boundary. A high link fence surrounds the village and its training tracks, and entrance from the outside world is only through one of its two forbidding gates, checkpoints for cars, where uniformed security guards note each coming and going. Strangers are kept out.

The village is a grid of one-storey buildings, most commonly white-frame barns with green shingled roofs. The roofs hang out, like the eaves of card houses, sheltering the paths that circumscribe each phalanx of stalls. Fences of two-by-fours, with their posts extended to the outer eaves, enclose the overhangs. These are the shedrows, where the horses plod off their exertions and the grooms do their work. The stalls are home, not only for the thoroughbreds but for the men who nurture them; here and there among the rows of stalls are rooms given over to office space, or the storage of tack, or two- or three-bunk dormitories. Many of the upper halves of the stall doors, and sometimes their lower halves too, are painted in the gay colours of individual stables. But the predominant shades of the shedrows are the browns and greys of dust and straw and weathered wood.

In the centre of the village, still only one storey high, are the brick administration buildings and the kitchen. The main administration building functions as a town hall. Each morning after the early workouts the trainers gather to make their entries for upcoming races and to check out possibilities for the future. But the social centre of the village is the dining hall, decorated with black-and-white photographs of past champions, and called, as at racetracks everywhere, the kitchen. In the mornings, the kitchen smells of coffee and frying bacon. The Greek brothers who man the till open for business at 5:30 a.m., when backstretchers line up for pre-sugared Styrofoam cups of coffee like heroin addicts awaiting their daily ration of methadone. By six, the long Formica tables ring with the clatter of china cups and spoons and the chatter of business: jockeys' agents seeking mounts, freelance exercise riders seeking work, all the villagers seeking information and swapping gossip. "You all right today?" goes the common greeting, phrased originally to ask if a jockey had a ride or a trainer had his horse in shape, but now used everywhere to enquire simply if the world is working as it should: how are your hopes? By their own Runyonesque nomenclature — Dirty Neck Helen, Dirty Foot Jim, Run-Down Ronnie, Bright Eyes, Coffee John — or by first names or function only, racetrackers all seem to know each other.

Across the road from the kitchen, just past the office of the Horsemen's Benevolent and Protection Association, and facing the pari-mutuel windows where backstretchers will make their afternoon investments, is the village shopping mall, a short block of permanently parked trailers, their backs to the road and their rear doors displaying neat, green and white signs of merchandise for sale: the trappings of harnesses, patent medicines and jockeys' silks.

The village's entire municipal design, from the soft dirt of the roadbeds to the architecture of the shedrows, has evolved for the convenience of the thoroughbred. The men sleep in rooms the same size as the stalls designed for horses. On the paths, the horse holds right of way over human traffic, like sail over steam in a crowded harbour, and no matter how urgent the transit of a veterinarian's panel truck or even of the coffee wagon that begins its rounds before dawn, vehicles stop when a thoroughbred prances by. The hours, too, are equine. The day begins early, long before the surrounding suburban freeways begin to hum with traffic, because horses work with less effort in the morning cool, and it will end at dusk, when the horses have been fed and watered and locked away to sleep.

Progress has left few marks on the life of the backstretch. Four-armed hot-walking machines, as stark as back-yard clotheslines, stand among the barns, waiting for the first horses to return from their sweaty workouts. But along the shedrows, old men with gnarled hands cough their way to wakefulness to begin chores as ancient as the sport: cleaning, shovelling, rubbing, washing, feeding, grooming, bandaging, and, for the trainers who still disdain the machines, walking their charges under the overhanging roofs. In a brick dormitory, safely separate from the male evils of the shedrows but still inside the high fence, young women with cheeks as bright as plums tumble from their beds and tie their hair in bandannas. Less than a generation ago, no female was allowed on the shedrow between sun-up and sundown, but now, in their blue jeans and rubber boots and with their tied-back hair, the young women quietly join in the timeless tasks. Owners in shiny cars inch down the road from the security gate, pausing as the first sets of lordly thoroughbreds head for the tunnel. In the biggest and shiniest of cars come the littlest of men, the jockeys, cocky princes of the backstretch, deigning to test a few favoured mounts — and to work off a few ounces before the real work of the afternoon. Trainers in elegant tweeds settle in by the rails of the practice tracks, and on their enclosed platforms above the courses, fat clockers light up their first cigars of the day and click their stopwatches to the ready.

The clearest sound on a backstretch morning is the tattoo of lightly shod hooves on the dirt of the main training track, from the allegro of the warm-up trot to the prestissimo of the driving gallop. Above the tattoo is a descant of snorts and whinnies. From first light on, huge jets drone up and over the backstretch from nearby Toronto International Airport; thoroughbreds that work at Woodbine have to learn to ignore the occasional roar of a 727 coming in upwind. More intimately, sparrows chirp along the shedrows, feasting on the recycled grain of the manure bins, huddling under the spacious eaves. Everywhere, as the village stirs to life, is the murmur of exchanged good mornings and the first salvos of hopeful banter.

The air smells as sweet as victory. The bouquet of the kitchen's coffee mingles with the perfumes of creosote and ammonia, of grass clippings and hot manure. Steam arises from the bins of used straw waiting for collection and from the hoses washing down the walkways. Fresh petunias and marigolds and geraniums have been planted in the flowerbeds and pots of fuchsia and impatiens hang along the rows. For the Queen's Plate, the most special of its special days, the backstretch dresses up.

The City Mouse Moves Back Downtown

from The Morningside Papers, *1985*

❦

I

On the morning of the first Saturday I moved back to the city, I went shopping. In itself, this was not a new experience for me, for in the past five years, while I have lived as a country mouse, I have often spent Saturday mornings shopping. I have jumped in my car and driven to the local bakery for a dozen sticky Chelsea buns and a copy of the morning paper, which lacked, because of my distance from its printing presses, the previous evening's sports scores. Later, if I have needed stuff, I have cruised the local merchants, chequebook in hand, and driven twenty kilometres to the nearest bookstore, where I have kept a charge account, or the provincial liquor outlet for another jug or two of the wine I know goes well with fresh sweet corn.

In the city, though, I needed no car, and my chequebook would have been only slightly less useful than a walletful of zlotys or a necklace of wampum. In the city you need hard, cold cash — or the 1980s equivalent of cash: hard, cold plastic.

In the city, I live downtown, on the edge of what my friend Harry Bruce, who has since moved to Halifax, christened the land of the white-painters. There are more BMWs on the street where I walk than there are trees. The houses are closer together than seats on a subway train. As evening falls you can hear the Jacuzzis flush as if in unison, and right around the corner there are more stores than there were in all of Rome. Without crossing the street I could buy, if I had the money, a Cuisinart or the *New York Times*, vitamin B12 or a quiche to go. There are three kinds of orange drink in my neighbourhood convenience store, and twenty-four kinds of doughnuts next door. I could have my suede cleaned, my fuel pump tuned, my walls hung or my aquarium stocked. If I did cross the street I could buy a silken kite or a Stilton cheese, a German knife, a Danish peppermill, a Swedish bar stool, a Hungarian table wine or a Mandarin orange. I could get egg bread or bread rolls, breaded veal or a well-bred parakeet. I could buy a marinated leg of lamb, a chocolate-coated cherry, Kiwi fruit, canned artichoke hearts, fresh lobsters, hot croissants and cold Heineken. I could take home a live Dieffenbachia or ice cubes made of glass, a wicker end table, the latest issue of a magazine I would not like my children to see me reading or a copy of the kind of book I used to carry under my arm at university, title-side out.

I could live my life in the neighbourhood I have moved to, I think, and never sample all its wares.

And yet, as Mordecai Richler says, and yet.

On Saturday morning I went to see if I could buy something that would make me a cup of cappuccino before I came to work. Cappuccino in the morning is one of my fantasies, although the only person I have met yet who can afford to drink it is Peter Pocklington. I went to my neighbourhood kitchenware store. (In the village I have just moved from, the equivalent is one corner of the Home Hardware, just behind the fertilizer.) A lady with a German accent came to help me. First she asked me how many cups I wanted to make, and when I just said one or two she gave me a one-sentence lecture about the need to entertain my friends. Then she showed me a machine that looked as if, were I to pull the right levers in the right order, it would leave in eight minutes for Brandon. When I said that was too complicated she showed me something automatic that, I think, would not only have made me a cappuccino but have served as the centrepiece for next week's exhibition on shapes of the future. When I demurred, my helpful storefrau led me to something that appeared to have been made for filling the gas tanks of model airplanes.

Nothing I saw cost less than $198.50.

And all I wanted was a cup of coffee.

I felt as my first-born son must have felt on the second Christmas of his life when, surrounded by half-opened packages and urged on by his loving parents to open more, more and more again, he burst into tears of sadness and being overwhelmed.

I went back to my rented house, past the parked BMWs, past the silent Jacuzzis, past the white-painted bricks, to my white-painted townhouse.

I had been gone for an hour and a half, window shopping in the casbah of the trendies, and I had bought . . . nothing. My plastic was intact.

II

On the first turn you take if you drive towards the city from the house I have been living in for the past five years is a pond. I'm not sure why it lies there; on a golf course it would be casual water, and you could move your ball from it, and on the prairies it would be a slough (a word unknown in the east). But beside Highway 7 in rural Ontario it is a pond; no river runs in, no stream out. A willow tree droops over one corner, and in the summer and early fall there are cat tails and bull rushes at its edges. Even when the wind is high, it is quiet and still.

On the last morning I drove in from the country, a tall blue heron posed a dozen feet from its shore.

I stopped my car to stare; the heron did not move.

If I had dared to predict, when I moved to the country five years ago, how much I would become intrigued by birds, my friends would have laughed at me. I was a total city mouse then; I rode taxis and ordered meals in, and for adventure took my kids to the zoo. In the country, blue jays jabber at me outside my kitchen window, and I jabber back, and run out with a handful of Thompson's wild bird food, $1.39 the four-pound bag, to pacify them. I am their servant. My mornings are better when they start with a brilliant male cardinal, tiptoeing in to get food for his lady. In the afternoons, an oriole pipes from the black walnut and I stop work. One summer evening as I sat with the latest P. D. James in the garden a hummingbird hovered over my teacup. I have seen grackles and juncos, bluebirds and warblers, woodpeckers and flickers, jays, buntings, larks and nuthatches, chickadees, thrushes, whippoorwills and enough sparrows to start my own cathedral — all outside my windows, or just over the first rolling hill. I do not always know what they are, for I am not always quick enough to find the right page in Roger Tory Peterson, my copy of which is now as well-thumbed as a family Bible. One magic morning I watched in wonder as a college of mourning doves waddled up through the early mists.

I am a sucker for all of this, and during the years I lived in the country my books, binoculars and birdseed have become as much a part of my life as backgammon once was, or Beefeater gin.

And now, I think I'm going to miss it.

There are compensations for all this, I know. Better shopping and faster taxis — or, in my case, taxis at all. Strangely, I can walk to work in the city, where I had to drive for anything in the country — or anything except work, most of which I did at home, next to the chattering blue jays. The snow won't shut me in this winter, and I don't have to worry about the well freezing or the door blowing off the barn.

The country surprised me when I moved there, and the city is surprising me again. This morning on my way to it I saw four sparrows, a starling and one of the last robins of the fall. But what I thought about was the blue heron, standing still near his private pond.

Reflections of an Unmade Bed

Canadian Living *magazine*

I am not, as my friends will tell you, the world's snazziest dresser.

People who write things about me, or put me on their worst-dressed lists (I tied for first in *Toronto Life* last year), tend to count this among my most notable characteristics. If I kept a scrapbook, I'm sure, the phrase "unmade bed" would appear almost as often as comments on my smoking or my sputtering speech. "Shaggy" would be there a lot, too. "Unkempt."

I do not dress badly on purpose. It's just that clothes and I don't seem to get along. Shirts sprout ink-stains on their pockets the day after I buy them, and their tails seek daylight every time I put them on. Sweaters unravel. Trousers wrinkle and droop. Cuffs fray. Socks get divorces in my drawers. Though I seldom wear ties or jackets, burns and coffee stains appear on those I do as if by magic, like frost patterns on a winter window. Belt-loops dodge my fumbling fingers. Zippers languish at an embarrassing half mast, and buttons fall from anything I wear like the leaves of an unwatered *ficus benjamina*.

I am not a pioneer of this sartorial lack of style. At least two of my heroes, in fact, Stephen Leacock and George Grant — though this is not why I admire them — were as carefree with their appearances as I am insouciant about mine.

Leacock, writes his biographer Ralph Curry, sometimes closed his waistcoat with a safety pin, and "wore his [academic] gown with the aplomb of a little boy playing baseball in torn trousers."

One year, Curry tells us, "a class that became particularly fond of him bought him a new robe. He thanked them generously, and thoughtfully wore the gown the next day. But it was not the same; it rustled. When he appeared the second day in his old robe, the class was not surprised . . ."

George Grant, philosopher, nationalist, guru to a generation, was no Beau Brummell either. "He used the tail of his fraying Oxford gown to wipe the blackboard clean," writes his biographer William Christian. "Inevitably, even the good students were distracted . . . not by speculations about justice and beauty, but by more mundane matters such as the large hole in his shoe, his trailing shirt-tail, or whether the necktie he was using as a belt would serve its intended purpose."

See? Two of the greatest thinkers Canada has ever produced kept the importance of clothes in perspective. Yet when someone like me comes along a few years later (I actually had the pleasure of interviewing Professor Grant a couple of times before he died, and Leacock, who was a friend of my grandfather's, is buried up the road from where I live at Lake Simcoe), people — even my friends — make sport of me. Last New Year's, after an evening in which, as is our tradition, we had plied a small circle of good friends with food and drink and conversation, we arranged for everyone to meet at the elegant neighbourhood resort called the Briars, for — again a tradition — brunch. Without much reflection, I put on my favourite plaid shirt (all right, it's missing a button or two), a Christmas sweater that was already showing a trademark burn-hole, some familiar flannels that may have lost their last crease about Thanksgiving and a pair of — well, two; they were *almost* the same colour but they weren't quite a couple — grey wool socks. Showing up last, I was greeted by a ripple of laughter.

"What is it?" I inquired as — oops — a forkful of scrambled eggs tumbled into my rumpled lap.

"Oh, it's just," said Peter Sibbald Brown, wearing his customary tweed jacket and cravat, "that you seem to be making such a . . . fashion statement."

Leacock, in particular, would have understood. I had, in fact, a perfect parallel to his favourite-gown story just last year. In October, I was in St. John's, and, as I always do, I dropped in at NONIA, the Newfoundland outport nurses' store on Water Street. NONIA, if they won't mind my saying so, run my kind of store, a crafts outlet that grew out of the old custom of using the wool from outport sheep to make beautiful, durable, hand-knit sweaters. I bought my first one in the seventies, a cable-stitched crew neck I came to call Old Blue, and which, along with a pair of jeans (I'm past jeans now), became my standard uniform for hosting *This Country in the Morning* for almost three years. Last fall, I found Old Blue's descendant, and from the day I bought it I wore it almost constantly — it was soft enough that I could wear it on weekends, without benefit of shirt — till Christmas. When, alas, I shrunk it in the washing machine (another skill I've never mastered), and donned the Christmas present I was soon to brand, my colleagues at *Morningside*, less understanding, apparently, than Leacock's students, issued a statement of relief.

"If you didn't change it soon, we were going to go on strike," they said. "We were just tired of looking at you in the same sweater *every* day."

Ah, well, I thought to myself, at least the new one doesn't rustle.

High Wind Off Antigua

Toronto Life, *December 1984*

We boarded *Vagrant* in Antigua. It was late at night and the four of us, still pale and tense from the Toronto winter, had to pussy-foot along the plank the skipper had laid out to her stern. Even in the dark, we could sense her loveliness — seventy-six feet, ninety if you counted her bowsprit, of oak and teak and mahogany and brass, long-lined and tapered, like a gull at rest, rocking comfortably under the Caribbean stars.

Below decks, she was redolent of history. A brass plaque at the foot of the companionway commemorated her long life under another name:

> *Queen Mab*
> *Designed and Built by Herreshoff*
> *Bristol, Rhode Island 1910*

As *Vagrant*, though, she had been born. Harry Vanderbilt, heir to the uncounted fortune of his great-grandfather, Commodore Cornelius Vanderbilt, commissioned her from the prince of American designers, Nathanael Greene Herreshoff. Herreshoff brought a da Vincian combination of practical expertise and lyric genius to his task. Among his contributions to the advance of the nautical arts was a catalogue's worth of valves, screws, boilers and engines. He designed the first folding propellers. He built seven torpedo boats for the U.S. Navy. He devised the first allowance tables for yachts of differing classes to race against one another. But it was for the smooth, efficient, graceful lines of his sailing ships that he was most celebrated — lines he is said to have worked out on the drawing board and then made into models for his brother, John Brown Herreshoff, blinded in a childhood accident, to caress and test with his craftsman's hands. Herreshoff yachts ruled the racing waves of the early century. Six times, Nathanael had been asked to design defenders of the America's Cup, and six times they had been successful.

Harry Vanderbilt chased sporting success as passionately as old Cornelius (who had launched his fortune with a small ferry service and gone on to run supplies in the War of 1812) had pursued money. Ashore one evening, dissatisfied with the rules of auction, Harry had invented contract bridge. At sea, he sought a marriage of luxury and speed.

These were not work boats, these early ocean racers. It was in response to their domination, indeed, that Nova Scotians had built the *Bluenose*, to prove that ships built along working lines also deserved a chance to race. The Herreshoff designs and their competitors were ancestors of the sleek, stripped-down, thoroughbred twelve-metre racing machines that now vie for the America's Cup, built to carry only their crew and their complex racing gear. What separated the early racers from the modern twelves was the belief that there was more to life at sea than checking a computerized compass or winding a triple-geared winch. On *Vagrant* and her contemporaries, the work was as hard and the return on skills as high, but there was no reason a man shouldn't have a bowl of strawberries and champagne before he turned in to his bunk.

The centre of gracious living below decks was the main saloon, into which the skipper, Hans Lammers, now escorted us, flicking light switches as he went. Overstuffed couches lined both bulkheads, the one on the starboard rounding the corner to provide two sides of seating for the large oak dining table. With chairs on the other

two sides, the table would seat eight of us, the four chartering guests
and an equal number of crew. On the bulkhead separating the saloon
from the fully equipped galley — gas range, fridge, cupboards and
work surface — was a bookcase chock-a-block with maritime lore
and history, including accounts of *Vagrant*'s own 120 racing victories. On the port bulkhead was a framed photograph of her under
full original rigging, and, in explanation of what she had once looked
like, Hans now turned to Herreshoff's description: queen staysail,
fisherman staysail, staysail, jib, numbers one, two and three jibs and
topsails — the number three, as Herreshoff had noted, usually called
"the baby." At the wheel of this splendid spectacle, in blazer, flannels and captain's hat, was the figure of Harry Vanderbilt himself.

Nathanael Herreshoff had brought the state of his art to *Vagrant*.
Among other distinctions, she was the first American yacht to have
what was called a Marconi rig on her mainmast, and in the morning
Hans would show us the distinctive metal fixtures, like tiny railway
lines, which still ran up the mast and gave the unique rigging its name.

Hans took us on the rest of our below-decks tour. Just aft of the
main saloon was the cabin my son, Peter, and his companion Heather
Black would share; across from it, their shower and bathroom and the
small space Hans used for navigation. Aft of that, across the full
width of the ship — tapering from about fourteen feet at that point
— was the master stateroom, with a raised bunk on either side and
above each, again, books. Unlike the younger couple, and as befitting
those who would sleep in the space of the Vanderbilts, Gill and I —
Gill is Gillian Howard, the lady in my life — would have a private
bathroom of our own. The cook, deck hand, and deck hand stew-
ardess would sleep ahead of the galley, under the foredeck. Hans
himself liked to sleep above, stretched out on a mattress in the
cockpit he had built around the wheel, accompanied by the ship's
cat, Puss, which he had brought aboard when he took possession.

Over one last rum, the skipper sketched in some of the rest of
Vagrant's history, finally explaining the matter of the two names. In
spite of *Vagrant*'s success at sea, Vanderbilt had become bored with
his first Herreshoff and, ever restless for new toys, had commissioned

a second, bigger design. To it, he took the name, and the original *Vagrant* had been rechristened *Queen Mab* by her new owners. For fully two generations she had sailed under that name, and many of the 120 victories had been so logged. Eventually, though, the second *Vagrant* had shown signs of age and been retired, and when Hans had finally bought *Queen Mab* in 1983, his first formal act had been to revert to the name she'd been given on Rhode Island seventy-three years earlier.

For Hans, the great, historic ship had been the completion of a dream he had first had as a boy in Holland. He had learned to sail from his father, begun work as a deck ape in the Mediterranean and bought his first yacht there while still in his twenties. His first ship was only a thirty-footer, and he had refurbished her to begin a series of upwardly mobile trades, like a young Toronto couple of the sixties who would buy a small house and live in it while they tore down walls and sanded floors. Three times, Hans and Barbara, the English girl he married, traded up, all the while chartering and taking whatever other commissions were available — not all of them, one could infer, totally legal — until finally in the Caribbean they handed over their shining fifty-footer for the run-down *Queen Mab*. All that first summer and into the winter, while Barbara worked ashore in Antigua and joined him in the evenings, Hans had laboured over his prize, stripping, polishing, painting. The only change in the original lines had been the low-slung cockpit. Otherwise, he had worked to make her as she was, though her rigging now took into account more modern materials of sail. He tore out the old decking, and covered her smooth decks with glowing teak, steaming, bending and gluing into the warm winter nights. One day he would like to replace her two tall masts, though timber of that stature — each stretched nearly a hundred feet — was harder to come by now than when the forests stood virgin. But that could wait, as could insurance; the insurance companies would take on a boat of *Vagrant*'s age, but first they wanted him to replace an old water tank, and to get at that he would have to pull up one of the giant masts. She had lasted seventy-four years as she was, Hans felt, and she would last at least one more season. He wrote to Mary Crowley, a sailor herself, who now ran a worldwide charter service out of Sausalito, California, called Ocean Voyages. As she does with all prospective charter skippers, Mary Crowley came to Antigua for a test cruise. She was delighted to add *Vagrant* to her catalogue, she said. Hans was in business. We were his third group of the winter, and each of the first two charters had gone well; the guests flew north tanned and relaxed, enchanted by the yacht and her history.

Hans leaned back on the overstuffed couch. Above his head was an oil painting that had hung in the saloon as long as anyone could remember. It was the scene of a storm at sea. On a storm-tossed sloop, the mast had shattered. On the afterdeck, a lone, muscular figure held the backstay in his hand, keeping the mast aloft against the forces of the roiling ocean.

• • •

I am not a sailor. In the 1960s, a friend talked me into going in with him on the purchase of a twenty-six-foot wooden yawl named *Tim Tam*. *Tim Tam* had had a long and happy career on Lake Ontario, but when we looked at her she was high and dry on the well-kept lawn of the Island Yacht Club at Muggs Island near Hanlan's Point. We decided to have her surveyed and, taking no chances, called Lloyd's of London and asked who did its work in Toronto. We hired its man, and for $110 he gave us five neatly typed pages, bound in blue, which spelled out apparently insignificant flaws that varied from some scraped paint on the bow to a missing screw in one of the hinges on the door to the head. At the end of the surveyor's report, though, was a proviso, not unlike the one accountants give you, which says they've done the best they can with what you've given them and if anyone's going to jail over all this it isn't them. We handed over our certified cheque anyway. A week later, as we tried to take the *Tim Tam* across Toronto harbour to the Queen City Yacht Club, where we'd arranged anchorage, she began to take water. When we started the engine to speed our journey, the flywheel hurled a spray of the bay's scummy contents into the air, an oily version of the rooster tail behind *Miss Supertest IV*. Only the bailing energy of the friends we'd press-ganged for our maiden voyage kept us afloat, until, half an hour later, we limped into the Queen City dock.

A batten across the stern, it turned out, which our high-priced surveyor had neglected to remove, covered dry rot you could sink your arm into above the elbow. My friend, feeling needless guilt, assumed responsibility for the *Tim Tam* and spent much of the next couple of years replacing her dry rot with epoxy resin, while I returned to the lubberly land.

Still, there was something about the sea. Over the years since our disaster, I had cruised a bit on the plasticized *Tim Tam* with other friends and, while the hours of carpentry and rope-coiling might have kept me away from sailing as a full-time sport, I understood its appeal. It is, or can be, both athletic and a way of life, and a spell of it — in touch with the sea and the wind and the tropical sun — seemed an appealing break from the ceaseless winter. Gill, furthermore, had spent some earlier vacations on the tall ships of the Caribbean and was enthralled by the life and the islands. Peter's Heather, an accomplished athlete — and like him an engineer — is good at everything she tries, and Peter himself, like all kids who did some growing up on the Toronto Islands, is as at home on a sailboat as uptown kids are on subway trains; he at least would be able to pitch in with the crew, and give our party of charter guests more in common with the Vanderbilts than the fact that we also play contract bridge.

To Mary Crowley of Ocean Voyages, these matters were germane. Mary's company — the first name comes easily after the briefest correspondence — is a young one, but she has already established a charter-yacht network that reaches from the Galapagos to the Greek islands. Her charters are not cheap; a fair average might be about $1,000 U.S. per person per week (some run substantially lower and some cost as much as the royal suite at the King Edward). But since all of them include meals as well as accommodation — pretty well everything, in fact, except airfare to get there and rum to drink on board — and since there is little to spend money on at sea, they are at least comparable to vacations in most reasonably priced winter resort hotels.

There are, now, a growing number of charter fleets speckling the southern seas, many of them offering bare-boat charters for experienced sailors — and good luck to them, I say. But Ocean Voyages is a syndicate of hospitable privateers, and Mary's role in it is halfway between that of a dispatcher of a company of independently owned taxis and a yenta; her principal service is one of matchmaking client to owner. After some preliminary exploration, she sends the prospective charterer a chatty letter, together with a form on which the client lists everything from sailing experience to dietary preferences, so that by the time the deal is settled — and paid for in advance — the pale strangers are greeted at the skipper's home port like welcome, if distant, cousins, about whom the skipper's mother has often talked.

Hans, as I said, met us at night — tall, blond, heavy-set and bronzed, with a pair of steel-rimmed glasses perched incongruously on his nose. Our charter did not start formally until the next morning, a Monday, but for a token extra charge, Mary had arranged for us to avoid hotel prices in Antigua and sleep aboard. Along with our guided tour of *Vagrant*, we spent the first evening getting to know the crew: our deckhand was Jim Tattersfield, a New Zealander not much older than Peter, skinny as bamboo, who, like so many of his compatriots, had set off to see the world. So far, he had made Egypt, the Mediterranean, Norway and British Columbia, and he had arrived in the Caribbean — this, too, is a common story in the yacht community — by sailing across from England. His mate on that voyage, and our deck hand-stewardess, was Joanne Maynard, a slim, lovely, British blonde with what appeared to be a permanent sunblister on her creamy nose, and the composure of a well-bred nanny. Jo, to Jim's dismay, planned to return to the U.K. before the winter was over to continue her study of music. Finally, our cook — Cookie to everyone — was Margy Denton (the "g" is hard), a blithe, effervescent South African who took quickly to teasing everyone and who, upon hearing what I do for a living and that, if all went well, I hoped to write a magazine piece about this trip, instantly christened me Papa, in honour of my old, grey beard.

Crews come and crews go in the Caribbean, as skippers such as Hans hire freelancers such as Jim and Jo and Margy, each looking for a stake to continue wandering, and only Margy had sailed with Hans before. But all four quite obviously liked one another, as we were quickly sure we would like them. An affectionate respect for the skipper united the younger three, but for all of them, it was evident, the star of the week would be *Vagrant*, and, restless to see her under sail, we turned in early. When we woke I wrote in my notebook: "This old girl is *alive*. We could hear her creaking and straining through the night."

· · ·

Antigua, as tourist brochures delight in boasting, has a beach for every day of the year — 365 of them, all, so far as I can attest, perfect half-moons of soft sands and double-blue waters. After a deck-top breakfast of fresh fruit and Margy's warm muffins, we spent much of our first day on *Vagrant* checking them out, cruising offshore but still in sight of land, ducking among the reefs and satellite islands. This was a shakedown cruise, but more for our city-tight bodies and habits than for the old schooner or her crew. Peter took to the work instantly, jumping in without waiting to be asked, and shortly after, the women and I found ourselves joining in. Charter guests, at least on a boat the size of *Vagrant*, are under no obligation to serve before the mast, but we found it more pleasant to work than watch, and well before lunch we were hauling lines and cranking winches, following Jim's easy responses to Hans's commands.

In point of fact, the work came easily, for once the awning that covered the cockpit had been tucked away and the heavy sails winched up the stately masts, *Vagrant* virtually sailed herself. Racing, of course, or in heavy seas or a stiffer wind, life would be different, but the only stress in our lazy cruise along the Antiguan shore was the question of what number sunscreen to apply to our shoulders and noses. By afternoon, Peter was taking occasional shifts at the wheel, with Hans maintaining an avuncular eye, and everything was so relaxed that Margy emerged from the galley, where she had been preparing the evening's meal of chicken, scalloped potatoes and a bewildering array of indigenous vegetables — Margy turned out to be to cooking at sea what *Vagrant/Queen Mab* had been to racing — to stretch out on the deck, Cat Stevens blaring silently into the earphones of what she called her walkperson.

In the peace of that first day, we began to develop the inside jokes and shared expressions that can mark a ship's company as well as they can a baseball team or a happy office: Jo's sun-blister, Puss's fierce protection of her cockpit space, Margy's infectious "all right, mon," to our every need, my own determination to honour Han's request not to smoke below decks. In the evening, coming into the bay where we would anchor for the night, we passed over the dark ghost of what appeared to be an old freighter. Hans, his Dutch accent making a rare appearance, pointed out "the vreck below," and "vreck" joined our vocabularies forever.

By Tuesday morning we were set for sea, and off we sailed for Barbuda, an Elysian island of a deserted beach and a nesting ground for frigate birds, some forty-three kilometres off Antigua. The sail across — my first real experience of the ocean — was exhilarating: old hat, I'm sure, to veteran sailors, but for me as thrilling as silent flight. *Vagrant* was close-hauled as we headed into the prevailing wind, but all her sails were up, the rigging groaning as she leapt through the water. She ironed the waves, as her skipper exulted, his "w" as clear as a CBC announcer's, his sun-browned face breaking into a grin of pride.

At one point, I remember, after Jim and I had bent our backs to winch the jib tight, he reached out and clasped the inch-thick sheet.

"Feel the force in her," he said.

Only briefly did my worst fears threaten to become reality. About an hour out from Antigua (we were making a good twelve knots), I began to feel queasy, but a few minutes below decks settled me, and I reappeared to see Peter, whose sailing experience had been on Lake Ontario, lifting his head from having leaned over the lee, and smiling sheepishly, while Heather stood in the wind and Gill, the Caribbean veteran, sat laughing in the spray of the bow pulpit.

That night, we anchored off the Barbudan beach, dined gloriously on Margy's cooking, toasted our good fortune with the French wines Hans had laid on in St. Maarten and, in the smoke-free air of the main saloon, played contract bridge at Harry Vanderbilt's old table until the ship's clock chimed four bells.

The masts came down at 3:05 the next afternoon, both of them, as suddenly and swiftly as if God had flicked them with His fingers.

To this day, like a man struck by a knockout punch — although, thank heaven, nothing hit us — I cannot tell you what it sounded like. There was a crunch, I think, and the sound of something rubbing and scraping on the cockpit roof. And then, instantly, silence, as if even the wind had stopped.

One minute the masts were there, holding straining canvas as we blasted back towards Antigua before the wind. The next, they were gone, and we were dead in the water.

Two things I remember. One: the look on Heather's face — dear, brave Heather, as she was to turn out to be in the hours that followed, but now, abjectly terrified. It was the only time I have ever seen anyone literally wide-eyed in horror, as Gill, who was to have her own moments of fear (as were we all) when the full realization of our plight set in, reached out to comfort her.

And the sudden recollection, which seemed to come to all of us at once, that Margy had been out on the deck sunning with her walkperson in her favourite place, which was . . . oh, God, *between the masts.*

"Are you all right, Margy?"

I don't remember who said it first.

And then, from amidst the strewn wreckage: "All right, mon."

Only later, when it was all over, would we fully understand how lucky we were. Six of us, the passengers, Jim and Hans, were in the cockpit. Jo was below, making the beds. As it turned out, and until she stuck her head out of the companionway, oblivious to what had happened.

Margy should have been dead. The masts had fallen forward and to starboard. One had fallen across the life lines, six feet forward of where she was sprawled; the other a few feet behind her. The force of their crash splintered the seventeen-foot wherry that rested on the forward hatches. The masts had ripped into the starboard life line with enough force to twist the bow pulpit into a nightmarish skein of metal. When the tape Margy was listening to was over, she told us later, she had planned to move to the pulpit, from where she would have been hurled into the rolling ocean.

"I'm all right, mon."

We were helpless. Hans fought the wheel to keep the lifeless *Vagrant* headed into the waves.

The waves had spelled her doom. The wind was a gusting fifteen knots, and, running before it, Hans had set only a staysail and one of the jibs. But the waves had been cresting at fifteen feet or more. After every lift, sixty tons of ancient ship smashed against a five-thousand-ton wall of water. One smash had been one too many. All the forces had lined up wrong. A bronze backstay, anchoring the rigging to the stern and supporting the two giant masts like the ropes on a tent pole, had snapped. The rigging went off like a snipped bow-string. The old, dry masts, thick as telephone poles, had crumpled as quickly as matchsticks, collapsing into a tangle of wire, rope, canvas, spars, rings, sheets, halyards, stays and, now floating on a cru-cifix of the upper half of the mainmast and its biggest spar, just yards away from our suddenly vulnerable hull, the great metal disc and box, as big as a sea trunk, of the ship's now useless radar.

The wind and the crashing waves filled the silence. The light was lowering. Rain was coming. We were almost exactly halfway between Barbuda and Antigua, nearly twenty-two kilometres of rising, angry sea in either direction. Either way, we could sputter along by motor — if, that is, the motor would start — with the craft Nathanael Herreshoff had designed to balance under sail now only an inert and awkward hull.

Land seemed a lifetime away.

• • •

Slowly, we began to act to save ourselves. On Hans's instructions, and even though it was highly unlikely there would be a ship in range of our aerial-less radio, Gill dialled the appropriate channel and began regular calls of "Mayday, Mayday," with *Vagrant*'s name and a one-sentence description of our plight; as Heather mastered her initial fear, Gill handed her the microphone. Having something to do brought Heather quickly to life. Then Gill, idle, began to tremble. As the light continued to fall and the rain began, the two shared the distracting and somehow comforting chore of repeating the un-answered call.

Instead of watching my life flashing before my eyes, I found myself pondering irrelevant detail. I wondered if either of them knew the origin of the distress call: "M'aidez, m'aidez — help me, help me."

Why wasn't my life flashing before my eyes?

I thought: *I was supposed to get an honorary degree this spring, and now I'm going to die without it . . .*

And I thought: *Peter's mother is going to be awfully mad if he doesn't come back from . . .*

Peter!

Hans had asked him to try to save the fibreglass dinghy we had been towing behind us, and on which we'd been sailing up the beach at Barbuda in the morning. It had rammed into *Vagrant*'s stern when we lost way, driven by the momentum of the heavy out-board motor chained, propeller up, to its backboard. The dinghy was taking water.

First, Peter had tried to pull it to *Vagrant*'s heaving lee, tugging on its thin painter. But when he'd been unable, he had secured the painter and scrambled into the small boat itself, where he was now trying simultaneously to bail and unleash the heavy motor from its chain. He was losing the battle when I noticed him, and the dinghy's stern was nearly under the waves.

"Let it go," said Hans, his voice tight against the wind.

Desperately, Peter continued to bail.

"Let her *go*," said Hans with more authority. "Heave the motor, if you can, but get out."

"For Chrissake, get out," I cried.

Peter clawed at the chain.

The stern was submerged.

"Too late," cried Hans, hauling on the painter. The dinghy swung against *Vagrant*'s hull. Hans reached down, and Peter, clutching at the skipper's wrist, clambered back aboard the mother ship. He was scarcely over the side when Hans released the painter, and the dinghy disappeared from view.

I clutched my first-born by his shoulders.

"Never mind," said Jo in her clear nanny's voice. "Even with the wherry smashed and the dinghy gone, there's still a rubber life raft that can comfortably take six."

We did not remind her till later there were eight of us on board.

Most of us who lived through the "vreck" of the *Vagrant*, as we eventually grew insouciant enough to call our adventure, will never know how close we really were to death that day. If that is not true of Jim and Jo and Margy, it is certainly of the four of us who were new to the sea. The terror we felt was more instinctive than rational, a simple and primitive reaction to the awesome power of the ocean.

For Hans Lammers, however, the dismasting, and the minutes and hours that followed it, were no time to succumb to instinct. The captain had to think, to weigh the possibilities, to act. The swift crunch of the falling mast signalled economic calamity for Hans. Uninsured, *Vagrant*'s tall masts would cost nearly $100,000 to replace.

The dream that had begun with his first command was over. But while the rest of us, privately or in the open, indulged our momentary fear, Hans, in the tradition of his calling, set boldly and decisively to work. I was Papa, perhaps; Hans was grace under pressure.

His first decision was to wait. Even his anxiety about the health of the motor would have to run unabated until he could be certain there was no rigging near the propeller. Twist the prop, he realized, and *Vagrant* would drift helplessly out to the open Atlantic.

His second decision was to free the wreckage. At whatever cost, and it was to amount to thousands more dollars in addition to the ruined masts, those of us fit and able to climb about the deck hacked and chopped, cut away priceless sails from their booms and sawed through bolts that had sat solidly for three score and fourteen years. With no time for sadness, we cut through the historic Marconi rig that now threatened to link the floating mast to the ship. During our work on the pitching deck — much of it one-handed, as we grabbed the nearest fixture — a taut cable Jim hacksawed through leaped at him like a cobra, shattering his front teeth. A few moments later, I took a scary tumble near the side, and the ship's knife I was carrying took a nasty slice out of my thumb. But like the Mayday calls that continued from the cockpit, the injuries Jim and I suffered served mainly to distract us from our fears.

Hans, at one point, looked up from his own labours and saw me pausing to wipe blood off on my shirt.

"Well, you have your story now," he said.

The masts, to add to our mounting misfortunes, had fallen to windward, and the crucifix of the shattered main, with its heavy spar and the radar, floated upwind, threatening with each thundering wave to crash into our exposed flank, its sharp end acting like a seaborn battering ram. As a result, Hans's third decision was to keep one of the experienced sailors, by turns Jim, Jo and Peter, at the helm.

Shortly before five o'clock we were — at last — cut free of the wreckage, and tentatively Hans went below to start the engine.

It caught.

Slowly, slowly, we turned downwind.

For the next six hours we huddled in the cockpit, the rain and the spray hiding our tears of relief.

Gill put a tape on the cockpit stereo, the radio being accepted as useless, and into the dark night came the strains of the singer declaring everything's going to be all right. Margy, until we sent Jo to stop her, was below in the galley, her bare feet set against the refrigerator door, trying to make tea.

As we limped sorrowfully into the nearest and most welcome of Antigua's 365 harbours and dropped our anchor for the night, Hans went below to find some kitty litter for his cat.

And then we broke out the rum.

We would, all four of us, do it again. Not get dismasted, of course (although I at least feel I have to take that chance to prove my first two experiences in sailboats are not the first two legs of a three-part maritime curse), but charter, not only a sailing ship, but most certainly a sailing ship from Mary Crowley and, should it be possible, with Hans Lammers at the helm. *Vagrant?* We would leap at the chance. And the chance may yet come about. Even in the days we lingered in Antigua after our misadventure, using the sad, crippled old beauty as a kind of floating hotel, and alternating between gorging ourselves on Margy's cooking and dragging our fellow veterans of the wreck to various shorebound occasions, the yachting community was rallying around Hans, offering him free-lance assignments as a skipper or pilot and generally spreading word of his plight to possible benefactors. (It is probably worth noting that one of the leading figures in the informal committee that began to work on Hans's behalf worked for one of the largest chartering chains, as if a Loblaw's executive had signed up to help save a mom-and-pop corner store.)

Hans remained stoic. He and Barbara spent the afternoon pre-ceding a large public cocktail party at English Harbour packaging splinters from *Vagrant's* masts, which together with a brief mimeo-graphed account of the disaster they proposed to sell for $10 each.

In the end, they decided to keep their souvenirs, but the idea was a perfect symbol of the mixture of rueful resignation and desire to get going again that characterized their mood.

Our mood, too. I am still, of course, not a sailor. But in my infinitely brief career at sea I have been both lucky and unlucky enough to feel the life and be near the death of a great vessel, and to learn, I suppose, that those two ideas are never very far apart.

Before we left Antigua I wanted to leave the crew some memento on behalf of the paying members of their company. Gill suggested T-shirts. I asked around. There was a young man — Jim would know him — who did airbrush designs from his small boat, which he too had sailed across from England. He was tied up behind a tall-masted training ship, a three-master, in English Harbour. To find him I would have to board the larger ship and hail him. I did so, found my man, commissioned my shirts — I SURVIVED THE VRECK, they would say, with the date — and had to return a few times to check on their progress, to pay and to collect my presents before our departure. In doing so, I developed at least a nodding acquaintance with the young men of the training ship whose decks I had to cross to make my rendezvous.

I think of those young men when I am tempted to make light of our own adventure, for the ship where I met them, and on which they left Antigua only a few weeks later, was the *Marques*, lost at sea in the summer, with nineteen of her hands.

A Couple of Memorable Meals

from The Morningside Papers, *1985*

I

One time I had a job of work to do in Prince Rupert. I'd never been to that part of British Columbia, although I knew about the rain, and I was not disappointed. One of the first buildings I was in had rain washing down the windows of one side and sun warming the bricks of the other.

The friends with whom I was working had a boat, big enough to fish salmon from. After our first half-day's work they asked if I wanted to go fishing. Sure, I said, finding it easier to overcome my work ethic than I might have feared.

On the way out of the harbour they threw three crab traps over the side, marking their location with buoys. The traps were baited with old salmon heads and tails.

For the next couple of hours we bobbed on the Pacific, in search of (or so we pretended) the giant salmon. We trailed a couple of lines over the stern and went to where my hosts were sure the salmon would be running. We got nary a bite. The highlight of the day was when a porpoise started to follow our boat and play hide-and-seek with it, frolicking in and out of the water. Since we figured he'd scare the salmon away, we tried to outrun him, but he was smarter — or faster — than we were. I think once, when he jumped in the air and I could see the sun sparkle off the flashing spray, that I could also hear him laughing.

Late in the afternoon we went back in. At the harbour mouth we picked up the traps. There were fourteen crabs in them. We threw back all the females and the young males, keeping five. Then we got in my friends' four-by-four and sped to the liquor store to pick up some white wine. Home, we stuck the wine in the freezer and put a cauldron of water on to boil. Someone had made bread that morning and brought it out now, with pots of sweet butter. That was supper. The chilled tart wine with sweat running down the side of the bottles, the sweet fresh boiled crab, eaten with our fingers, the warm bread.

I can taste it now, and hear the porpoise laughing.

II

I didn't see the Arctic until 1971, when I had already edited two national magazines. I've been there seven or eight times since, and each time have been moved and affected by it, but I still don't know it. I am a southerner. The north may be a part of me (its presence in our consciousness, I believe, helps define us as Canadians), but I am not a part of it.

For that reason, I approach the story I want to tell now with some trepidation. It's possible, I know, for southerners to romanticize the north. I remember years ago, on the radio, when one person was celebrating the joys of making her own bread — in contrast, she said, to buying the plastic bread of the supermarkets — and someone else who'd grown up on the prairies when you had to make bread or go hungry wrote in to say that that was "plastic romanticism." And I remain leery of people who can have modern conveniences limning the joys of the primitive life. Choice is one thing, necessity another.

Given that, though, the most memorable meal I have had in my life was eaten in Inuvik, in the Mackenzie Delta, and many of the foods that comprised it were the same as those that have been eaten the same way for thousands of years: *muktuk*, which is hacked with an *ulu* from just under the skin of the whale and chewed raw; *mipgoo*, dried whale meat soaked in *oksuk*, which is oil; slivers of raw, frozen caribou; splits of dried fish; and some other parts of wild animals and marine life I do not care to discuss at this time of a southern morning. To be quite frank, there were foods in this unforgettable feast — and it *was* a feast — that I would not eat again by choice unless my life depended on it (just as some of the people who shared this repast with me call what many of us eat every day "dead meat"), but there were delicious tastes too: rich roasted caribou — surely the single best meat in the world — dressed with a sauce of small, tart delta cranberries; ptarmigan; fried bannock; a seasoned steak of well-hung bear; the dark meat of goose; pemmican; and the exquisite flavour of arctic char.

I was travelling through the north with a CBC crew, trying to learn something and reflect it on the radio. I'd ridden a dogsled up the Peel River to Archie Headpoint's cabin; talked whaling in Tuk with Vince Steen; danced through the night in Aklavik; and gone the next morning to watch Don McWatt's baby christened in Inuktitut. It was a high time: Bob Ruzicka was with us, singing songs of his own earlier days in the Arctic; the boys of Ryan's Fancy (still cherished friends) and the enchanting Angèle Arsenault were there too, absorbing the land and the people and paying their way with concerts. We capped our trip with the final feast, at Nellie Cournoyea's house in Inuvik. Nellie is a territorial councillor now, returned this winter by acclamation, but she was with the CBC then, giving her people a northern voice, and she had assembled some of her friends to help bake, roast, fry, serve and make the pots and pots of tundra tea. There was too much food to go on the table: samples of muskrat, duck, seal, whitefish and herring pâté and kippers, steaks and flanks. We spread our plates on the floor, and crouched to dine. One dish of reindeer meat, I remember, was served sweet and sour; some dried caribou meat had been fried white-man's style, with onions, but many of the other dishes were raw, smoked or preserved, bursting with strong flavour, rich in fats and energy. For dessert: *ukpik* — sweet yellow berries — and Inuit ice cream, whipped from ambrosial fat and speckled with dried meat.

Romanticized or not, our belly-stuffing feast left an indelible impression on all of us: of a land as rich in its natural food as in its customs, of a way of life that had flourished without us, but welcomed us in, however briefly.

Hard — impossible — to forget. It is a complex, changing, changeless, wonderful land.

A Sprinkling of Canadian Living

from Canadian Living *magazine, 1989-1998*

<u>I</u>

When Arlene Perly Rae, who is an ardent crusader for literacy and children's books as well as the wife of one of Ontario's several living former premiers, asked me a while ago to write up a little something for a project she's been working on, I had only one condition. Her project will be a book about books — various people's reminiscences of works they read as children or teenagers which, as Arlene wrote to her potential collaborators, "woke you up, stirred your soul or changed your life" — and my condition was that I get to write about J. D. Salinger's *The Catcher in the Rye*, which had done all of that (and more) for me when I'd first read it, and which, because I figured a lot of people would feel the same about, I wanted to get first dibs on.

I've always had a special feeling for *The Catcher in the Rye*. I was seventeen when it was published, just a year or so older, as I recalled, than Holden Caulfield, its protagonist and narrator, and I was just finishing up at a boarding school in Ontario that bore a lot of resemblance to the prep school where he was going in Pennsylvania — except, of course, Holden runs away in the book and I never did, although, to tell you the truth, I thought about it a couple of times. Books had been part of my life as long as I could remember — my librarian mother had made sure I knew Winnie the Pooh and Dr. Doolittle before I could throw a ball — but nothing had ever hit me the way Holden and his tale did. Right from the opening words ("If you really want to hear about it . . ."), I found something I had never found before: someone on the printed page who was of my age, who thought the same things were funny as I did and the same things crazy, and who said aloud (or in writing) things I could only imagine. It changed forever the way I thought about school, about honesty, about families — I longed for someone in my life like Holden's sister, Phoebe — and about books and the people who wrote them, and in every way, it seemed to me, it fit the criteria Arlene was looking for.

I had, however, a couple of small problems. One was that I was still slightly troubled by the fact that I'd chosen an American book. Over the years, the work I do has put me into the middle of what we now realize has been the golden age of CanLit, and I've spent too much of my life in the world of Canadian writers and writing not to want to push them any time I get a chance. Furthermore, dozens of those writers — heck, hundreds — from W. O. Mitchell to Mordecai Richler, from Alice Munro to Dennis T. Patrick Sears, the author of a little masterpiece called *The Lark in the Clear Air*, and so many other Canadians have been important to me in ways that even Salinger was not. But *The Catcher in the Rye* was the book of my adolescence, and this time, I figured, I could leave my cultural chauvinism in the drawer.

My other problem was more practical. As I sat down to write, I realized I didn't have a copy of the book, and I needed to look up such matters as Holden's exact age and the name of his school. Well, I thought, I'll just amble down to the local library, which I use all the time and whose environs, not only because they remind me of my mother, I always enjoy.

The librarians were busy. I ventured an encounter with the computer. To my surprise, I found both J. D. Salinger and his masterwork with no difficulty. But the copy in my village had been checked out a year ago and the one down the road, in Pefferlaw, was simply "lost."

"This happens all the time," a librarian said when she became free. "Books on the school reading lists are taken out and never returned."

"Nuts," I said, explaining what I wanted it for.

"Well, we do have the Coles Notes," said the librarian.

"Coles *Notes*?" I said. "I'm a serious man of literature. I can't be seen leaving here with . . ."

"Use it here," she said, bringing forth a copy.

"I . . . well, I . . ." I said, and opened the familiar yellow-and-black-striped binding at the list of characters. Hmm. Holden was sixteen, just as I remembered. The school? Pencey. In Agerstown, P.A. And . . .

"And do you do *all* your writing with Coles Notes?" said the man next to me at the counter, laughing.

"Sure I do," I said. "They're Canadian, aren't they?"

II

Halfway through my little after-dinner talk to a very congenial group in Edmonton, a lens pops out of my glasses and clatters onto the podium. This isn't a rare occurrence in my life — I really should get my glasses fixed — but I never know what triggers it or when it's going to happen. Sometimes I jar it a little as I push my specs higher on my nose, but sometimes it just takes off on its own. Once, in the Arctic, I was peering out over the railing of a hotel verandah when it fell spontaneously into a snowbank below my vantage point, but after a moment of worry I managed to spot its landing place and track it down. Another time I was simply getting out of my car when it landed in the gravel where I was parking. And so on. The weirdest time of all was right at home, when I was sitting on my bed one morning and pulled on a sweatshirt with a tightly fitting crew neck. When my head emerged, though I hadn't felt a thing, the world was suddenly blurry. The crew-neck must have knocked my lens out. I started patting down my lap, the bedclothes, the carpet. Nothing. (One of the problems, of course, is that without both lenses in I have trouble seeing clearly enough to search.) I began to panic. Patted down everything again. Lifted the duvet and shook it out. Patted some more, groped, crawled under the bed. Nothing. My lens had just disappeared. Got up to find a phone, though even if I could make out the numbers, I didn't know who I could call. Felt something rubbing on my waistband — and, lo, there it was, wrapped in a fold of the offending sweatshirt.

Here in Edmonton I have a different problem. The lens is right in front of me, but until I can wipe it off and snap it back into the frame, I can't read the notes from which I've been speaking. I hit on a diversionary tactic. As I work on fixing my glasses, I tell the story — true — of another discombobulating moment in my public-speaking career.

"In those days," I say, "I used to like to recite a list of Canadian inventions, just to remind people what an innovative country we are, and how we never brag about what we've done. A Canadian invented the telephone," I would go on, "although the Americans have claimed him the same way they claimed Lorne Greene. Two Canadians discovered insulin, another invented Pablum. Canadians came up with the humidex, invented basketball, the green garbage bag, the snowmobile (though not the Zamboni), Marquis wheat, Social Credit, the Bloody Caesar, Trivial Pursuit, and . . .

"'And,' someone had yelled from the audience, 'you forgot the zipper.'

"This," I say in Edmonton, "is not a good thing to shout at a man standing on a platform in front of you."

People laugh; my lens is back in and I return to my notes to finish the evening.

The next night is both an honour and a pleasure for me. I have been invited to read and tell a story or two with the Edmonton Symphony, one of Canada's most imaginative musical institutions. For the occasion, which calls, of course, for formal dress, I've written an account of my life as a music critic, which began — and ended

— in Timmins, Ontario, where I was the greenest reporter on the *Daily Press*. For reasons not clear to me then (or now) I was given what we used to call the culture beat, writing about the local amateur theatre group, music festivals and other odds and ends of Northern Ontario life.

To cover music, for which I was even less qualified than any of the other arts, I worked out a little trick. A young woman I was dating — I'd have said girl then — was a piano teacher, as well as the daughter of one of Timmins' most popular piano entertainers. When I had a musical event to write about, I would either take my young teacher with me or, if she couldn't make it, talk over the program with her.

My career as a critic reached its climax — I am reading about this now, perched on a stool on the stage of the magnificent Winspear Theatre, with the symphony players arrayed behind me — when I was scheduled to review a string quartet concert that would be held in Timmins under the auspices of *Jeunesses Musicales*, an admirable organization that used to send classical musicians all over the country.

With a copy of the evening's program in my hands, I called for my piano teacher early. We decided we'd go listen to her father play in a local hotel while we talked over the concert, and I could pick up some appropriate technical terms.

What with one thing and another, we stayed too long listening to her father's lively stylings, and before I even noticed, we'd missed most of string quartet's performance.

Ah, well, I thought, and after seeing my companion home made my way to the *Daily Press* office to type up my notes.

Early next morning, the phone rang at my desk. "Can you tell me," said the caller, "why the *Jeunesses Musicales* concert was cancelled last night?"

I sidled to the front of the office, managed to retrieve my "review" from the in-basket, and as I tell the symphony audience at the Winspear, adding a comment or two about critics in general, came to the end of my career in the arts.

The audience applauds warmly. Relieved and appreciative, I rise from my stool to take a bow.

Oh, good heavens, I think as I look down at my formal trousers, *this* is the night I needed someone to shout out about my zipper.

III
—

There's always plenty to do in Yellowknife on Canada Day, but since about 1989 — even Pat McMahon, who was mayor at the time, isn't exactly sure of the date — things haven't been the same. That was the year the Feds, as everyone in the North calls the federal government, decided, well, okay, if you *really* don't want fireworks, we won't send them to you.

The problem was one northerners have grown used to. The North, it's been said (by me, at any rate), is to the rest of us as all of Canada is to the United States: remote, mysterious, taken for granted. Most of us know about as much about our own arctic regions (quick now, what's the capital of Nunavut, and where is it?), as the Americans who cross the border in July with skis on their car roofs know about Canada — except in the North it works the other way: tourists arriving in February in blue jeans and hiking boots, not knowing that the only way people have survived the arctic winter is by dressing for it, in layer upon layer, of skins if that's possible, and footwear that's made for the cold.

So much of the North seems old; in European terms it's prehistoric. The presence of people can be traced back at least four thousand years, and some sites suggest that figure might be more like ten thousand. There are such mysteries as the human-shaped stone figures called *inukshuks* that easily predate the arrival of what southerners call civilization. Yet much of it is also dramatically new. The North, surprisingly, is the most wired part of the country, and there is cutting-edge technology in mineral exploration and extraction, in navigation (using a device that bounces its signals off a satellite, you can now locate a snowmobile on the frozen tundra within a couple of metres of where it sits) and in communication. Its political institutions are as fresh as this morning's newspaper. It's only since 1967, for instance, when Yellowknife became its capital, that the N.W.T. has had anything resembling an elected government. (The capital was in Fort Smith before that, if you're interested, although the old appointed council used to meet in Ottawa, where most of its members lived, and the capital of Nunavut is Iqaluit, which is at the head of Frobisher Bay on Baffin Island.) In so many ways, the south is having difficulty coming to terms with northern reality. In many remote communities, to take just one tragic example, fresh milk, vegetables and other perishable goods that have to come by sea-lift or air freight cost more than double what you'd pay in Victoria or Fredericton. Yet in the few places where there are still government liquor stores, the price of booze, which is a blight in the north, is no higher than in Edmonton.

So I guess no one should have been surprised some years ago when the Feds, in a magnanimous gesture to all the territories and provinces, decided to send them fireworks for Canada Day.

Except in Yellowknife you couldn't see them. Yellowknife, like Whitehorse, the capital of the Yukon, doesn't *quite* get twenty-four hours of sunshine in the summer; you have to be a bit farther north to find that. But around the middle — and Canada Day, don't forget, is just ten days after the solstice — you may not be able to read a newspaper at midnight but you can easily make out the headlines. And at eventide, the traditional time to launch fireworks, all you'd get would be loud bangs in the bright and endless sky.

"We told them and we told them," laughed Pat McMahon when I ran into her this spring. "We even passed a motion in council saying, for heaven's sake, please . . ."

And so, at last, Ottawa saw the light. There are fireworks every year now, but they go off during Caribou Carnival, the festival of dog races and other celebrations that's held in Yellowknife towards the end of March.

And on Canada Day there's always the Midnight Sun Golf Tournament, which attracts entries from all over the continent, and tees off at two a.m. The fairways are made of sand (you drag a little mat around to hit from) and the greens are imported fake grass. But if a raven flies off with a ball, thinking it's a missing egg, there's no penalty. You just put a new ball down, and laugh at people who don't know the special rules.

IV

Minutes before they are due to arrive, I call Anne-Marie. It was she, after all, who got me into this. She called me about a month ago, saying her brother, a pipe major in the air force, was producing a recording to celebrate the force's seventy-fifth anniversary, and wanted me to read a poem for it. He would set it to bagpipe music. He was too shy to ask me, she said, so he'd recruited her to do the enlisting. "You'll enjoy it," she'd said. "You know the poem, I'm sure. 'High Flight,' by John Gillespie Magee, the young RCAF pilot who was killed so early in the Second War; he was only nineteen."

"'High Flight?'" I said. "I don't think I . . ."

"Sure you do," said Anne-Marie, and began to recite:

> *"Oh I have slipped the surly bonds of earth*
> *And danced the skies on laughter-silvered wings . . ."*

Even from the opening lines, I realized I did recognize it — a lyrical sonnet that seems, even to those of us who've never sat in the pilot's seat, to capture the exaltation of flying. President Reagan read it for the people who went down in the *Challenger* tragedy, I seemed to recall. But as I listened, even over the phone, I was loath to interrupt her. Anne-Marie — she is the Cape Bretoner Anne-Marie MacDonald, in case you haven't guessed — is one of my favourite actresses, known best, I suppose, for her role in the film *I've Heard the Mermaids Singing* (she was nominated for a Genie) but also a star of such television movies as *Where the Spirit Lives* (she *won* a Gemini). On top of that, of course, she is an accomplished playwright — her drama *Good Night Desdemona (Good Morning Juliet)* won the Governor General's Award and has been performed all over the world — an opera librettist and, with the publication, in 1996, of her first novel, *Fall On Your Knees*, which was short-listed for the Giller Prize and stayed on the best-seller list for the better part of a year, one of our most celebrated young authors. And whatever her achievements (I don't imagine anyone has ever won so many awards in so many varied fields so early in their career), I could listen to her all day.

> *"Sunward I've climbed, and joined the tumbling mirth*
> *Of sun-split clouds — and done a hundred things*
> *You have not dreamed of . . ."*

"Of course," I admitted at last. "I guess I just didn't know what it was called."

"And you'll do it?" said Anne-Marie.

"Well, I'm pretty intimidated," I said, her own softly eloquent reading still echoing in my mind. "I'm no actor, you know."

"But John-Hugh — that's my brother — really wants you. He'll arrange to get you to Trenton, where he's stationed, and show you around the base, and all you'll have to do is read the poem and . . ."

And now, a month later, John-Hugh — Pipe Major John-Hugh MacDonald, C.D., B.A. (Mus.) — is on his way to my apartment in Toronto, along with his recording engineer. We've been unable to find a mutually convenient date to meet in Trenton, and he, graciously, has agreed to come to me. And now, I'm more scared than ever. Although Anne-Marie, in our original conversation, was able to soothe my fears — enough, at least, that I've agreed to do it — the day before John-Hugh's arrival I've had another experience that has me quaking again. I did an interview for television with the film actor Donald Sutherland, in the course of which, and with some nudging from me, he launched into a recitation of T. S. Eliot's "The Love Song of J. Alfred Prufrock." This was a poem I'd studied at university, but Sutherland, one of the premier screen actors of our times, turned it into a whole new work for me; he *spoke* it, rather than performing it, so magically that sometimes I wasn't sure if he was quoting Eliot or just talking to me with unusual grace. All that craft, I thought. All that *artistry*.

"Hello." Anne-Marie, thank heavens, is home. I tell her about Sutherland. I tell her there's no way I can play in that league. I say I know it's too late to tell John-Hugh I can't do it, but I wonder if . . .

"Relax," she says, laughing her throaty laugh. "That's how you do *Eliot*. He's conversational. 'High Flight' is different. You just let the words carry you."

I ask her if she'll read it to me again. As she does, and I hear the lyricism in the words once more, her calm relaxes me. We talk a bit about what the poem means, about how it builds from image to image to what Anne-Marie calls its "punch line":

> *"And while with silent lifting mind I've trod*
> *The high untrespassed sanctity of space*
> *Put out my hand and touched the face of God."*

Just as she finishes, there is a beep on the line.

"They're here," I say. "I'll have to go. But, hey, thanks for this — I guess."

She laughs again.

"And know what else?" I say. "'I've heard the mermaids singing.' Know where that's from?"

"Sure," says Anne-Marie MacDonald. "It's T. S. Eliot. 'The Love Song of J. Alfred Prufrock.' Say hi to John-Hugh for me, eh?"

V

The first time I was ever upstairs in a hotel with Margaret Atwood, the earth moved. Really. This was the Friday afternoon last fall when a minor earthquake, which started somewhere near Hamilton, rumbled through Toronto, and Ms. Atwood and I were in a seventh-floor suite in a comfortable downtown hotel when something shook. (It was so gentle I didn't know till I listened to the radio later on what had happened.)

Ms. A. and I — I've never been quite comfortable calling her Peggy — weren't alone. Also in attendance was the Saskatchewan novelist Guy Vanderhaeghe. We had gathered in the suite, away, as someone said, from the prying eyes of the media, for the happy but daunting task of going through the list of more than sixty books that had been submitted for the fifth annual Giller Prize for literature, and choosing from among them a short list — the rules allowed us to pick as many as six — of those we liked the most. A few weeks later, on the very day of the sumptuous gala that has now become the social highlight of the Canadian literary year, we would meet again to select the single winner, who would, in turn, pick up a cheque for $25,000 that evening.

In both style and substance, the Giller is a reflection of the grace and generosity of one man, Jack Rabinovitz, a Montrealer who made a fortune in development before moving to Toronto. Jack, as everyone calls him, set up the prize five years ago, as a memorial to his late wife, the much loved literary journalist Doris Giller. He pays for everything, from the long-stemmed roses that arrive with each of the coveted invitations, to the expenses of both judges and nominees, to the lavish dinner with its garland of short but eloquent films on each of the finalists to, of course, the prize itself. He stays out of the selection process entirely, deliberately keeping himself so in the dark that he actually writes cheques for all the finalists and tears up all but the winner's only when he, like everyone else, hears the announcement at dinner. So being asked to be one of the three jurors, as I first was a couple of years ago (no one has served for more than two years), is, I knew from the start, both a thrill and an honour.

It's also as intimidating as an audience with the Queen. From the start, both good manners and custom have made it an iron-clad if unspoken rule that Giller jurors never discuss their deliberations outside their sequestered rooms, which precludes, among other things, the kind of messes other awards have fallen into when one of the judges expresses public disagreement with his colleagues' choices. Still, I think I can say without breaking my vow of *omerta* that in the sessions I've been part of there have been some disagreements — why else have three judges, for heaven's sake? — but they've been settled without rancour or, so far as I know, hard feelings.

No, the intimidation comes not from the gifted and dedicated writers who read all the submitted books with such care and acuity and then lock themselves up with you to make some choices. It comes, in my case anyway, from having to make the choices in the first place. I'm just not good at saying no, and in spite of the celebration (and extra book sales in the thousands) bestowed on everyone who makes the short list, not to mention the generous cheque that goes to the winner, the jury — you — are still saying no to the more than fifty writers whose books *don't* make the final round.

Oh, I know I shouldn't make too much out of this. In the end, nothing can detract from the joy and comradeship of the Giller evening. The writers who attend, and not only the nervous nominees, really do remind you of what Margaret Laurence used to call "The Tribe," and the shouts of pleasure that ring out when the winner's name is announced — Alice Munro in '98, Mordecai Richler before that and Pegg . . . oops, Margaret Atwood before Mordecai — are profound honours in themselves.

Still, so many of the books I read in preparation for our meeting in the hotel suite seemed to me to be worthy of some accolades.

Maybe, though, the earth wouldn't have moved when we reached any other decision.

How to Ruin Your Golf Game — and Teach a Whole Lot of People to Read

from Reading the Greens, *1998*

I know it's hard to believe some twelve years after it all started, but I didn't set out to ruin my golf game.

Not that there was all that much there to ruin. I'd played as a kid, beginning as a caddy, as I still believe every young golfer should (if there still were caddies), at the Waterloo Golf and Country Club on the outskirts of what was then Galt, Ontario (it's Cambridge now), where my stepfather was a member. I don't know how much golf I learned there, though the pro, Art Hunt, was kind to me, but I did get my first lessons at bootlegging. From caddy — twenty-five cents a round, twice that if you carried double — I moved up (or down) to a job in the basement snack bar, beside the men's locker room. It was pretty grim, to tell you the truth, picking up soggy towels in the shower room, wiping out smelly ashtrays, slugging cases of Orange Crush and Dentyne chewing gum, but it did pay a cool two dollars a day, seven days a week, and on Saturdays, when the canteen offered cold beer, I got to stand behind the pop cooler and snap the green bottles open. It couldn't have been too illegal, come to think of it; the Galt chief of police, who had a belly as impressive as his handicap, was one of our best customers.

Later I started to play myself. Mr. Hunt let me while away some of my off-duty hours hitting bags of balls with a borrowed 5-iron, and by the time I began spending summers at Lake Simcoe I could keep my head up (mostly by keeping it down, I guess) in the family foursome. They had all started about the same time, my grandfather, the Colonel, my aunt and my uncle, just after the Colonel bought his cottage on the Black River. They loved it, though they seldom broke 50 on the Briars' original nine holes. With the suppleness of youth, I quite quickly became the long driver of the family (all of us seemed to have a natural slice) though the Colonel, frustrated by his own inability to knock it more than 150 yards as he watched his grandson's drives grow ever longer, would urge me to hit while the foursome ahead was still in range — or did until the day I landed a 7-iron on the shoulder of the local (and his personal) dentist. I could putt a bit in those days, too, not yet having learned how hard it was, and posted some satisfying scores, including a landmark 39, whose scorecard was posted on the cottage wall, right beside the Colonel's certificate, thanks to Canada Dry, having racked up a hole-in-one one day on what was then the Briars' seventh.

Ah, youth, though along with Chi Chi Rodriguez, I'm pretty sure the older we get the better we used to be.

I never did do well in tournaments, soaring to 105, as I remember, in a qualifying round for the Ontario Junior, and never making it past the semi-finals of even the Briars' friendly junior championships. With university, marriage, fatherhood and other distractions my interest waned, though the memories of the pleasures and the companionship stayed with me.

In the early 1980s, now ensconced as the host of CBC Radio's *Morningside*, I returned to Lake Simcoe and the Briars. Gill — Gill Howard — and I bought a modest cottage on the first fairway, not far from the sand trap that used to gather in our family's banana-shaped drives, and I returned to the game of my boyhood, this time dragging Gill along. As we began, all I seemed to have retained from my adolescence was the family slice. But gradually, things came back to me, and while I never again broke 40 for nine — or

80 for eighteen, the Briars now having grown to full size — my handicap crept slowly downwards.

Mostly, though, I was finding in golf something that even our family foursomes had seldom provided. Under Gill's tutelage, I learned to enjoy not only the game but its environs: the songs of birds, the feel of the sun on my neck, the dewy freshness of the morning air. The good shots I hit — arcing through the wind to fall softly on the Briars' undulating green — stayed with me; the bad were just interred with my post-game Scotch. It was fun.

In the summer of 1985, I wondered if we might find a way to spread the pleasure around. I still remember the scene. The sixth hole — the eighth, as it had been when I was a kid. I had hit it on the screws, and as Gill and I walked to our drives, I said, "Do you think we might have a little tournament next year?"

What followed, of course, changed my life. I called John O'Leary at Frontier College, who had approached me about recruiting what he called "The Morningside Army" to work for literacy. I had said I couldn't do that, but if we held a golf tournament . . .

I still remember that first one. 1986. Scrambling to think of who I knew who might play golf, worrying about the weather, trying to come up with some rules. Then being astonished at how well it all worked. Ken Dryden in shorts, leaning on his unfamiliar putter in that unforgettable stance. Bill Ardell, with Coles the book people then, outfitting his foursome in yellow sweatshirts. O'Leary with his threat of a prize from Lovecraft. Bill Buxton of the Frontier board riding up on his motorcycle, and, on the fourth hole of golf he had ever played, smacking a drive and yelling for all the world to hear, "It's airborne!" David Peterson, the premier of Ontario then and a former labourer-teacher, being followed by the TV cameras until he scuffed a 6-iron with a divot the size of his riding, which made, of course, the six o'clock news. Lorne Rubenstein of *The Globe and Mail* with a swing as smooth as his prose. Michael de Pencier of Key Publishers, snaking in a twenty-five-foot putt to win a playoff. The classical music of the Bowkin Trio, playing through the badinage of lunch. And Dennis Lee's poem, somehow squeezing in the name of Larry Zolf, who wasn't there but who provided a happy rhyme, and setting a standard that, well over a hundred works later, still holds its own.

Right from the start, I knew we were on to something. Our gathering brought together so much that mattered to me: friends, laughter, poetry, music and, in the game itself, some of the happiest memories of my youth. And most of all, somehow signalling underneath it all that everything was about reading and writing.

The cause of literacy was new to me then, though as soon as I decided that that's where any profit we made should go, I knew how appropriate it was. I am, after all, a librarian's kid, and books have been part of my life as long as I can remember. But when I began with the PGIs, I can confess now, I could hardly comprehend how many people have to get along without books — as well as without the more fundamental needs that an ability to read answers, from making out an instruction manual to trying to follow a recipe. The tournaments, and the stories they brought together, taught me everything. John O'Leary and his colleagues in the literacy movement urged me on. I became caught up. The more I learned, as I've said so many times, the more I wanted to do, and the more I did — or my friends and colleagues did — the more I learned.

Twelve years. A hundred and some odd tournaments. A network that stretches from sea to sea to, as I am proud to say, sea. A partnership that, through the generosity of our family of corporate sponsors, leverages the seed money from the public purse into, now, millions of dollars to make a better world — a partnership that may well be a model for an everchanging country.

And, at the same time, a thousand friends, a hundred thousand memories, and who knows how many people who have learned to read or write or just make their lives a little better.

So much accomplished, and so much still to do.

And oh, yes, my golf game.

Much of its deterioration, I blush to say, is because of the spirit of generosity that pervades the PGIs. Not long after Michael de Pencier sank that wonderful putt, we started playing scrambles, which seemed like a way to bring people together and make a place for golfers almost as bad as I was becoming. The people who organize our tournaments have tried to make my life easier by putting me, invariably, with good players. As a result, I've learned to coast. Out of bounds? Who cares? One of my partners will save the day. Miss a putt? Doesn't matter; someone will go to school on my errant path. I haven't won anything, to be sure, though I did come close in the Yukon once (my, that's a lovely course, isn't it?) and my son was in the winning foursome at the Briars in '98 (leading Shelagh Rogers, our poet, who knows about the genetic Gzowski slice, to suggest that Peter C. was probably adopted), but I've also only been "most honest" twice, in P.E.I. once and, as I remember, Ottawa. Mostly I've just stood around, soaking up the sunshine, laughing with my friends, thinking of people who will learn to read, and watching my game regress to where it all began.

Caddy anyone? When we're finished, I could crack you a beer.

Murray

Foreword, Getting Out of Here Alive, *1998*

"Scots wha hae wi' Wallace bled," I'd written — well, Robbie Burns had written and I'd cribbed for the occasion — "Scots wham Bruce has aften led," and then, taking off from the original, that being as much as I could dig out of my childhood memory anyway, I went on,

> *Murray McLauchlan is nae dead —*
> *Just growing older.*

The occasion was Murray's fiftieth birthday party. It was early summer, and he was finishing this lovely book, though no one at the party knew how lovely it was, except maybe Denise, who said (not at the party) that she'd cried at some of the passages he'd read to her, and, to some extent, me, since I'd read by then most of what the editors at Penguin had been able to wring out of him (I don't think I cried, though I certainly laughed out loud a few times). We were gathered in the garden of Murray and Denise's house, over-looking one of Toronto's verdant ravines — a motley group, whose very motleyness, I suppose, reflected Murray's remarkable history: musicians; a poet or two; the novelist Alison Gordon (Murray's partner in his triumphant appearance on CBC Television's *Great Canadian Quiz*); no painters so far as I knew, though the landscape artist Doris McCarthy, unable to attend, had sent along a painting as a birthday gift, but some aviation people; some radio people; me; my life partner Gillian Howard, who likes Murray and Denise as much as I do; Murray's brother Calvin; Denise's Mom; a few cousins and aunts; the music entrepreneur Bernie Finkelstein; and quite a few people whose identity (introductions not being a major part of etiquette at gatherings of this sort) I had no idea of, all drawn together on a glorious summer afternoon to pay tribute to a man we liked, admired or — in many cases — loved. I went on:

> *Like flats, Labatt's or orange bills,*
> *He, at fifty's o'er nae hills,*
> *He still needs nae Viagra pills*
> *(Or so he's told her).*

Flats, for the uninitiated, are — or were — flat fifties: tin boxes of cigarettes you could buy for about a quarter when Murray and I were learning to smoke, something he's been much better than I at learning not to do. (He has, in fact, turned into something of an antismoking zealot.) Labatt's, of course, is a reference to Labatt's 50 (it's still around, isn't it?) and orange bills . . . well, pink has only one syllable. But the poem was for Murray, and he'd get it.

This was actually Denise's suggestion. I'd been wracking my brains for something to bring along to the party, which in my case, as usual, meant huddling with my incomparable assistant Shelley Ambrose and wracking her brains, and Shelley had called Denise, who was producing the party as a surprise for Murray (it worked, too), and Denise, without wracking anything, said what he'd like most of all from me was something I might write for him.

Hmmm. On the one hand, exquisitely appropriate. High on the list of things Murray has done for me over the years are two pieces of writing. One, indeed, was a poem. Not a parody, either, but a clever and original work, which he composed for one of the golf tournaments that are now held in my name all over the country to raise money for literacy, and of which, typically, he's been a generous supporter. One of the traditions of those tournaments is to have a poet laureate, who spends the day with us and finishes our closing ceremonies with a poem written on the spot. Dennis Lee started it all a dozen years ago, and we'd had all kinds of other distinguished writers since, from Margaret Atwood to (bless her memory) Bronwen Wallace — a Who's Who of Canadian poesy. But I was sure Murray could handle it. I remembered the first time I met him, when, still in his early twenties, he came shuffling into the old CBC building on Jarvis Street to be on the program then called *This Country in the Morning*, and, as well as singing, presented a poem or two. Besides, just read some of the songs he's written since. Maybe not "wiping his face like a shoe," whatever that means, but much else that sticks in the head. Anyway, he was a smash hit, though I think the pressure kind of spoiled his golf that day, and the only line I can remember from his epic was about golf really being "flog" spelled backwards.

The other occasion when he wrote something for me was more ostentatious. In 1995, I was asked to accept a Governor General's Award for the Performing Arts (the capitals are His Excellency's). This both astonished and delighted me — astonished, since I considered myself neither performer nor artist (the award was for work I'd done on radio) and delighted because it sounded like a splendid occasion. Among its splendours was a gala evening at the National Arts Centre in Ottawa, where a concert would be held in the recipients' honour, and it was up to the award winners to choose both who would perform for us — the other anglophone honourees that year were Anne Murray and Maureen Forrester — and who would read and write our citations. I thought immediately of Murray — for both roles — and Gill, when I consulted her, agreed enthusiastically. But the more I thought of it, the more I thought, singing is work for him — and he's already done so much of it on my behalf, at literacy concerts everywhere from St. John's, where he sat at the piano and did one of the elegant 1940s ballads he seems to write so well since Denise has come into his life, to Yellowknife, where I can still see him doing, of all pieces, "Farmer's Song" ("wiping his face . . ." and all) —

and virtually every kid in the place, most of whom had never even seen a farm, singing along with all the familiar words. Besides, I wanted the world to see the Murray I knew: thoughtful, articulate, honest (not unlike this book, come to think of it). So I arranged for Ashley McIsaac and Laura Smith to perform, and asked Murray if he'd honour me by doing the citation. As he had with the golf poem, he either felt or feigned intimidation when I asked him. But he wrote an eloquent and touching piece, and when I heard him read it at the ceremony, I may well have reacted as Denise did to parts of this book.

Later on, on a visit to our home in the country, he brought along the manuscript, which he'd signed and had framed. I'm not sure I'd like the Governor General to know this, but I treasure that memento as least as much as — maybe more than — the sumptuous gold medal that now sits in its velvet-covered case on our mantelpiece.

On the other hand, I am to poetry what Newfoundlanders are to swimming — smart enough to stay out of the water. Ah, well, if Murray could do it . . .

> *Now's the day and now's the moment,*
> *Raise your glass in Murray's gloamin'*
> *Join the wishes of the poem 'n'*
> *List' the piper.*
>
> *Och, the frost's nae on his punkin,*
> *His stride is bold, his cheeks not shrunken.*
> *He's young at heart like Bonnie Duncan,*
> *Just somewhat riper.*

Though I'm kind of proud of turning Murray and Denise's meandering and enchanted garden into a "gloamin'," and though, as it turned out, advising people to "list' the piper" was a prescient thing to do, since there were a couple of pipers waiting in the wings at the party, I will confess that much of those two verses was constructed with an eye — or ear, I guess — on Duncan, Murray and Denise's son.*

---

*I know I'm overexplaining, but think of all the work I'm saving Ph.D. students of the future. Wouldn't it have been nice if Burns himself had been so considerate?

I have quite a few friends who are on their second marriages. I'm on my second myself, if you count living contentedly with the same woman for fifteen years marriage. (If there's a better ode to that part of life than Murray's "Second Time Around," by the way, I'm not aware of it.) And more than a few of them have young children. I imagine all those second-time fathers are determined, as I would be if Gill and I had decided to have a family of our own, to do for their second families what they were too busy or too stupid to do for their first. This doesn't mean they — we — were bad fathers the first time; from what I know of Murray, both before and after reading what he has to say here, quite the opposite was the case, for he dotes on his daughter, and is as proud of her nightingale's singing voice as of anything he has achieved himself. But none of the second-chance fathers I know come anywhere near Murray in passion and determination. He loves Duncan in a way that puts the rest of us to shame — spoils him even, but why not? — and his young son, as well as Denise, has inspired new music from him — including, notably, "The Old Tin Star," as sweet and poignant a Christmas song as anyone anywhere is turning out these days.

Murray will be sixty-five when Duncan is the captain of his university football team, in his seventies when Duncan stars in his first movie and even older when he wins the Nobel Prize for literature. But he's fifty now, and, yes, that's him on the front of the toboggan, laughing even louder than his diminutive, beautiful passenger.

> He's poet, pilot, painter, bard
> Too much for one wee business card.
> For thee and me he stands on guard,
> Yet still at ease.

In a longer poem, or if Burns had set the metre differently, I could probably have gone on with my list. Chiropractor? Well, probably not, but I remember once when Murray and Denise showed up at our cottage for some golf and my tricky back had hobbled me, Murray ordered me onto the floor and drill-mastered me through a series of exercises from which, miraculously, I rose like Lazarus. (Around our house, this routine is still called "doing your Murrays.") Or chef, maybe, though I've witnessed only his prowess on the barbecue. Or Scrabble player. Golfer even, for he hits the ball an astonishingly long way, even though, like his life, it may not always go in the direction he's planned. Certainly debater could have been in there; one of the most memorable dinner gatherings Gill and I ever assembled featured Murray and Denise and Bob and Arlene Rae, when Bob was premier of Ontario, with Murray and the premier in full conversational — and enjoyable — flight for most of the evening. Bob won, I think, but he was up against a formidable opponent — who'd have been even more formidable if he'd been arguing with someone he actually disagreed with.

But poet, pilot, painter, bard will do. The poet we've already established. The pilot, as you'll learn in these pages, is a man possessed. My guess is that when people who don't know Murray hear that he flies, they think, Oh, sure, he goes up and tools around sometimes as a lark. Well, maybe. But he's a folk singer who's licensed to fly anything up to twin-engined jets (see his adventures with our Armed Forces) and who finds a Saint-Exuperian ecstasy in being above the clouds, and, when he's aloft, he is as meticulous and professional as he is on stage. He loves everything about planes, and if I have any warnings about becoming friends with him, they would be: (1) Don't sit with him when he's a passenger on a small aircraft, as I did one sunny day when we were going from Halifax to Cape Breton — Murray kept up a running commentary, not all of it complimentary, on every wind current and flying manoeuvre — and (2) Don't let him start to show you the videos he's made of the latest air show he's been to — they go on longer than the search for Amelia Earhart.

But if he offers to take you up, go with him. You'll see flying as you never have before. One day, he picked me up in a float plane in Orillia, near where I live, and we soared up and over Muskoka, banked left to Georgian Bay to overfly Calvin's cottage and came back along the Severn River, drinking in the lakes and the rivers and the forests, reliving memories of summers past, gazing down at the Lilliputian rich people of Muskoka and the ant-like cars along the byways, laughing and chortling to ourselves, and for a couple of hours I knew what it was like to be an eagle — or at least an eagle's lucky friend.

He's almost as good a painter. Maybe, in fact, better. As I read through his early years in Toronto, I thought from time to time, Hey, Murray, stick with this. Listen to Doris McCarthy — painters as great as she is don't take an interest in just anyone. But maybe if he'd just painted, we wouldn't have those songs. In any case, he's painting again now: big, bold, colourful canvases that capture the spirit of the land — or, in the case of one that holds pride of place in his living room, of flying.

And bard? He practically defines the word, Celtic origins and all: a national minstrel, a spinner of tales, a recorder of people and places. Surely one of the most remarkable things about him is that the kid from Toronto has come to understand not only the landscape of the wilderness but what it means to us. For all the genius of "Down by the Henry Moore" or "Honky Red" or his other sketches of urban life — or even the unforgettable "Farmer's Song" — my own favourite among all these songs, for what it's worth, is the haunting "Beyond the Timberline," which describes, accurately, where the real Canada begins. And for all the impact of all his music, I wonder if the truest thing he ever created wasn't the film he put together a few years ago, flying his plane across the country he loves, dropping in to share songs with friends, drawing together his flying skills, his musical gifts and his painter's eye in a statement about the land, which is, I think, what I was thinking about when I wrote about Murray standing on guard. He really cares about this place, and knows and loves it well.

And know what? The son of a bitch can write, too.

> So lay the proud usurpers low,
> As Burns would have it did he know,
> And wish him fifty more to go
> With fair Denise.

And then, in the summer air, the pipers began to play.

Life After Smoking

50+ Magazine, *June 2001*

Nearly all the lessons of your early life, from tying your shoes to parallel parking to knowing which wine to order with dinner (not just before you take your parking class, I hope) are about things you're figuring out how to do as you grow up. Not only how to do but that you can do them, sometimes well, occasionally with some profit, and often just because you love doing them. From knowing your skills and dreaming of where they can take you, you begin to figure out not so much who you are, as they used to say in the 60s, but who and what you'd like to be when, if ever, you grow up.

But there's another part of the process too: learning — and accepting — what you *can't* do, or sometimes what you used to do but can't do any longer Some of that's just aging, accelerated, in my own case, by fifty years of smoking cigarettes — a tyranny I've been free of for well over a year now (thank God, the patch, Zyban and some wonderful professional help) but for which I am still paying a heavy price. But some of it's been going on for a long time too, and I realize now, hell-bent for seventy, and still with some growing up left to do, I'm beginning to understand that the limitations I'm facing up to now really aren't that different from those I've had to deal with all my life.

I was only about twelve, for instance, when it became clear that Elizabeth Taylor wasn't going to marry me, and not much older when I saw from the expression on the choirmaster's face as he listened to me run through some scales that I should probably give up my dream of succeeding Bing Crosby.

I held on a bit longer to the idea that I'd play in the National Hockey League some day. I had, after all, scored dozens of goals in the Stanley Cup finals, many of them in overtime — you could hear Foster Hewitt yelling my name as I broke down the wing of the outdoor rink in Dickson Park. "The Kid from Galt has done it again," Foster would shout over the roar of the crowd, even though he and I — or his voice and I — were all by ourselves in the winter morning.

Actually, I never stopped thinking there'd be a place for me in the NHL. Playing big-time hockey is the one ambition that draws all Canadian males together, and though I couldn't prove it I'd be willing to bet that if Chris Hadfield had been a better skater he might never have walked in space or if James Orbinski of Montreal had had a harder slap shot he might never have become the president of Medicins Sans Frontieres, which won the Nobel Peace Prize last year.

About thirty years after everyone else had given up on my hockey career, I spent a season hanging out with the Edmonton Oilers. Ostensibly I was writing a book about them, but in my heart I was just looking for a chance to show my stuff. It came one day at practice. The team had been playing well, and Glen Sather, their coach and general manager, set up a game of old-fashioned shinny. I borrowed some gear, joined in, and managed for a shift or two to become a winger on Wayne Gretzky's line. At one point I wobbled to a place in front of the opposition goal. Wayne set up behind the net — in his office, as we reporters liked to say. He dug out the puck, feinted once, and flipped it right onto my stick. I took dead aim at the empty corner, cocked my wrist and . . .

Oh, well, maybe I wasn't cut out for the NHL after all — though I almost hit the net.

Hockey, crooning, or marrying movie stars aside — not to mention breaking a quarter horse, flying my own jet or swimming the Strait of Juan de Fuca and other dreams that have faded as I've aged — I've had a pretty full life. On radio or television or with a pencil in my hand, I've got to meet the Queen, eight prime ministers (nine if you count Margaret Thatcher, who had a cold and couldn't hear my questions but kept on answering what she'd have liked me to ask anyway), four governors general, two chief justices, two Nobel Prize winners, the world yodelling, whistling and bagpipe champions (all Canadians) and every winner and most of the runners-up of the Giller Prize for Literature. I've danced with Karen Kain (well, I made a lifting motion and Karen sprang in the air, light as dandelion fluff), sang with Leonard Cohen (well, Leonard sang and I chanted along to "Tower of Song"), played chess with Boris Spassky (I moved, he moved, I asked if he wanted to resign, he grinned, said sure and we shook hands), golf with George Knudsen, cribbage with Gordon Sinclair and — well, sort of, as we've seen — hockey with Wayne Gretzky.

And I'm a long way from finished. I need oxygen most of the time now, and without my walker — a kind of baby carriage without the baby — I'm pretty well confined to barracks. On radio, which I still love, I sometimes sound a little breathier than I'd like to, and if I'm asked to make a speech, I need to know there aren't too many stairs to the platform.

But, I've learned, once you accept your limitations you can deal with them. Travel is hard for me now, but if I plan every move as carefully as I can, ask for rooms near elevators and make sure the airlines know I need oxygen, I can get to most of the places I want to go. Even around the city where I live, I've learned to call restaurants in advance to make sure washrooms are on the main floor. I've taken to — and hugely enjoy — having friends in for lunch rather than going out. I'm way ahead on my reading, and writing more than I have for years. I've bought a treadmill to keep myself as active as I can. I'd like to learn some Inuktitut — there are lessons, believe it or not, on the Internet — and I'm wondering if I could try a little watercolour sketching.

Elizabeth Taylor? I'd probably still be standing in line.

Acknowledgements

⟨ornament⟩

The essays in this book originally appeared in the following publications, to which grateful acknowledgement is due:

"A Perfect Place to Be a Boy" from the foreword to *Images of Waterloo County* by Richard Bain, Quarry Press, 1996.

"My Grandfather Leacock" from an unpublished address at the Leacock home, summer of 1989.

"Peter Brown's Schooldays" from the introduction to *A Sense of Tradition: An Album of Ridley College Memories, 1889-1989*, Hedge Road Press, 1988.

"A Taste of the Wild Frontier," originally published in *Maclean's*, November 2, 1963, as "The Last Frontier — Wabush, Labrador." Reprinted with permission from *Maclean's* magazine.

"First Splashes of Printer's Ink" from *The Private Voice*, McClelland & Stewart, 1988.

"The Graduation of a Canadian Sex Symbol" Convocation Speech on the occasion of receiving an honorary degree from the University of Toronto, June 19, 1995.

"The School of Heady Mistakes" from *The Private Voice*, McClelland & Stewart, 1988.

"The Editorial That Changed My Life," originally published under the title "Suffer Yourselves to Hang" in *The Varsity*, Thursday, January 24, 1957.

"Greenhorn in the Heartland," originally published in *Maclean's*, July 25, 1964 as "Canada's Heartland — Saskatchewan." Reprinted with permission from *Maclean's* magazine.

"Portrait of an Intellectual Engagé," *Maclean's*, February 24, 1964. Reprinted with permission from *Maclean's* magazine.

"The October We'll Never Forget" from *Peter Gzowski's Book About This Country in the Morning*, Hurtig, 1974.

"A Prince in the Revolution," originally published in *Maclean's*, July 14, 1962, as "The Cardinal and His Church in a Year of Conflict." Reprinted with permission from *Maclean's* magazine.

"And the Man We'll Always Remember" from *Trudeau Albums*, Penguin, 2000.

"Racism on the Prairies," originally published in *Maclean's*, July 6, 1963, as "This Is Our Alabama." Reprinted with permission from *Maclean's* magazine.

"Gordie," originally published in *Maclean's*, December 14, 1963, as "A Profile of Gordie Howe." Reprinted with permission from *Maclean's* magazine.

"A Hockey Writer's Last Stand at *Maclean's*," originally published with the title "The Time the Schick Hit the Fan and Other Adventures at *Maclean's*" in *The Canadian Forum*, October, 1964.

"Why *Maclean's* Still Matters," *Globe and Mail*, March 31, 2001.

"In the Days of the Seven-Day Hour," *The Nation*, July 11, 1966.

"And F— as a Dirty Word," originally published under the title "How You Gonna Keep 'em Down on the Farm After They've Said **** You" in *Saturday Night*, May, 1969.

"How CBC Radio Made Me a Canadian" from *The Private Voice*, McClelland & Stewart, 1988.

"And How Being Canadian Helped Make *This Country*," from *Peter Gzowski's Book About This Country in the Morning*, Hurtig, 1974.

"The Rules of Hopscotch" from *Peter Gzowski's Book About This Country in the Morning*, Hurtig, 1974.

"Why Summer Never Lasts Long Enough," *Canadian Living*, August 2000.

"But Winter Can Still Happily Surprise Us" from *Peter Gzowski's Book About This Country in the Morning*, Hurtig, 1974.

"Why All My Teenage Romances Ended in December" from *Peter Gzowski's Book About This Country in the Morning*, Hurtig, 1974.

"The Complete Works of Pete Gzowski, Lyricist, as Recorded by Ian and Sylvia, the Chad Mitchell Trio and — Seriously — Bob Dylan" "Song For Canada," by Ian Tyson and Pete Gzowski © 1965 (Renewed) Warner Bros. Inc. All Rights Reserved. Used by permission Warner Bros. Publications U.S. Inc.

"The Abbreviated Memoirs of an Abbreviated Talk-Show Career," *Toronto Life*, October, 1978.

"Meeting Rhonda," originally published as "Rhonda's Big Day: Tears of Happiness" in the *Toronto Star*, December 18, 1987, and "Don't Feel Sorry for Rhonda," December 19, 1987. Reprinted with permission — the Toronto Star Syndicate

"Life in the Big Leagues I: Behind the Bench" from *The Game of Our Lives*, McClelland & Stewart, 1981.

"Life in the Big Leagues II: How Gretzky Does It" from *The Game of Our Lives*, McClelland & Stewart, 1981.

"The World of the Racetrack I: The Fans" from *The Private Voice*, McClelland & Stewart, 1988.

"The World of the Racetrack II: The Backstretch" from *An Unbroken Line*, McClelland & Stewart, 1983.

"The City Mouse Moves Back Downtown" from *The Morningside Papers*, McClelland & Stewart, 1985.

"Reflections of an Unmade Bed," originally published in *Canadian Living*; reprinted as "Making a Fashion Statement" in *Friends, Moments, Countryside*, McClelland & Stewart, 1998.

"High Wind Off Antigua," *Toronto Life*, December 1984.

"A Couple of Memorable Meals" from *The Morningside Papers*, McClelland & Stewart, 1985.

"A Sprinkling of Canadian Living" from *Canadian Living*, 1989-1998.

"How to Ruin Your Golf Game — and Teach a Whole Lot of People to Read" from *Reading the Greens*, ABC Canada, September 1998. Reprinted with permission from ABC Canada Literary Foundation.

"Murray," from the Foreword to *Getting Out of Here Alive: The Ballad of Murray McLauchlan*, Penguin, 1998. Reprinted courtesy of Murray McLachlan, all rights reserved.

"Life After Smoking," *50+ Magazine*, June 2001. Reprinted with permission from CARPNews Fifty Plus.

OTHER TITLES FROM
DOUGLAS GIBSON BOOKS

PUBLISHED BY McCLELLAND & STEWART LTD.

HATESHIP, FRIENDSHIP, COURTSHIP, LOVESHIP, MARRIAGE
by Alice Munro
This latest collection by one of the world's great writers deftly combines the familiar with the unexpected, and surprises us, as only Alice Munro can, with unforgettable characters and "the small narrative brilliance of each individual story." *Quill & Quire*

Short Stories, 6 × 9, 336 pages, hardcover

LIVES OF MOTHERS AND DAUGHTERS: Growing Up With Alice Munro
by Sheila Munro
"The book will thrill anybody with a serious interest in Alice Munro." *Edmonton Journal* "What Sheila Munro says about her mother's writing could be just as aptly applied to her own book; you trust her every word." *Montreal Gazette*

Biography/Memoir, 6 × 9, 60 snapshots, 240 pages, hardcover

THREE CHEERS FOR ME: The Journals of Bartholomew Bandy, Volume One *by* Donald Jack
The classic comic novel about the First World War where our bumbling hero graduates from the trenches and somehow becomes an air ace. "Funny? Very." *New York Times*

Fiction/Humour, 5½ × 8½, 330 pages, trade paperback

THAT'S ME IN THE MIDDLE: The Journals of Bartholomew Bandy, Volume Two *by* Donald Jack
Canadian air ace Bandy fights at the front and behind the lines in the U.K., gallantly enduring both German attacks and the horrors of English plumbing. "A comical tour-de-force." *Montreal Gazette*

Fiction/Humour, 5½ × 8½, 348 pages, trade paperback

RAVEN'S END: A novel of the Canadian Rockies *by* Ben Gadd
This astonishing book, snapped up by publishers around the world, is like a *Watership Down* set among a flock of ravens managing to survive in the Rockies. "A real classic." Andy Russell. "Irresistible." *Edmonton Journal*

Fiction, 6 × 9, map, 5 drawings, 336 pages, hardcover

THE GRIM PIG *by* Charles Gordon
The world of news is laid bare in this "very wicked, subversive book . . . it reveals more than most readers should know about how newspapers – or at least some newspapers – are still created. This is exceedingly clever satire, with a real bite." *Ottawa Citizen*
Fiction, 6 × 9, 256 pages, hardcover

THE CANADA TRIP *by* Charles Gordon
Charles Gordon and his wife drove from Ottawa to St. John's to Victoria and back. The result is "a very human, warm, funny book" (*Victoria Times Colonist*) that will set you planning your own trip.
Travel/Humour, 6 × 9, 364 pages, 22 maps, trade paperback

AT THE COTTAGE: A Fearless Look at Canada's Summer Obsession *by* Charles Gordon *illustrated by* Graham Pilsworth
This perennial best-selling book of gentle humour is "a delightful reminder of why none of us addicted to cottage life will ever give it up." *Hamilton Spectator*
Humour, 6 × 9, 224 pages, illustrations, trade paperback

FOR YOUR EYE ALONE: Letters 1976-1995 *by* Robertson Davies
These lively letters, selected and edited by Judith Skelton Grant, show us the private Davies at the height of his fame, writing family notes and slicing up erring reviewers. "An unmitigated delight." *London Free Press*
Belles lettres, 6 × 9, 400 pages, facsimile letters, notes, index, trade paperback

RED BLOOD: One (Mostly) White Guy's Encounter With the Native World *by* Robert Hunter
The founder of Greenpeace looks back on a wild, hell-raising career. "Hunter acts. He does things. . . . In all his adventures humour is a companion, but he can also write angry political commentary." *Globe and Mail*
Non-fiction, 6 × 9, 280 pages, trade paperback

BROKEN GROUND: A novel *by* Jack Hodgins
It's 1922 and the shadow of the First World War hangs over a struggling Soldier's Settlement on Vancouver Island. This powerful novel with its flashbacks to the trenches is "a richly, deeply human book – a joy to read." W.J. Keith
Fiction, 5⅜ × 8⅜, 368 pages, trade paperback

A PASSION FOR NARRATIVE: A Guide for Writing Fiction *by* Jack Hodgins
The classic Canadian fiction writing guide. "One excellent path from original to marketable manuscript. . . . It would take a beginning writer years to work her way through all the goodies Hodgins offers." *Globe and Mail*
Non-fiction/Writing guide, 5¼ × 8½, 216 pages, updated with a new Afterword, trade paperback

INNOCENT CITIES: A novel *by* Jack Hodgins
Victorian in time and place, this delightful new novel by the author of *The Invention of the World* proves once again that "as a writer, Hodgins is unique among his Canadian contemporaries." *Globe and Mail*
Fiction, 5⅜ × 8⅜, 416 pages, trade paperback

CONFESSIONS OF AN IGLOO DWELLER *by* James Houston
The famous novelist and superb storyteller who brought Inuit art to the outside world recounts his Arctic adventures between 1948 and 1962. "Sheer entertainment, as fascinating as it is charming." *Kirkus Reviews*
Autobiography, 6 × 9, 320 pages, maps, drawings, trade paperback

ZIGZAG: A Life on the Move *by* James Houston
This "remarkable account" (*Books in Canada*) ranges from the Arctic to New York and beyond and tells of Presidents, hunters, glass factory gaffers, leopards, walrus, movies, bestselling books and 10,000-year-old meatballs.
Memoir/Travel, 6 × 9, 288 pages, drawings, trade paperback

HIDEAWAY: Life on the Queen Charlotte Islands *by* James Houston
This gentle book is a song of praise to the rainforest magic of Haida Gwaii, its history, its people, and the little green cottage the author loves. "James Houston finally writes about his own backyard." *National Post*
Memoir/Travel, 6 × 9, 272 pages, 40 b&w illustrations, map, trade paperback

THE SELECTED STORIES OF MAVIS GALLANT *by* Mavis Gallant
"A volume to hold and to treasure" said the *Globe and Mail* of the 52 marvellous stories selected from Mavis Gallant's life's work. "It should be in every reader's library." *Fiction, 6⅛ × 9¼ , 900 pages, trade paperback*

W.O. MITCHELL COUNTRY: Portrayed *by* Courtney Milne, Text *by* W.O. Mitchell
A beautiful book for all seasons, showing prairie, foothills, and mountain landscapes. "Milne's photographs are as dramatic, as full of colour and as moving as Mitchell's best writing." *National Post*
Art/Photography, 10½ × 11½, 240 pages, 200 colour photographs, hardcover

AN EVENING WITH W.O. MITCHELL *by* W.O. Mitchell
"A collection of 31 of Mitchell's favourite stories ... which he regularly performed with ebullience and dramatic flair to delighted audiences across the country." *Toronto Star* "An excellent performance." *Saskatoon StarPhoenix*
Anthology, 6 × 9, 320 pages, 30 photographs, trade paperback